68-59/39 Dec 19, 1976

Wayland

HUNGARY'S WAY TO WORLD WAR II.

by Nandor A. F. Dreisziger

Hungary's Way To World War II.

by Nandor A. F. Dreisziger

An essay awarded the 1967 Helicon Prize
in Hungarian History and Literature

Published by the
Hungarian Helicon Society, Toronto, Ontario, Canada

FOREWORD

This book examines the origins of Hungary's involvement in the Second World War. The starting point for the story is the end of World War I, when out of the ruins of the defunct Habsburg Monarchy a number of independent states emerged, among them Hungary. The closing date is 26 June 1941, the day when that country joined Hitler's invasion of Soviet Russia and thereby became irreversibly involved in the world conflict.

The story presented here is, in many ways, a tragic one. It is the tale of the tribulations of a small nation struggling for a place in the sun in the restless and hostile world of Europe of the interwar period. And it is a story which does not have a happy ending. Hungary's entry into the war proved to be the prelude to a German and then a Russian occupation resulting in the loss of the country's independence.

Attention in this study is focused on the years immediately preceding the events of the summer of 1941. In particular, the book describes that process by which Hungary was forced to align her foreign policy with that of the Third Reich without the actual intervention of German arms. Hitler's military triumphs have been examined many times. His diplomatic conquests, of which Hungary is a classic example, have received less attention. This is perhaps unfortunate, since it is the latter that provide a more fascinating story and a more profitable field of study. Military tactics and strategy become outdated as a result of changes in technology. The methods and means of diplomacy are more constant. As a result, they tend to have more pertinence to the present.

In the writing of this book an endeavour has been made to use some documentary material which, only a decade ago, was presumed to have been destroyed during the war. Efforts were made also to use recently published memoirs and historical literature, often not available in English, to throw new

5

light on many aspects of independent Hungary's foreign policy, as well as on the personalities of those connected with its making.

I would like to take this opportunity to express my thanks to Professors H. G. Skilling, H. I. Nelson, P. Brock, R. C. McNeal and N. C. Field for having been my me tors during my studies at the Centre for Russian and East European Studies of the University of Toronto. I am especially grateful to Professor Nelson for his comments on an earlier version of a part of this essay.

I would also like to acknowledge my indebtedness to all those without whose help, advice and e icouragement the completion of this work would have been impossible. In particular I want to tha k Professor S. Borbely, Br. J. Bottlik, Drs. S. Szoczy, J. Torzsay-Biber and F. S. Wagner for reading and criticizing my manuscript. I am grateful to the Hungarian Helicon Society for making the publication of this book possible.

Finally I wish to emphasize that I am alone responsible for all opinions expressed in this book, as well as for any errors of fact, style or interpretation.

Ottawa 1968.   N. F. D.

CONTENTS

INTRODUCTION

The historical development of almost every nation has been periodically interrupted by tragic events of great magnitude. The growth of the German states was greatly retarded by the Thirty Years War of the Seventeenth Century. The Battle of the White Mountain in 1620 rudely interrupted the evolution of the Czech nation. The development of Poland was delayed for generations as a result of the Partitions of that country by its neighbours in the second half of the Eighteenth Century. The emergence of a French state in North America was nipped in the bud by the victory of General Wolfe's Redcoats at Quebec in 1759.

Throughout its history, the Hungarian nation has often been beset by great calamities. The last one of these has been the Second World War. The military struggle caused extensive destruction in Hungary. In the wake of the hostilities, moreover, an alien political order was forced upon the Hungarian people. Centuries-old traditions were uprooted in the country. The straightjacket of Marxist-Leninist dogmas was imposed on the arts, humanities and sciences. As a result, free intellectual development was stifled. The Magyar nation, furthermore, was forcibly isolated from Western influences, and its energies were harnessed to serve alien causes.

There are few prospects for a basic change in this state of affairs even today. Although the fierce winds of the Cold War have died down, and revisionist tendencies continue to prevail in the councils of the communist regimes of Eastern Europe, the established order, based ultimately not on popular consent but on Soviet Russian power, will probably continue its existence for a considerable time to come.

It has often been asked how did Hungary become involved in the war that had such unfortunate consequences? This question has been answered in many different ways.

During the Second World War it became the commonly accepted view in the Western World that Hungary entered the military struggle on her own volition, that her leaders abandoned the country's independence in order to aggrandize themselves in league with Adolf Hitler, the leader of Nazi Germany. Such an opinion was intimated, for example, by the contemporary journal, *The Central European Observer*. This publication asserted, even before Hungary's involvement in the hostilities, that the "Holy Crown of St. Stephen has become a mere satellite of the swastika."[1] This view was also expressed, in no uncertain terms, by the British historian and publicist A. J. P. Taylor. In a book which appeared during the war, Mr. Taylor concluded that the aristocratic rulers of Hungary were "the agents and principal promoters of German imperialism."[2]

With the passing of years and the dissipation of the passions aroused by the war, historical opinions in the West slowly began to change. The famous American scholar, Professor Henry Roberts, for example, exempted the countries of Eastern Europe from the ultimate responsibility for their own misfortunes. "This unhappy area," he wrote during the early 1950's, "by its history, its geography, and its low economic and industrial level, was scarcely in a position to maintain itself against external aggression or internal strain."[3] This view, of course, did not gain universal acceptance. Writing a few years later, Professor Stephen Borsody, an expert on East European diplomatic history, expressed a diametrically opposite opinion. According to him the fate of these "nations was of their own doing. Their energies were consumed in wrangles . . ."[4]

The problem of Hungary's share of the responsibility for the tragic outcome of events was examined by Professor C. A. Macartney of Oxford University. In his books, this veteran student of Hungarian history argued that the allegations about the Hungarian leadership's wilful collaboration with Hitler did not, on the whole, stand up in the light of historical evidence. After a prodigious amount of research on the subject, Professor Macartney concluded that while Hungary's leaders had their faults, the country's "doom" was "dictated by forces far exceeding Hungary's own."[5]

The evolution of historical opinion on the subject of Hungarian entry and participation in the war presents a different picture behind the Iron Curtain. There, communist historians have steadfastly clung to the view that Hungary became involved in the war as a direct result of the irresponsible and adventurous policies of her "reactionary" and "fascist" leadership. At first these theories were not buttressed by substantial documentation. Indeed, little evidence could be marshalled in support of such arguments since historians in communist Hungary were not in possession of most of the pertinent historical documents. By about 1960, however, many of the important state and foreign policy papers of the pre-1945 Hungarian Government had been returned to Hungary from the Soviet Union. Using this new documentary material communist historians began publishing, in all the major European languages as well as in Magyar, articles and monographs by the score on the topic of Hungarian diplomatic history before and during the Second World War. Although these works pretended to be of the highest scholarly calibre with extensive documentation, their message was still the same. Their chief purpose was still the condemnation of the Hungarian leaders of the interwar period. The author of one of these books, the Soviet historian A. T. Pushkash, for example, dismissed Professor Macartney as the "apologist of the Hortyite regime."[6] The Hungarian historian Magda Adam, writing in the Soviet journal *Voprosy Istorii,* accused the rulers of interwar Hungary of conducting a "revanchist" policy against the country's neighbours.[7] Finally, another historian of communist Hungary, Gyula Juhasz, in a detailed study of Hungarian diplomacy during 1939-1941, concluded that "beginning from 1935 the chief line of counter-revolutionary Hungary's foreign policy was the alliance and co-operation with fascist Germany."[8] To support their interpretations the communists did not rely solely on the writing of books and articles. They also published bulky volumes of the new documentary material which came to light in recent times.[9]

It is the purpose of this study to show that the historical evidence available, including the carefully edited collections of documents published in the past few years in Hungary, does not, on the whole, support the findings of communist historiography.

True, Hungary's foreign policy in the years under consideration here was highly nationalistic. It was, moreover, full of inconsistencies and contradictions. However, this is not unusual. Every serious student of international relations knows that the foreign policy a state is based primarily on nationalistic considerations, and that a foreign policy without contradictions does not exist. In the external relations of a country there are no single and constant objectives. At best, there are only "red threads", that is, aspirations which are given priority most of the time, and aims which are sought with greater than average determination. Although Hungary's external policy prior to the country's involvement in the Second World War had been characterized by many shifts and turns as well as the pursuit of often incompatible ends, it is possible to discern in it such "red threads" or main lines. These, however, are not the ones that communist historians purport to find.

Of course, it cannot be denied that one of the primary goals of Hungarian diplomacy during the years prior to the war was the revision of the peace settlement which had followed the First World War. Apart from this, however, the chief aims of Hungary's foreign policy were not *"revanche"* and "alliance and co-operation with fascist Germany" but the maintenance of the "free hand" in international relations and the avoidance of the country's involvement in a major European military conflict. The story how Hungary lost her freedom of action and became involved in the Second World War in spite of these aspirations, is the theme of this essay.

PART I

A BURDENSOME HERITAGE

1. *War, Revolution and the Dissolution of Historic Hungary, 1918–1919.*

If wars are the watersheds of history, then World War I has been the greatest turningpoint in the evolution of European civilization. This war caused fundamental changes not only in the social, economic and political structure of Europe, but also in its entire philosophical outlook. The senseless slaughter of millions of human beings deeply shook that unbounded faith in the power of human reason to guide the destinies of mankind to ever ascending heights of achievement which had characterized the Nineteenth Century. The war, however, weakened not only this belief in the march of progress through history, but it also lead to the questioning some of the other underlying principles of the European political mind of the pre-1914 era: those of liberty, equality and fraternity. It is no wonder that in the wake of the war movements came to flourish on the continent which abandoned these lofty ideals.

The immediate effect of the First World War was the collapse of the old European political order. The four years of unceasing military struggle brought exhaustion and ruin to large historic states. As a result of the war the Habsburg, Romanov, Hohenzollern and Ottaman empires disappeared from the stage of history. The political transformation brought about by the war within these countries was more than just a change of regimes, or the simple disintegration of dynastic empires into their constituent elements. It was a change which had deep repercussions upon the political development of every nation affected. This was particularly true in the case of Hungary, a country whose historical evolution took a fundamental turn as a result of the First World War.

At the time the war broke out in 1914, Hungary was not a fully independent country. She was part of the ancient multinational empire of the Habsburgs which occupied much of East Central Europe. More precisely, she was one of the two states which made up the Dual-Monarchy of Austria-Hungary. In this unique constitutional arrangement, which had come into being with the famous Austro-Hungarian Compromise of 1867, Hungary was linked with the Austrian half of the Habsburg realm through a dynastic link. The ruler of the Habsburg Monarchy, the aged Francis Joseph, was the Emperor of Austria and, at the same time, King of Hungary. Besides this dynastic link, Austria and Hungary shared, through a complex constitutional setup, the administration of foreign affairs, imperial defence, finance and some other matters affecting the interests of the Dual-Monarchy as a whole.

Hungary became involved in the great European conflict when the imperial government of the Habsburg realm declared war on Serbia in July of 1914.[1] The four years of struggle exhausted the economic and human resources of the Dual-Monarchy and greatly increased the tensions among the many national groups which lived within the ancient realm. The end came suddenly and unexpectedly. In Hungary the public had not been prepared for the news of defeat. The enemy had not entered the country; the war did not appear to have been lost in October of 1918. Yet defeat came all the same. By fall, the position of the Central Powers and especially of Austria-Hungary became untenable. Vienna, the imperial capital, was starving. The various nationalities were demanding self-government or even independence. Unrest was rife in many provinces as well as in the big industrial centres. On the fronts the situation was worse. In September Bulgaria capitulated. Soon Turkey followed suit. By the end of October an allied army made up of a French expeditionary force and many Serbian divisions seemed ready to march on Budapest. Meanwhile, the Austro-Hungarian army was in a process of

14

disintegration. Many of its units, exhausted by the seemigly endless struggle, had already disbanded or mutinied.[2]

When Count Istvan Tisza, Hungary's Prime Minister, admitted defeat, the news was greeted with general consternation. The result was disastrous. "The bewildering fact of military defeat", wrote of this period a prominent political figure of the day, Count Istvan Bethlen, "threw the older and established classes of Hungary, together with the bourgeoisie, into a state of torpid lethargy."[3] Before these classes recovered from the shock of defeat, the country was swept by revolution.

At first came the so-called October Revolution.[4] A new government was soon formed under the leadership of Count Michael Karolyi, an aristocrat of strong socialistic leanings. As Karolyi himself put it later in his memoirs, the whole "October Revolution was based on ... a half-hearted alliance ..." of his own party and the country's Social Democrats.[5]

Karolyi and his followers were, what in the Canada of today would be called, "separatists". For many years they had advocated the severing of the constitutional link with the Austrian half of the monarchy. Accordingly, they declared the independence of Hungary. Their act was more than just the work of blind nationalism. According to the American historian Professor Low, Karolyi and his associates abandoned the link with Vienna because they hoped that this would save their nation from the vengeful treatment that the victorious Entente Powers were expected to mete out to Austria. By declaring independence, the Hungarian leaders hoped to strengthen their position at the peace negotiations. "Cutting ties with Austria seemed to them an act of self-preservation."[6] How naive their expectations were, was indicated when Karolyi, as the head of a newly independent state, felt obliged to seek a separate armistice agreement. The terms of the armistice he got were much more onerous than those which had been accorded to the Habsburg Empire as a whole just a short while before. But this was only an indication of things to come.

On November 16, 1918, the revolutionary government proclaimed Hungary a republic, and thereby severed the last tie, the dynastic link with Austria. The magnitude of the problems that faced the new Hungarian Republic has been effectively outlined by Professor Low:

> The whole political and administrative organiza-
> tion of the country was in a state of collapse and
> its economic situation, in the wake of the dissolution
> of the Austro-Hungarian economic realm and in
> view of further threatening territorial losses, was
> appalling. The railroad system had virtually broken
> down. Hundreds of thousands of ragged and war-
> weary soldiers were streaming back from the front.
> From the neighboring countries tens of thousands of
> Magyars were seeking refuge in a truncated country
> against which the Entente continued to maintain its
> blockade...[7]

The Karolyi government was particularly ill-equipped to handle the situation. The members of his cabinet had little if any experience in political leadership on the national scale. Moreover, they were idealists, newcomers to the game of *Realpolitik*.[8] Nor did Karolyi's revolutionary movement have the backing of the majority of the country's population. "The older and established classes", to use the words of Bethlen, began to rally against the revolutionary cause as they recovered from the shock of defeat. The radical left, increasingly under the influence of communist agents who made their way into the country from Soviet Russia, began fomenting disorder in preparation for a takeover of the revolutionary leadership. Nor did the national minorities, always distrustful of the government in Budapest, have more faith in Karolyi and his regime than they had had in that of Tisza and his predecessors.

The Karolyi government began its short-lived existence under these very difficult circumstances. It is not surprising then that only a few of its measures had any success at all, and some of them proved outright calamities.

The most disastrous step of the Karolyi regime was its decision to disband the remaining units of the old army.

16

Perhaps the move was the result of simple blundering on the part of the new revolutionary leaders. Perhaps it was a deliberate measure designed to demonstrate to the victorious Entente Powers the anti-militaristic character of the new Hungarian Republic. There might have been still another reason why the leaders of the October Revolution disbanded the country's armed forces. Only a year ago in Russia, Lenin and his bolshevik followers had done everything in their power to dissolve the old Russian army. In the fall of 1918 Karolyi and his Minister of Defence, Bela Linder, did the same. Their reason was probably the same as Lenin's: they feared that the remnants of the army might be turned against them by officers who did not approve of the revolution. The result of Lenin's work was the Peace of Brest-Litovsk.[9] The consequence of Karolyi's act was the Treaty of Trianon. There was, however, one difference: Russia could hope to reverse the verdict of an unjust peace settlement; Hungary, a small power, could hardly expect to do so.

It would be unfair to say, of course, that the Karolyi regime made no attempt to delay and to ward off the dismemberment of the country by its insatiable Rumanian, Czech and Southslav neighbours. Karolyi's Minister of Nationality Affairs, Oscar Jaszi, directed most of his talents and energies precisely to the achievement of this end. For many years prior to the war, Jaszi had advocated a nationality policy which went a long way to meet the cultural, social and economic needs of Hungary's numerous non-Magyar minorities.[10] Now, at the end of October 1918, he announced the new government's policy on this vital issue. Jaszi's proclamation promised the country's nationalities autonomy and self-determination within a reorganized Hungary. By offering such fargoing concessions, he hoped to allay the grievances of the minority groups and thereby to retain their loyalty to the new Hungarian Republic.

During the next few weeks Jaszi worked hard to put his programme into effect. He began negotiations with the leaders of Hungary's Slovak minority who, during these troubled times were being urged by the Czechs to separate from Hungary and join in the formation of the new state of Czechoslovakia. The Karolyi regime offered the Slovaks a certain degree of autonomy with provision for a Slovak National Council under the Hungarian Ministry of Nationalities. This body was to have some say in the cultural, fiscal and economic affairs of districts inhabited by Slovaks. After some wrangling over the details of this offer, the negotiations were discontinued.[11]

In his discussions with the representatives of the Rumanian minority who, much like the Slovaks, were being called upon by their fellow nationals in Rumania to leave Hungary, Jaszi was similarly unsuccessful. He failed in spite of the fact that he was prepared to make even greater concessions to them than he made to the Slovaks. He offered complete cultural, economic and administrative autonomy to Transylvania, the large eastern portion of the country where most of Hungary's Rumanian subjects lived, provided that this province governed itself through an arrangement based on an alliance of the three ethnic groups inhabiting the region: the Rumanian, Magyar and the German-speaking Saxon.[12] His offer was not accepted. The Rumanian leaders apparently considered Jaszi a Hungarian nationalist who wanted to perpetuate Magyar rule over them by token concessions and promises made in bad faith. At the same time, Jaszi was accused by many of his Magyar opponents of betraying the interests of his own nation by deliberately promoting the disintegration of historic Hungary.[13] What the Minister of Nationality Affairs really wanted was neither a Magyar-dominated centralist state nor a truncated Hungary, but a federated Hungarian Republic which could have served as a focal point for a larger political unit, a confederation of all the small nations of East Central Europe. A few years later, when Hungary's dismemberment had been completed by the Treaty of Trianon, Jaszi wrote rather bitterly: "(in 1918) I believed and still believe that a Hungary reorganized on the model of Switzerland, closely united in federal bonds with the neighbour states, would have been a better guarantee of democracy, of economic progress and of peace, than a mutilated Hungary, robbed of the means of existence, embittered and pursued by the dreams of revanche . . ."[14]

18

It is safe to say that under the circumstances of the fall of 1918 Jaszi's schemes had little if any chance of realization. During the immediate aftermath of the war the political atmosphere was not condusive to coolheaded reasoning and lengthy bargaining at the conference tables. Jaszi, it seems, wanted to continue his efforts into the winter, but by December new events made his and his country's position much more difficult. This change came about mainly as a result of external political developments.

The evolution of the international situation in Central and Eastern Europe during 1918-1919 had its immediate roots in the policy that the Western Powers adopted toward this area in the latter part of the war. It is a well known fact that by about the middle of 1918 most leaders in France, Britain and the United States had accepted the idea of Austria-Hungary's dissolution after the war into several small national states. Other Allied Powers, such as Serbia, Rumania and even Italy, had definite expectations of territorial gains at the expense of the Habsburg Monarchy as a reward for their contribution to Western victory.

After the conclusion of the hostilities came the time of laying the foundations for the planned changes in East Central Europe. The armistice conventions concluded with the Viennese and Budapest governments had, in part, already served this end. Anticipating the break-up of both Austria and Hungary, these agreements provided for the occupation of sections of these countries by allied forces. In the case of Hungary, the areas first assigned for allied occupation were, relatively speaking, not very extensive. After the armistice, however, at the insistence of the country's neighbours, the Allied Powers repeatedly advanced the lines of demarcation allowing for the occupation of more and more Hungarian territory by Rumanian, Serb and Czech troops. The Karolyi government protested on each occassion, but its protests went unheeded. The Western Powers cared little for Karolyi in spite of his long known pro-Western sympathies. Nor could they do much for him even if they had wanted to, since by this time the initiative in this part of Europe had passed into the hands of the governments at Belgrade, Bucharest and

Prague. Once the Serbian, Rumanian or Czech armies had decided to make still another advance into Hungarian territory, the Allied Powers could do nothing but inform Budapest of the change in the demarcation line. The Karolyi government in vain argued that the occasion for a territorial rearrangement was the peace conference, and the method for it was a plebiscite; Hungary's neighbours insisted on laying their hands on as much Hungarian territory as possible. No doubt they considered military occupation a much surer way of territorial aggrandizement than diplomatic bargaining or democratic elections.

The effects of these developments on Hungary have been well described by Professor Low:

> *The results of this continuous shrinking of Hun-garian-controlled territory were devastating, judged from the economic, the political, as, well as the psychological point of view. The loss of valuable natural resources and industrial regions, and of non-Magyar and Magyar population, paralized the Hungarian nation: it shattered its morale and undermined the rapidly diminishing prestige of the democratic and pro-Western government of Michael Karolyi.*[15]

During the winter the step-by-step occupation of the country continued. The government offered no effective opposition, as indeed it was in no position to do so, having dissolved the army the previous fall. This irresponsible decision now began to bear its bitter fruit. By March 1919 the political situation became hopeless. At home the government was attacked from the left and right. Yet "the final blow" to use the words of Professor Low, "which actually swept it from office originated in Paris."[16] At the end of February, the Entente Powers decided to call upon the Hungarian Government to evacuate another huge tract of an almost purely Magyar-populated area in the East. The decision was conveyed to Budapest only on the twentieth of March. Karolyi resigned in protest. In the resulting confusion power fell into the hands of a hastily established coalition of socialists and communists. However, the new government soon came under the control of the bolshevik leader Bela Kun and his followers.

With the beginning of the Commune, the darkest hours of Hungary's troubled post-World War I years had arrived. The Country's communist leaders, more impatient and daring than their Russian comrades, attempted to establish socialism in Hungary by decree. In all disrespect for the teachings of Marx, they wanted to convert Hungary from a largely pre-bourgeois society immediately into a socialized state. In total contempt of the Russian revolutionary example they national-ized the land of the nobility instead of dividing it among the peasants, and instead of seeking peace they prepared for war.

This is not the place to give a detailed account of the in-glorious record of the Hungarian Commune. To be sure, with the advent of Kun to power, the fatal defeatism of the Karolyi period had ended. Yet the four months of communist rule did irreparable damage to the country.

The coming of communism to Hungary, which in the troub-led days of 1919 raised the spectre of the spreading of the bolshevik revolution from Russia into Central Europe, brought about a further deterioration in the country's international position. The fact was that, from the spring on, the victorious Entente Powers had one more reason to take away from Hungary as much territory as possible. Limiting the country's size now not only served the purposes of satisfying the de-mands of the Rumanians, Czechs and Serbs, and of building up a group of successor states in Eastern Europe to act as a bulwark against Germany, Austria and Hungary, but it also helped to curtail the spread of communist revolution. The leaders of the victorious powers, assembled at this time in Paris to deliberate over the terms of a peace settlement in Central and East Central Europe, could hardly be expected to favour a country that had fought against them in the war, and now raised the flag of proletarian revolution. Accordingly, when a newly organized Hungarian army regained eastern Slovakia, pressure was applied on Budapest, and the area had to be abandoned.[17] In the West, moreover, Hungary was forc-ed to cede a long strip of territory to Austria.[18] The experi-ment in communism finally led to the occupation of most of the country by Rumanian troops. These came on the pretext of stemming the tide of revolution. As a result, Hungarians were liberated from Kun and his followers. They were also freed of some of their wordly possesions which the occupying army carried away as "war reparations" owed by Hungary to Rumania.[19]

Actually, the collapse of the Kun regime was due as much to internal developments as to external intervention. The fact was that, by the early summer, the government's policies precipitated a strong reaction, particularly in the countryside, against the whole proletarian revolutionary experiment. The emergence of rural opposition to the communist regime was no surprise. The government of Kun, with its urban-proletarian, atheist and internationalist roots, and predominantly Jewish leadership,[20] was not the ideal candidate to win the sympathies of the conservative, nationalist and staunchly religious peasant masses. The experience of the Russian Revolution of 1917 had shown, however, that it was possible for the dictatorship of the proletariat to gain and retain power without the support of the peasantry. Lenin had been shrewd enough to realize the implications of the problem and managed to eliminate serious rural opposition to the establishment of bolshevik supremacy by sponsoring a distribution of the land among the Russian peasantry. Kun and his associates refused to follow Lenin's example. It has been suggested that, by attempting an immediate socialist transformation of the countryside, they wanted to prove the inherent superiority of European communism over Russian bolshevism.[21] Thus, to the disappointment of the peasant masses, the communists simply nationalized the *latifundia* of the Church and the nobility instead of dissolving them.[22] Kun's "Red" regime, moreover, had to resort to periodic requisitioning to support its war effort against the Czechs and Rumanians. The peasants occasionally expressed their displeasure through violence. The Reds retaliated with terror. Punitive detachments were dispatched to the scene of the disturbances with orders to execute those suspected of disloyalty to the proletarian dictatorship. In the end it was the communists who lost. Their war effort collapsed as a result of an increasing lack of support by the masses. Kun and his associates fled the country.[23]

The experiment in communism had cost Hungary much in terms of a further disruption of her economy and a deterioration of her international position. But its greatest and perhaps most lasting damage was sociological and political. The violent days of the Commune and its aftermath left bitter hatreds behind. For, when the collapse of the Kun regime came, a popular reaction set in. Communists and their sympathisers were hunted down by the "Whites", groups of self-appointed avengers of the nation's sufferings. The treatment their victims got was not unlike that which was accorded to Nazi collaborators by the people of some German-occupied countries during the closing days of the Second World War. As the leadership of the Commune had been largely Jewish,[24] the White reaction to the Red regime acquired strong anti-Semitic overtones. After this, relations between the Jews and Gentiles of Hungary were never the same as before.[25] This too, was part of the burdensome heritage bequeathed to Hungary in the troubled days of 1919.

All in all, the revolutionary *interregnum* of 1918-1919 had lasting and deep-going effects that would be difficult to assess accurately. At home, this dark period of Hungarian history discredited not only leftist radicalism, but also all forms of socialist and, to some extent, even liberal ideologies. The fact that the Karolyi era had passed into the Commune seems to have been ample proof to many in the country that liberalism and parliamentary socialism were just forerunners of bolshevism, and therefore just as dangerous. In a political atmosphere dominated by such beliefs there was a natural tendency for a full swing of the pendulum in the opposite direction.

In the realm of international affairs, this period of haphazard experimentation and civil strife witnessed the dismemberment of the country by its neighbours with the approval of the victorious western powers. The Karolyi and Kun regimes failed to limit or to delay this process largely because of their ineptitude and lack of experience in diplomacy and national leadership. The naive pacifism of the former and the inordinate militancy of the latter did not enable either to handle an extremely difficult situation which required determination, firmness yet a capacity to accept a compromise. Under the circumstances of 1918-1919 no government in Budapest could have preserved historic Hungary unchanged and intact. Yet a vigorous leadership able to command broader popular support with a consistent foreign policy should have been able to better handle the situation and to prepare the ground for a more equitable peace settlement. Lacking such a leadership, the revolutionary regimes in Budapest committed blunder after blunder and the country encountered calamity after calamity. By the summer of 1919 Hungary was reduced to the capital and the surrounding central plain of the Carpathian Basin. What was left of her, moreover, was under temporary occupation by foreign troops. National morale was at an ebb. The collapse of the country's economy was complete and chaos reigned in the field of politics. Prospects for the future looked very dim indeed.

2. Search for a Place in the Sun, 1920–1929.

By 1920 the revolutionary period of interwar Hungary's history was over and the dismemberment of the ancient Kingdom of St. Stephen was legalized by the Treaty of Trianon of 4 June 1920.

The losses inflicted on Hungary by this treaty were staggering. The country was reduced to less than one-third of its former territory. As a result, close to sixty per cent of her inhabitants were transferred to the neighbouring countries. Hungary also lost some of her most valuable natural resources. Nearly all of her ore deposits were taken away, as well as close to ninety per cent of her waterpower.[26] Gone were most of the country's extensive forests. Hungary was left, for example, with less than three per cent of her former pine stands.[27] As a result of the Treaty and war reparations about seventy five per cent of the country's rolling stock was also lost.[28] Hungary was deprived of many essential industries, while most of those that were left were deprived either

24

of their sources of raw material or of their markets, and in many cases of both. The country's flour milling industry, which used to supply the markets of the Habsburg Empire, rapidly decayed after 1920.

The overwhelming majority of Hungarians could never acquiesce in the judgement of Trianon. Time and again their spokesmen argued against the injustices of the Treaty.[29] They pointed out that since its provisions were arrived at without Hungary having been consulted, it could hardly be called a treaty, but only a "ukase". They argued that the principle of self-determination of nations was not adhered to, first of all because the people involved in the transfers of territory had never been consulted,[30] secondly because the Treaty left nearly one out of every three Magyars outside the country, and that the boundaries of the new Hungarian state were "unintelligible, both from the geographical and also from the ethnographical standpoint."[31] They pleaded that there was neither historical nor economic justification for dissolving Hungary which had existed, with some interruptions, for the past thousand years,[32] and which had a high degree of geographic unity because of its location within the Carpathian Basin.

Today, only a few of those familiar with the facts of the peace settlement in East Central Europe would deny the validity of many of these arguments. Viewed from a historical perspective of almost half a century, the provisions of the Treaty of Trianon cannot but seem "cruel and unjust", to use the words of Jaszi.[33]

At the time of the peace settlement the treatment meted out to Hungary was justified on the following grounds: first, that the idea of self-determination of all nations had to be adhered to; second, that the nation states established in place of the Habsburg Empire had to be economically viable; third, that boundaries in that part of Europe had to be militarily defensible and last, that the future stability of the area had to be assured as far as possible. It seems, however, that the peacemakers used these principles only when they worked to the disadvantage of Hungary.

The doctrine of the self-determination of nations was only

applied to make sure that as few non-Magyars were left to Hungary as possible.[34] Many important regions were taken away from Hungary to assure the economic viability of the successor states, while no one cared if these losses permanently disrupted the Hungarian economy. Strategically defensible borders were drawn only where their establishment served as a justification for detaching additional Magyar populated regions from the country. The argument for the need to assure future stability in East Central Europe was adhered to only when it resulted in the further weakening and disarming of Hungary. At the same time the prospect of internal peace within the successor states was dangerously prejudiced by the inclusion of large Magyar and other minorities in each of them.

In June of 1920, however, Hungary had no choice but to accept this peace teraty,[35] and to begin the arduous work of reconstruction. This task fell to a group of leaders greatly different from those who had been in power during the revolutionary interlude.

In the days of Karolyi and especially those of Kun, the opponents of the revolution fearing for their own safety and desirous of changing the political situation in Hungary, gathered together in places beyond the reach of the regime in Budapest. Many prominent aristocrats and leaders of the pre-revolutionary era fled to Vienna. Here they rallied around Bethlen. A somewhat different group of men assembled in the town of Arad in southern Hungary. Those who came here were men with various political and social backgrounds: members of the nobility, career soldiers and right-radicals. They were united by their desire to change the pitiful state of affairs in Hungary, and by their hatred and contempt of Kun and his Commissars. The "counter-revolutionaries", as they were called, organized a rival government, and chose the nearby city of Szeged as their headquarters. Here, under French aegis, they began their preparations for a takeover of power in Hungary.

The leadership of the new movement was assumed by Admiral Miklos Horthy. The choice of Horthy as leader was an ingenious one. A member of the Magyar nobility who attained many distinctions and a very high rank during his long service in the imperial armed forces of the Habsburg Monarchy, he was the ideal candidate to attract the support of both the advocates of the restoration of the old Empire, and the believers in Hungarian independence. Horthy was a naval officer. Thus his choice also eliminated the emergence of acute rivalries which could have ensued had one of the many army officers of the Szeged camp been selected as leader.

Horthy also commanded considerable respect. He had distinguished himself during the war. As admiral of the ill-equipped Adriatic fleet of the Habsburg Monarchy, he had, on one occasion, succeeded in breaking through the British naval blockade in the Straits of Otranto. Wounded in the midst of the engagement, he had refused to be carried below deck. Although Horthy was not made into a national hero, a "Hungarian Nelson", until after his accession to power in Hungary, the Otranto incident probably also played some role in his becoming the leading figure of the Szeged government.

In November 1919, after the withdrawal of the Rumanians from Budapest, Horthy entered the capital at the head of a small army.[36] From this event is dated the beginning of the so-called Horthy Era of modern Hungarian history. This label, of course, is a misnomer when applied to 1919-1920, just as it is a mistake to name Hungary's interwar years after this man who did not exercise predominant influence until after the storm of World War II had burst upon Europe.

Hungary's post-revolutionary era began with rather short-lived and ineffective coalition governments.[37] A change came, however, in July 1921, when a new government was formed under the leadership of Bethlen.

Count Istvan Bethlen came from a historic Transylvanian family. His studies had taken him to Vienna and England. In 1901 he had entered Parliament. Bethlen was to remain active in Hungarian politics for more than four decades. In politics he was a realist. A shrewd but vain man, Bethlen possessed a political *finesse* which has perhaps not been equalled in recent Hungarian history. As most of his aristocratic compatriots, he was a conservative. In 1919, as it has been mentioned, he had been the leader of the more conservative Vienna group of counter-revolutionaries. During the ten years of his rule, according to Professor Macartney, Bethlen succeeded to a remarkable extent in imposing his will and ideas on the political, social and economic system of Hungary.[38]

Bethlen distrusted all forms of revolutionary ideologies and extremisms whether they came from the country's socialists or some of the right-radical members of the Szeged group. He allegedly began his term of office by declaring that the "revolutions and counter-revolutions were over." The threat of radicalism from the Left had been crushed during the days of the White reaction to the Commune. Now it remained to disarm the pra-military organizations of the far-Right. This task Bethlen achieved with dispatch as soon as a sufficiently powerful police force had been organized. Subsequently he made sure that the work of peaceful reconstruction was not disturbed by communist or fascist, urban or rural radicalism.

With Bethlen then, a long period of stability began in Hungary. True, the political system that came to prevail under him was not a democratic one — a fact which the Prime Minister himself admitted.[39] Yet the Hungarian Parliament continued to function throughout the 1920's and there was even a modest attempt made at land reform. Nor was there a complete return to the old order of things in the issue of the restoration of the monarchy. While a monarchical form of government was re-established, no one came to occupy the throne. In fact, Habsburg attempts to regain the Hungarian crown were resisted by force. Instead, Horthy was elected Regent. Indeed, Hungary of the interwar period was contemptuously referred to as a kingdom without a king ruled by an admiral without a navy.

Horthy, the hero of Otranto and the leader of the Szeged group, was a traditionalist in politics.[40] In his younger days he served as an officer at the imperial court in Vienna. Horthy's ideal was his old master Francis Joseph, and there is every reason to suppose that the Regent's ideal of a social and political order was not far removed from the one which prevailed in pre-war Austria-Hungary. While he accepted the inevitable change of times, the new ideologies of the twentieth century, so irresistible to some of his younger contemporaries, seem to have made no impression on him whatever. This made him an unlikely candidate to sponsor, or even to support a radical transformation of the country's political and social system.

In the 1920's, however, Horthy could not have initiated major changes in Hungary even if he had desired to do so. Although he was the head-of-state and the commander of the country's small army, he did not exercise a great deal of influence in politics. As one observer put it: under Bethlen, Horthy "had to keep quiet".[41]

It was to this regime, headed in reality by Bethlen rather than Horthy, that the task of reconstruction fell. The difficulties that had to be overcome were enormous. The sad state of the country's economy has already been described. To these problems were added those of unemployment and a housing shortage caused to a considerable extent by the continuing influx of people displaced from their homes as a result of the peace settlement. On top of all this the country experienced a severe inflation.

This, however, was not all that stood in the way of reconstruction. For there was another problem, one quite different in nature from the others. The source of it was Hungary's emigrees.

During the turbulent months of revolution and counter-revolution thousands had left Hungary. Many did not return, indeed could not return to the country of Bethlen and Horthy. Among these were some prominent people including Count Karolyi and his associates. They, for many years, conducted a campaign of vilification against Hungary and her government.

The chief figure of the propaganda campaign against "counterrevolutionary" Hungary was Karolyi's one-time right-hand man: Jaszi. An effective publicist, he was able to inflict enormous damage on the Bethlen regime's international reputation.[42] Jaszi's articles appeared in many periodicals, and his book: *Revolution and Counter-Revolution in Hungary* went through several editions in different languages.[43]

29

It might be asked why a man like Jaszi insisted on castigating the government and political system of his country when this hurt not only his political foes but also did a great disservice to his nation as a whole? The fact was that Jaszi, who possessed all the sensitivity of a proud and highstrung intellectual, left Hungary as a greatly disillusioned and offended man. To the Whites he could not forgive their treatment of the Jews, to the aristocrats who ruled the country, their stifling of progressive (i. e. leftist) political movements, and to his compatriots, their rejection of his dream of a federated, democratic Hungarian state. Thus, for many years Jaszi heaped invectives upon Hungary and her regime. In his anger he extolled the political systems of her enemies: Czechoslovakia, Yugoslavia and Rumania. He contrasted the "liberalism" and "pacifism" of the governments of these states with the "militant nationalism" of that of his own country.

With the passage of time, however, Jaszi's bitter resentments gradually dissipated. After a visit to his favourite succession states in 1935 he admitted that these were plagued with the same nationality problems as Austria-Hungary had been only two decades ago. What went on in Eastern Europe at the time, according to Jaszi, was "a hidden *bellum omnium contra omnes.*"[44] By this time he saw that no one in Eastern Europe was immune from the bacilli of chauvinism. After 1945 Jaszi went even further in admitting how unfair he had been to his country and countrymen during the early years of his exile.[45] All this, however, could not undo the damage he and his colleagues had inflicted upon Hungary in the 1920's.

The adverse international publicity had done a great deal to hinder the Bethlen government from attaining its foreign objectives particularly during the early 1920's. The country was isolated. With the exception of Austria, her neighbours formed an alignment known as the Little Entente whose primary purpose was to prevent Hungary from attaining a revision of the Treaty of Trianon. Thus, the country was surrounded by hostile powers ready to pounce down at the first false move.[46] Nor were the suspicions of these countries without foundation. During these years it was the aspiration of probably every Magyar to end the sad state of affairs imposed upon them by the peace settlement.[47] It is no wonder then that revisionism, as the movement for the alteration of the terms of the Treaty of Trianon was called, became a very important factor in Hungarian politics. It also became a declaration of faith, a measuring rod for every Magyar's patriotism and loyalty. The most ardent and outspoken revisionists were usually those men whose ancestral homes had been transferred to alien rule as a result of the peace settlement. Many of the nation's leaders belonged to this category. To serve as an instrument of this cause the "Hungarian League for Revision" was organized. The League collaborated with the influential British politician and newspaper magnate Lord Rothermere, who conducted a personal campaign for the peaceful revision of the Treaty of Trianon.

By the end of the 1920's the Bethlen government openly associated itself with this gathering movement for revision. The campaign, however, led to little if any visible success. The international reputation of the country and its regime could improve only very slowly and, as a result, revision had very small prospects. The lack of notable success in the field of external affairs, however, was counterbalanced to some extent by the Bethlen government's positive achievements in the field of internal reconstruction.

First to recover was the agrarian sector of the economy. Exports of agricultural produce, for example, more than doubled from 1920 to 1923.[48] Next, the country's finances were put in order with the help of an international loan extended to Hungary as a part of a League of Nations reconstruction programme. Recovery came last to the industrial sector of the economy largely because it had suffered the greatest dislocations in 1918-1920. Yet, during the second half of the 1920's, improvements came here also. This was in no small degree the result of the fact that internal political stability and a policy of tariff protection and budgetary equilibrium made for an increased investment of local as well as foreign capital in manufacturing. Commenting upon the "outward aspect" of the economic situation in Hungary at the end of the 1920's, Professor Macartney had the following to say:

> The currency had been stabilized and order re-introduced into the national finances. Foreign trade had increased considerably. Prices were at a high level, and the farmers had enjoyed some years of prosperity. In industry, the desire to achieve self-sufficiency had led to something like boom conditions. A superficial observer might have supposed that Hungary had succeeded in establishing an economic modus vivendi within the limits of the Treaty of Trianon.[49]

3. Politics in the Great Depression, 1929-1933.

Into this newly reconstructed, yet basically very fragile economic structure the World Depression brought havoc and destruction. Being an exporter of agricultural produce, Hungary was particularly hard hit. The market prices of food declined sharply. To make things worse, Czechoslovakia and Germany, the country's best customers for grain, livestock and the like, embarked on a policy of agricultural protectionism and thus shut their doors to Hungarian exports. Hungary's plight was aggravated by the fact that she was a debtor nation having borrowed considerably on the international money market, often at high interest rates, during the period of reconstruction.

The nation's increasing economic hardships, manifesting themselves in both urban and rural unemployment and in a general slump in production and business, had their definite effects on political life also. As in many other countries, the Depression caused growing political discontent in Hungary. Bethlen, after battling in vain the onslaught of bad times for more than a year, resigned his office. Leadership was taken over by Count Gyula Karolyi, who continued to combat the depression by orthodox methods, namely by an economy drive. His policy was quite ineffectual. Dissention grew within the ranks of the ruling party and demands were made for Karolyi's resignation.[50]

Meanwhile political unrest in the country increased. Faith in the value of orthodox policies to cure the problems declined. Because of the hopelessness of the situation, the political atmosphere became revolutionary by 1932.[51] To avoid an outright catastrophe, the leaders of the ruling party looked for a candidate for the Prime Ministership who could wield a firm hand in the critical hours and could better command the loyalty of the restless elements of the population. Their choice was Captain Gyula Gombos.

Gombos had an active, almost turbulent political past. Not once in his past he had been associated with leadership of militant nationalist organizations. In 1919 he had been a member of the Szeged government. Two years later he took a prominent part in foiling a legitimist coup to restore Charles Habsburg to the Hungarian throne. In 1928 Gombos once again entered the government as Minister of Defence. This position he retained almost till his death. According to Horthy, Gombos was an excellent officer, a gifted orator and a flamboyant politician.[52] Captain Gombos, however, had definite authoritarian inclinations. He was an admirer of Mussolini, whom he even resembled somewhat in personality and appearance.

If in looks Gombos resembled the Italian leader, his accession to power reminds one of Hitler's ascent to leadership in Germany a few month later. Like the Nazi leader, Gombos was pushed into the forefront of national politics in a time of crisis by people who hoped to retain real power for themselves behind his back. In fact there is evidence that Horthy and his closest associates called upon Gombos to head the government with the expectation that he would be crushed under the weight of the enormous economic difficulties of the day. They hoped that the Captain's appointment to office would not only serve to let off some steam in an unstable political situation, but would bring to an end the career of the loud and over-ambitious soldier-politician. They had even picked a successor to him: Count Kuno Klebelsberg, a prominent politician and an intimate of Bethlen and Horthy. "Gombos got one year to rule," remarked Klebelseberg to a close friend of his at the time.[53]

Like his more notorious German colleague, Gombos disappointed his masters. Once in office, he displayed a remarkable talent for political survival. Horthy seems to have thought he could manipulate Gombos.[54] In reality, however, the situation was almost the reverse, at least in the first period of Gombos' term of office. For the new Prime Minister, in considerable contrast to Bethlen, flattered Horthy by consulting him in policy decisions and by making him appear important in the eyes of the public.[55] Even luck was on Gombos' side at first. His secret heir-apparent, Klebelsberg, died in a few months.

Historical parallels, however, are never complete. Although Gombos' accession to power might resemble that of Hitler, there were important differences. The German leader had a disciplined and vigorous movement to back his ambitions. The party Gombos came to lead in 1932 was still basically Bethlen's party. It was not till 1935 that Gombos organized a party and attained a Parliament more to his liking. Even more significant was the fact that Horthy, though quite old, and somewhat susceptible to flattery, was not a senile Hindenburg. Most important of all, fate was to put an early end to Gombos' life.

October 1, 1932, the day of his appointment as Prime Minister, however, still ushered in the beginnings of a change in Hungarian politics. General Gombos, (he soon promoted himself), took every opportunity to place his followers into higher positions within the government party, the civil service and the army. At the same time he drove out undesirables by the score. He and his followers, incidentally, were instrumental in the revival of anti-semitism in the country. The hatred of the Jews, wrote the contemporary politician Miklos Kallay, was the "Trojan horse" for fascist influence and ideas in the Hungary of the times.[56]

These developments soon caused the crystallization of opposition to Gombos and his programme. Bethlen himself, and Kallay, who was then the Minister of Agriculture, left the

34

government party.[57] Intellectuals, conservatives, Church leaders and Jews alike rejected the new administration's policies. In opposition circles Gombos' programme was openly attacked by prominent political figures of the day: Tibor Eckhardt and Endre Bajcsy-Zsilinszky.[58] The new Prime Minister was contemptuously called "Gombolini" for his imitation of the Italian leader's politics.

The advent of Gombos to power also had its repercussions in the realm of foreign policies. The Prime Minister's authoritarian inclinations and admiration for the Italian and post-1933 German patterns of politics tended to give an even stronger pro-Rome and pro-Berlin orientation to Hungarian diplomacy than had been the case before this time. One of Gombos' foreign policy aspirations was to iron out the frictions which existed in the relations of Italy and Germany. He has rightly been regarded as the earliest advocate, the "father" of the Rome-Berlin axis. Behind this aim, however, there were more than simple rightist sympathies. Hungary had nothing to gain from a war between the two great powers of Central Europe. After such a conflict Hungary would have probably become the vassal of the victor regardless of whether she took sides in the struggle or not. In fact, it was in the interest of the country that she should not have to choose between Berlin and Rome. Friendship with both, moreover, could bring the definite advantage of ending the country's isolation.

Gombos' attitudes toward foreign policy were not shared by Horthy and some of his most influential advisers. To be sure, all Magyar leaders at the time agreed on the desirability of a change in the onerous terms of the peace settlement. They also shared a common aversion to bolshevik Russia.[59] All of them harboured deep antagonism toward the leaders of Czechoslovakia, whom they considered to be the real authors and perpetuators of the Trianon *status quo*.[60] Agreement, however, ended there. The feelings of these men conflicted considerably when it came to the question of relations with Germany and England. Gombos, it has been mentioned, was a pro-German. Bethlen, Horthy's close friend and adviser, in contrast, was an anglophile. Horthy himself might not have had any feelings against Germany and the Germans; but being a naval officer, he respected and even admired Britain for her navy.[61] Here he differed from men like Gombos, whose idea of greatness and power was the Prussian Army rather than a fleet.

Hungarian foreign policy in the mid-1930's, however, was not made by the Regent and his advisers on the one hand, and the Prime Minister on the other. For there was the figure of the Minister of External Affairs.

Hungary's Foreign Minister for the years 1933-1938 was Kalman Kanya. A man of exceptional gifts,[62] Kanya was a veteran diplomat. His father, a member of the gentry, provided his son with an excellent education designed to enable him to enter Austro-Hungarian diplomatic service. Kanya's first assignments took him to posts in the Balkans and Russia. Eventually, he rose to be the head of the Press Department. In 1913 he was assigned as Minister to Mexico, where he stayed until the demise of the Dual Monarchy.[63] In 1919 he offered his services to the Government of Hungary. During the next few years he had a lion's share in founding and organizing the now independent Hungarian diplomatic service. From 1925 to 1933 he was the Hungarian representative to Berlin, where he worked to attain friendly relations between his country and Weimar Germany. Throughout the twenties, testifies Andras Hory, one of his younger colleagues in the Foreign Office, Kanya was an open advocate of a German orientation in Hungarian foreign policy.[64] Probably because of these views he was brought into Gombos' cabinet early in 1933.

In his conduct of the day to day routine of Hungarian diplomacy Kanya was no innovator. Having been brought up in the traditions of the old Viennese school, he had little faith in the methods and institutions of the post-war diplomatic world: slogans, mass propaganda and the like.[65] What share Kanya had in the making of foreign policy is difficult to determine. The mere conflict of personality between himself and the Prime Minister inevitably led to frictions if not over aims at least over the methods of policy. Kanya was a professional in his field with an aristocratic contempt for amateurs. Gombos was a soldier-politician, impatient in his conduct of affairs and quite indiscreet in his foreign policy ut-terances.[66] Horthy testifies that the cautious Foreign Minister often clashed, but in the end usually went along with the sweeping Prime Minister.[67] Kanya's sphere of authority in the realm of foreign relations increased considerably only with the illness and subsequent death of Gombos in 1936. Two years later, Gyorgy Ottlik, a prominent journalist of the time, felt justified to write that in recent years Kanya has had an "absolutely decisive part in shaping our foreign policy".[68]

This then was the situation in Hungary at the height of the Great Depression. The recovery the country had made since the troubled days of 1918-1919 was quickly undone by the economic crisis. In politics, too, the stable atmosphere of the 1920's was gone. With Gombos' accession to office radical tendencies increased within the nation's leadership. At the same time, the division of national opinion on issues of im-portance became sharper. The making of governmental policy, both internal and external, was the domain of a few men whose *de facto* relationship to each other and to the final product was indefinite and changing. The complexity of the picture, however, was not entirely disheartening. The conflicts of opinion and approach among the country's policymakers were not strong enough to give rise to political crises or upheavals. If anything was really disheartening in the Hun-gary of the mid-1930's, it was the enormity of the external problems which were about to confront the nation's leader-ship.

The change in the international situation in Europe began with the coming of Hitler into power in Germany in 1933. From this point on the pace of events on the continent quickened. With the state of affairs being in a constant flux, the problems of external relations came to occupy a more and more important position in the life of European nations. In countries most affected by the revival of German power: Austria, Czechoslovakia and Poland, foreign affairs began to dominate the realm of politics almost to the exclusion of everything else. It was not long before the same was true of Hungary.

PART II

FOREIGN POLICIES IN THE GOMBOS ERA

1. The Rome Protocols.

For many years after 1919 one of the prime objectives of Hungary's leaders was to break out of the isolation in which their country found itself in the world of European international relations of the 1920's. By the second half of the decade this aim was partially realized with the attainment of a *rapprochement* with Italy. Mussolini's interest in Hungary, especially his public rejection of the Treaty of Trianon, was warmly welcomed by the Hungarian Government. In 1927 a pact of friendship was signed between the two countries.[1] Italo-Hungarian amity intensified in subsequent years. Soon Austria became a partner to it. The three states eventually joined in a loose bloc based on economic and, to a lesser extent, political co-operation. The factors which led to this development were manifold. Although the three countries had many objectives in common, each also had its own peculiar reason for joining hands with the others.

Mussolini desired to extend his influence in the Danubian area. At the time he was still hoping for the disintegration of the crises-ridden multinational Yugoslav state. Such an event, he probably thought, would enable Italy to gain a foothold in the Balkans, and to increase her influence in the Danube Basin, particularly in Croatia.[2] The Italian leader told Starhemberg, the Austrian politician, on the latter's visit to Rome early in 1933, that Italy needed a friendly Danubian hinterland composed of Austria, Hungary and Croatia to prevent Italy from being "forced to play the insignificant role of a peninsula on the edge of Europe". Mussolini added that speedy action was needed in connection with this, for Hitler would not wait.[3]

Ever since the triumph of Nazism in Germany, Dollfuss, the head of the Austrian Government, desperately needed support against Hitler and the National-Socialists of Austria. He decided to seek this support for his internal and external position through establishing closer relations with Hungary and Italy. The way for this was cleared during his visit to Budapest early in March, 1934.[4]

The Hungarians had various ideas in mind when they moved toward closer co-operation with Austria and Italy. To a few the Rome bloc meant an anti-Nazi alignment designed to keep Hitler out of Austria.[5] The Regent apparently regarded the idea of friendship with Vienna and Rome as primarily an anti-Little Entente policy. "In a sense" writes Horthy in his memoirs, the protocols signed at Rome in the spring of 1934 were "an answer" to the Pact of Organization concluded by the Little Entente with the Balkan League early that year.[6] Gombos probably sought success in foreign policy to buttress his internal position against his opposition.[7] Still another consideration behind Hungarian support for the establishment of the Rome bloc was probably that of economics. This is evident in the terms of the protocols and the history of trade relations among the three countris in the mid-1930's.

The protocols defining the friendly relations which had developed among the three states were signed in Rome on March 17, 1934. The first protocol called for consultation among the signatory powers on matters effecting all or any of them in international politics. The second dealt with economics and problems of reconstruction in the Danubian region, in the spirit of, and according to the decisions of a number of international agreements, among others the Stresa Conference. It called for promotion of mutual trade, encouragement of grain exports from Hungary, better transit facilities for each other's commerce, agreement on the use of Adriatic seaports, and the establishment of a board of experts to hep solve trade problems affecting the three countries. The third protocol dealt with economic matters affecting Austria and Italy.[8]

Undoubtedly, the economic implications of the treaty meant a lot to Hungary, especially in the years 1934-35. One student of economic relations among central European states in the interwar decades went so far as to say that, for Hungary, the regulations concerning the marketing and valorization of her wheat was the "backbone of the agreement".[9] Hungarian wheat, for example, was sold to Italy at about double its free market price. Trade among the three countries increased considerably and Austrian and Hungarian exports to Italy increased greatly. As a result, Italy became seriously indebted to her junior partners. This situation eventually led to frictions within the bloc.[10]

The political history of the Rome Protocols during the remainder of Gombos' Prime Ministership is that of futile attempts to enlarge the bloc and of somewhat more successful efforts to put more teeth into the political provisions of the agreement. During the two years following March 1934 various suggestions were made for the enlargement of the group by adding to it Poland, Germany and even one or the other of the Little Entente countries. It seems that German entry was opposed by the Austrian Chancellor, Schuschnigg.[11] Gombos appears to have made the idea of bringing closer the Rome and the Little Entente blocs conditional on the consent of the German Government.[12] He was upset by the attempts of some Austrian circles to come to better terms with Prague with the probable aim of associating Czechoslovakia with the Rome group.[13] Mussolini seems to have been the most favourably disposed toward the idea of both enlarging and strengthening the block. At least on one occasion he suggested a customs union, alliance or at least a solid entente.[14]

The attempts at further consolidation bore their fruit at the Rome meeting of the three heads-of-state in March, 1936, when supplementary protocols were adopted to the Rome agreements of 1934. In these, the already existing ties among the three states were reaffirmed and the need for even closer co-operation was acknowledged. The signatory powers expressed their determination not to negotiate with outside governments on any major Danubian political issue without consulting first with the other two members of the block. They also agreed upon the desirability of extending economic relations with other Danubian states but only on the basis

40

of bilateral agreements. Most important of all, the supplementary protocols provided for the creation of a permanent organ of consultation made up of the foreign ministers of the three countries. This body was to meet periodically when the three governments deemed it desirable.

The immediate advantages to Hungary of the Rome Protocols were significant. In the field of politics they strengthened Hungary's position *vis-à-vis* the Little Entente and particularly Yugoslavia, a fact which was especially appreciated during Marseille murders crisis about which more shall be said later. The economic provisions of the agreements probably had a lot to do with helping Hungarian agriculture out of the worst of the Depression. The Protocols also contributed to the prolongation of the life of an independent Austria,[15] a development generally welcomed by Hungarians who were not anxious to see a vast German empire on their borders.

The long range heritage of the Rome Protocols, however, does not seem to have been beneficial to Hungary, nor for that matter, to the cause of European peace.

The idea of the Rome bloc worked well as long as Italy was willing to put the weight of her influence against that of Germany in the Danube region. Once she declined to do so the Protocols were hardly worth the paper they were written on. The apparent success and prosperity of the Rome bloc in the first two years of its history, moreover, strengthened Mussolini's determination to embark on his Ethiopian campaign, a venture which did much to bring Europe closer to disaster. Lastly, the Protocols probably reinforced the crystallization of the states of the Danube region into two antagonistic camps. The fact that in the years 1934-1936 the various government in this area continued to buttress their security by offering their friendship to two different West European capitals, namely Paris and Rome, was not conducive to the emergence of a friendlier political atmosphere in the Danube Basin. In short, the Rome Protocols made Danubian co-operation less necessary and more difficult. In a sense, their real beneficiary was perhaps Germany, the country against which, in part, the Protocols were aimed in the first place.

2. Early Contacts with Nazi Germany.

Simultaneously with the establishment of friendly relations with Italy, Hungarian diplomacy sought closer contacts with Germany. Friendship with Berlin strengthened the position of Budapest *vis-à-vis* the countries of the Little Entente. It made the complete dependence on Italy unnecessary. Germany, moreover, had always been a natural outlet for Hungarian agricultural produce. The feeling of resentment against the entire Versailles system was shared by Hungarian and German politicians. Kanya, as has been mentioned, worked hard to improve relations with Germany during his assignment to Berlin from 1926 to 1933. Gombos was an admirer of the new order in the *Reich,* particularly its economic system. He had come to power with an economic programme based on a studious examination of the ideas and theories of Schacht.[16] The enthusiasm of Hungary's leaders for the idea of friendship and collaboration with Germany, however, was by no means unqualified. Horthy's dislike of Hitler, the Austrian ex-corporal, is well known.[17] Kanya got along reasonably well with his German counterpart Neurath; disaster came to the personal relations of the two countries' Foreign Ministers only with the coming to office of Ribbentrop. Even Gombos could not be blind to the danger of an overwhelmingly powerful German Empire.[18] "We knew the Germans well enough" writes Horthy in his memoirs "to be chary of too close a friendly embrace."[19] The Rohm purge of the night of June 30, 1934, and especially the murder of Dollfuss a month later, inevitably strengthened the suspicions of Hungary's leaders towards the Nazis.

Fear and distrust of the Germans was not the only major factor which retarded the establishment of close contact with Berlin, for Hungarian-German relations throughout the thirties were plagued by the problem of the German minority in Hungary.

As most countries in the Danube Basin, Hungary too, had a sizeable German minority. This was the result of migration of groups of agriculturalists or of individual townspeople from the various parts of the Germanic world into the Danube region in the historic past. Some of these newcomers had been assimilated by the local population. Others, however, had clung tenaciously to their ethnic heritage. The resurgence of German nationalism and the re-emergence of Germany's power on the international scene in the mid-1930's proved to be too much for some of these people to accept calmly and peacably.

The situation was further aggravated by the appearance in the German communities of visitors from the Reich, often disguised as students, tourists or researchers who, intoxicated by the spirit of the "new order" in Germany, spread the doctrines of National-Socialism and Pan-Germanism among the inhabitants.

The activities of the various organizations of the German ethnic groups were heavily subsidized by Berlin, often without the knowledge of the Hungarian authorities. The Budapest government periodically protested about the behaviour of these organizations to Berlin. These protests had partial success only. In August of 1933, soon after a visit of Prime Minister Gombos to Berlin, the German Government decided to inform the leaders of the German minority in Hungary that it was desirable that hostile relations should not develop between the German ethnic community and the Hungarian public and authorities.[20] The problem was not solved. The frictions continued. The secret payments of money continued to flow from Berlin even after August 1933. A Foreign Office memorandum, probably by a lesser official of the Wilhelmstrasse, years later still argued that for the sake of an atmosphere of confidence in German-Hungarian relations minority interest should be ensured through diplomatic channels and not by secret financial aid to agitators.[21]

If the minority problem was a considerable hindrance to the development of closer relations, the economic situation which prevailed in the Hungary of the early thirties was a strong enough factor in favour of friendship with Germany to override distrust generated by frictions between the ethnic Germans and Magyar officials of the country.

As has been mentioned, the impact of the Depression on Hungary's agricultural economy was particularly severe.[22]

The exports of food produce to Germany declined drastically during the early 1930's. The reason for this was the fact that Germany responded to the economic crisis by adopting very high protective tariffs.[23] As a result, Hungary exported, for example, only 9.3 per cent of her cereal crop to Germany in 1931, in contrast to 17.9 per cent four years earlier.[24]

As the Depression lingered on, there was a reaction in Germany to this policy on intense protectionism. The policy of restricting agricultural imports caused German business many hardships, consequently it became unpopular. Economists sought solution to the problem in the theory of the *Grossraumwirtschaft*. They advocated the development of extensive trade within a mid-European economic sphere composed of Germany and the countries of East Central Europe. These theories soon acquired political overtones. The "sphere" came to be talked of as the "German sphere" and its establishment was now justified by reference to the need to liberate the German economy from its dependence on other great powers, and the necessity to counterbalance French influence in the Danube Basin. It was the Nazis who seized upon these ideas with great alacrity. The theory of the *Grossraumwirtschaft* became a basic feature of the economic programme advocated by the German economist Hjalmar Schacht.[25]

Meanwhile, the agricultural sector of the Hungarian economy continued to suffer from the lack of sufficient outlets for its produce. The agrarian interests, who had very powerful lobbies in the government and Parliament, clamoured for the securing of markets. Gombos, who came to office on a Schachtian programme aimed at putting business back on its feet,[26] was anxious to prove that his new policies for combating depression were a success. As a result, Budapest put out feelers to Berlin in the winter of 1933-1934 inquiring about the possibilities of establishing closer economic ties.[27] These attempts came to success at the end of February 1934, when economic relations between the two countries were strengthened by a Supplementary Agreement to the already existing German-Hungarian Commercial Treaty, and the new Confidential Agreement on Promotion of German-Hungarian

Trade.[28] The provisions of these agreements probably did not meet the expectations of the government in Budapest, yet the news of the extension of the Treaty was received with great enthusiasm and approval by the agricultural and land-owning interests.[29]

Although at the time these agreements did not rival in importance those concluded at Rome a few weeks later, they served as a basis for later expansion of Hungarian economic relations with Germany. Trade between the two countries came to be co-ordinated by government committees. Trade quotas were steadily expanded in subsequent years.[30] Like Italy, Germany also paid higher than free-market prices for Hungarian produce, especially livestock.

Hungary's policy of developing close economic ties with Germany was motivated primarily by a desire to improve the country's economy. It was facilitated by a change in German trade policy from one of protectionism to one of seeking extensive commercial contacts with the countries of the Danube area. The fact that trade talks were conducted simultaneously with both Italy and Germany, makes it evident that Hungarian diplomacy tried to avoid becoming one-sidedly dependent upon either country in economic affairs. Here, the policy of trying to make the influence of the two Central European great powers cancel out is already evident. This policy was often to prevail in the realm of politics also.

While the problems of trade and, to a lesser extent, the minorities had a large part in Hungarian-German discussions during this period, often other issues, more closely connected with the international situation, also came under review. Usually these were the problems of Austrian-German relations, Hungarian revisionism and political affairs in the Danube region in general.

Diplomatic relations between Hungary and Nazi Germany began early in 1933. Gombos was first to congratulate Hitler on the latter's coming to power. In June he stunned the Hungarian public and his own foreign Minister by making a sudden visit to Berlin. Here he argued with the Germans for the expansion of mutual trade, an Austrian-German *rapprochement,* the improvement of economic co-operation among Germany, Italy, Austria, Hungary and later Rumania, and for preventing a Habsburg restoration in Austria.[31] The reasons for this trip, besides the economic ones, were probably the suspicion on the part of the Hungarians that Dollfuss, in his fear of *Anschluss*, might resort to drastic measures such as restoration, or worse, a *rapprochement* with the Little Entente. The former many Hungarians opposed, the latter all of them dreaded. Restoration in Austria would have caused political unrest in Hungary; while an understanding between the Little Entente and Austria would have completed her encirclement. It was because of such preoccupations that Gombos went to Berlin to counsel, not for the last time, better political understanding and closer economic ties between Austria and Germany.[32]

During 1934, the Austrian problem loomed large in German-Hungarian discussions. In May Horthy offered his personal services to Berlin to mediate between Austria and Germany and thus help to end the existing hostility between the two countries. The overture was rejected.[33] Horthy repeated his offer soon after Dollfuss' murder. He sent Kanya to Berlin as a special envoy to plead for an improvement in German-Austrian relations. Hitler did not seem to have been impressed.[34] By the end of the year Hungarian-German relations themselves became quite cool with little prospect for improvement.

During 1935, contacts, often shrouded in the greatest secrecy to the extent of bypassing diplomatic channels, were resumed. In May Hitler asked that Göring be received to discuss "what cannot be discussed in letters."[35] During the ensuing talks the German official seems to have urged the Hungarians not to direct their revisionist efforts against Yugoslavia but to try to work out a *modus vivendi* with that country. This advice was well taken by Gombos in particular; on the occasion of his next visit to Berlin he talked of Hungarian revisionist claims being least weighty in the south, and of detaching Yugoslavia from the Little Entente thereby improving the chances of revision in other directions.[36] Upon his return from the German capital, he informed his cabinet that Hitler had told him that Germany was seeking good relations with Italy and Britain, wanted a Hungarian-Yugo-slav detente and was determined to solve the Sudeten prob-lem.[37] The latter issue, among others, came up for discussion at an informal but lengthy discussion of German and Hun-garian staff officers in May of next year. Here mutual pro-mises were exchanged for co-operation in propaganda and "other fields" against the Prague government's policies of a Russian alliance and stepped-up internal military security.[38] The Czechoslovak question was to come up again and again in talks with the Germans after the summer of that year. By that time, however, Gombos, because of his failing health, was no longer associated with the making of foreign policy.

Relations between Hungary and Nazi Germany during the Gombos era were on the whole cordial. Some issues, like the question of mutual trade, were resolved to the advantage of both countries, or at least so it seemed at the time. Others, foremost among them the minority problem, continued to be an obstacle to the creation of a friendlier atmosphere. Better relations between Vienna and Berlin, so insistently advocated by Budapest, failed to materialize. Hungary's policy of op-posing *Anschluss,* therefore, was a failure. Of course, *An-schluss* did not take place yet, but that was certainly not the achievement of Hungarian diplomacy. Some vague statements were dropped now and then about the cause of Hungarian revisionism, but no commitments amounting to importance were made by either side. In fact, in spite of all these con-tacts with Germany, the policies of the Gombos era toward Berlin were those of friendship but non-commitment.[39]

Indeed the aim of Hungarian foreign policy under Premier Gombos was not direct alignment with Nazi Germany. Rather, the chief aspiration of the country's policymakers was to attain a balance of power situation in Central Europe favour-able to Hungarian interests. To attain their goals they sought, at first, to bring in the economic and political weight of Germany to counterbalance Italian influence in the Danubian basin. Later, when the rapid growth of German might threat-ened to upset the Central European balance of power, Hun-gary's leaders strove to strengthen their ties with their Rome bloc partners. Through this, and through their attempts at mediating between Vienna and Berlin, they hoped to head off a German annexation of Austria, an event which would have exposed Hungary to the danger of expansion of Nazi influence and power into the Danube Valley.

This policy of cultivating the friendship of Italy and Germany, and at the same time making their influence cancel out in the Danubian realm, offered definite benefits to Hungary. It ended the country's diplomatic isolation and strengthened its position with respect to the states of the Little Entente. It ensured a much needed market for her grain and other agricultural produce. It did all this seemingly without necessitating the alignment of her foreign policy to that of a single great power and thereby incurring the loss of her freedom of action.

This apparently ingenious policy, however, also carried grave risks. Association with fascist Italy and Nazi Germany was bound to strengthen the influence of extreme rightist ideas in Hungary. There was an even greater threat: the possibility that one day one of these great powers would find itself in a position in which it was no longer able or willing to assert its influence in the Danube region, and the country would find itself dangerously exposed, and dependent on the other. Judging from a vantage point of hindsight this peril was very real indeed. This was evident only to a few contemporaries. The author of a German foreign policy memorandum dating from this period ventured to forecast that with Italy engaged elsewhere, and Hungary increasingly dependent on armaments from Germany ,she would have to look to Berlin for support.[40]

In view of the risks and dangers which were implicit in Gombos' foreign policy, it is not surprising to find that the country's participation in the Rome bloc, coupled with its cultivation of Germany's friendship, created as many new problems as it solved. Fate, however, had prevented Gombos from having to tackle these problems. The task of reaping the rather bitter harvest of the General's political activities fell to others.

3. The Threat of Austria's Annexation and Other Problems.

By the summer of 1936 Gombos was very ill. Some groups were already voicing the view that the General should hand over power to someone else. Horthy, who by this time had developed a dislike for the Prime Minister's political behaviour, asked Gombos to resign. Although the latter refused to do this,[41] effective power slipped from his hands after he agreed to enter hospital. Early in October he died. "His death," writes the contemporary American Minister to Hungary, seemed "no cause for regret"; most responsible people "from the Regent down" were "relieved".[42] Others, especially Gombos' political followers, undoubtedly regretted the premature passing of this "Hungarian aspirant to Führerdom".[43]

Gombos was succeeded by Kalman Daranyi, a landowner, agrarian expert, and a much less colourful and less assertive personality than his predecessor. Kanya retained his post of Minister of External Affairs in the new cabinet. The Daranyi administration shouldered the task of formulating the country's internal and external policies amidst mounting difficulties.

One of the problems of the period was primarily internal in nature. The eighteen months of the Daranyi administration witnessed the growth and proliferation of extreme rightist groups and organizations in the country. Although this development was already noticeable in the Gombos era, especially in some ethnic German communities, it was the strength of the movement which was new after 1936 .The reasons behind this turn of events are far too complex to be analyzed here in detail. Suffice it to say, that probably all of these groups were German inspired. Some of them, particularly those among the German minority population, were actively supported from Germany. Others thrived on the example of Nazi success and strength, which was in great contrast to the cautious and less energetic politics of Hungary. All of them cashed in on latent sentiments of anti-Semitism, and on dissatisfaction with the prevailing "semi-feudal" conditions in the country. The cry against exploitation by the landed aristocrats and Jewish capitalists netted many followers for these groups. The desire for social betterment and land reform were harnessed to the advantage of rightist extremism.

Although the situation was not nearly as bad as in neighbouring Austria, the government was somewhat alarmed. The matter, however, was handled in a dilettantish manner. Outright Nazi organizations with German emblems were abolished. Reluctant to make martyrs out of the chief figures of the movement, however, the government refused to put these men permanently behind bars. The resulting half-way measures, temporary imprisonment of leaders, closing down of some subversive publications, and so on, probably helped the movement more than harmed it.[44]

New problems emerged in the realm of economics, namely in the field of commercial relations with Italy and Germany. Although the two cases were very much different, there was one common aspect about the tensions of trade with these two "friendly" great powers. The problem in each case was not too little trade but too much of it.

During 1936 the volume of Hungarian as well as Austrian exports to Italy increased over that of previous years. Due to the dislocations in the Italian economy caused by the Ethiopian affair, Italian exports of industrial products to her Rome bloc partners lagged behind. Italy became more and more indebted to Austria and Hungary. Repayment became increasingly difficult, and Italy showed little interest in solving these difficulties.[45] Much to the disappointment of the Viennese and Budapest governments, in August, 1937, Italy abandoned the preferential exchange system which thus far regulated the three countries' trade relations.[46] This loosening of the economic ties among the Rome Protocol states inevitably involved the political weakening of the bloc.

In the same period Hungary's trade with Germany also expanded. From both the political and economic viewpoint this development was unhealthy. According to the German-Hungarian commercial agrrements of 1931 and 1934, Germany was to pay for her imports of Hungarian foodstuffs and raw materials in kind. Consequently, Hungary could export only if she was willing to accept almost anything the Germans were willing to offer.[47] As a result of the expansion of mutual trade, moreover, the country's external commerce became increasingly onesided, increasingly dependent on the policies of the Berlin government. The Germans soon acquired a position in which they were able to exercise influence "even with regard to the kind of new industries that were to be established in Hungary."[48] Thus, the economic agreements which in the first half of the thirties helped Hungary to escape the worst of the Depression, gradually, and to most contemporaries imperceptibly, led to a situation in which the nation's economic and political independence became increasingly impaired.

The most serious problems of the Daranyi government, however, were not internal affairs, not even the realm of foreign trade, but the international situation which prevailed in Europe at the time. There were several developments in 1936 which considerably affected the balance of power in Central Europe. Hitler's reoccupation of the Rhineland in March of that year strengthened Germany's military and political position. Although the signing of the supplementary Rome Protocols a few weeks later by Italy, Austria and Hungary, and the Austro-German agreement in July might have seemed at the time to have neutralized Germany's gains, by the end of the year the factors which could have prevented the tipping of the balance in Germany's favour began to lack. The chief reason for this was the increasing disinterest of Italy's leaders in the affairs of the Middle Danube region. Before his Ethiopian campaign Mussolini still protested his intention to bring back his army to the Brenner within a year.[49] The Abyssinian affair, however, split the Stresa front.[50] With the outbreak of the Spanish civil war in the summer of 1936, Mussolini found more dramatic use of his troops than the vigil on the Brenner. And, on October 15, just a few days after the formation of the Daranyi government, the Rome-Berlin axis officially came into existence.

If these developments caused some doubts in the minds of Hungary's leaders about Italy's readiness to put her full weight into the scales to preserve the Central European balance of power *vis-á-vis* Germany, the attitudes of some German and Italian politicians to this problem should have caused further alarm in Budapest. The day after Gombos' funeral, Göring, in a conversation with Kanya, asserted that *Anschluss* would have to come one day, although Germany had no plans for Austria's annexation in the near future.[51]

The Hungarian Foreign Office was also aware of the Italian leaders' increasing disappointment with Austria. It was known, for example, that Mussolini had been outraged by the hostility which the Italian National "all-stars" were accorded at a soccer match in Vienna during Easter of 1937.[52] On a visit to Budapest some weeks later, Ciano, the Italian Foreign Minister, told Kanya that *Anschluss* had to come. Italy would make efforts to delay Austria's annexation, but she would "not move her armaments again."[53]

In the Gombos era the threat of the expansion of German influence to the southeast was combated by the triple policy of proffers of friendship to Berlin, attempts at minimizing Austro-German friction and most important of all, alignment with Italy and Austria in the Rome bloc. In view of the changed international atmosphere and situation of 1936 it was doubtful that these policies would serve their purpose in the coming years. It was unlikely that the ever more daring Nazi leaders would listen to Hungarian appeals for moderation in Austro-German relations. Moreover, as a result of the evolving Italian attitude to the Danube area, the effectiveness of the Rome Protocols as an instrument to contain German aggrandizement probably greatly declined. If Hungary was to escape the adverse economic[54] and political effects of *Anschluss,* if she was to avoid the emergence of a situation in which she was the immediate neighbour of a German empire not effectively counterbalanced by some kind of an international alignment, if she was to retain at least some freedom of action, her leaders had to find more effective policies for the containment of German power than those of the Gombos government. Either new life had to be put into the old Rome front, or an alternative solution had to be found for the buttressing the country's position *vis-à-vis* Germany.

There were many proposals regarding the ways and means of containing the Nazi tide. At home politicians, soldiers, civil servants advocated various solutions. From abroad advice came from all quarters of Europe: Vienna, Prague, and even distant Moscow and London were anxious to give counsel. Of the alternatives suggested to the policies of the Gombos era, three deserve attention. In brief, one was the idea of strengthening Austria's ability to resist German pressure through helping that country to restore the Habsburgs; the other was the creation of some sort of a Danubian bloc; the third was a Czech-Austrian-Hungarian alignment. All of these were essentially Danubian solutions envisaging political change in the Danube Basin designed primarily to forestall the undue growth of German influence in this part of Europe. No such solution ever materialized. Some of the plans for resisting the Nazi onslaught by changes in the political set-up of the Danube Basin were much too idealistic. Others could not be realized because of that atmosphere of mutual distrust which prevailed in the diplomatic relations among the countries of the Danube Valley.

Before turning, however, to the story of the attempts at a Danubian solution and that of Hungary's relations with her immediate neighbours in general, one incident, which had momentous influence on the diplomatic history of the Danube countries in this period, will have to be examined. This incident was the international crisis which followed the murder of the Yugoslav king at Marseille in 1934.

PART III

THE SEARCH FOR A DANUBIAN SOLUTION

1. The Marseille Affair

On October 9, 1934, King Alexander of Yugoslavia and Barthou the French Foreign Minister were assassinated during their visit to Marseille. The incident set off an international crisis which had a lasting effect on relations among the states of the Danube region.

Soon after the murders it became known that the terrorist organization responsible for the crime had had contacts with Hungarian authorities in its past. Although the Italian Government probably had an even more direct complicity in the case,[1] and this might have been suspected at the time, out of consideration for the fragile nature of Italian-French relations the blame was directed against Hungary. The excitement in Yugoslavia ran particularly high. Public opinion, especially in Serbia, demanded satisfaction, and the Chetniks, Serbian military irregulars, clamoured and prepared for armed retaliation against Hungary. Leading circles in the Little Entente countries and France realized that it was advisable to satisfy the excitement caused by the crime. They also hoped to destroy the international standing of the Hungarian Government.[2] Yugoslavia brought the matter before the Council of the League of Nations, accusing Hungary of having violated the League Covenant by training terrorists for political purposes. At the same time she expelled thousands of her Hungarian residents.[3]

The truth was that revisionists in Hungary, among them some government officials and army officers, at the time still believed that the best chance for a change in the Trianon status quo was in the South. Suspecting that Mussolini was working for the disintegration of Yugoslavia, they maintained contacts with members of the Ustasi, a terrorist society of Croatian separatists. The government itself did in fact finance separatist agitation in Croatia, through its relationship to the Ustasi group itself is not clear. The press of the times was also vociferously anti-Yugoslav. The most controversial action of the Hungarian authorities in connection with these activities was the establishment of a camp for Croatian political refugees at Jankapuszta in southwestern Hungary. The Budapest government maintained that this was a place set aside for men who fled Yugoslav persecution and had no means yet for supporting themselves in Hungary.[4] The Yugoslavs asserted, and in vain attempted to prove, that the camp was a training-ground for political terrorists.[5] The truth probably lies somewhere in the middle. Jankapuszta did become a meeting place for the members of the Ustasi and other anti-Serb activists. It is unlikely, however, that the Hungarian Government was aware of the nature of their plans. Moreover, the leading figures of the Marseille conspiracy had not been to Hungary and the plot itself was not hatched at Jankapuszta in the first place.

All the same, the Hungarian Government found itself deeply involved in an international dispute. Rumania and Czechoslovakia became co-sponsors of the Yugoslav resolution. Germany left Gombos and his friends in the lurch and used the occasion to woo Yugoslavia. Arriving for Alexander's funeral, Göring made some public comments against Hungary's revisionist foreign policy,[6] and had lengthy discussions with the Yugoslav leaders. Only Italy and Austria sided with Hungary in the dispute.

In Hungary the situation was regarded as extremely grave. In a memorandum to Horthy by one of his advisers argued that it might be necessary to appease the excited international sentiment by sacraficing Gombos and Kanya upon whom the attacks were concentrated. The author of the memorandum suggested that lest the public at home should resent the making of such concessions to the enemy, an excuse was needed to form a purely internal crisis. The government could sponsor, for example, a democratic reform of the elections act, which would arouse opposition within the government party and would end in the defeat of the Gombos administration in Parliament.[7] He advised further that for the sake of the friendship with Italy the blame must not be shifted on her. The memorandum ended in a pessimistic tone. Its author saw little chance of escape from economic blockade by the Little Entente, and the further deterioration of the country's currency. Germany, he argued, would further its *Anschluss* policy by supporting Yugoslavia in the crisis.[8]

The quarrel, however, was resolved without a resort to arms, sanctions or other drastic measures. In this the attitude of the great powers played a considerable role. Laval, the new French Foreign Minister, wanted no conflict between the Rome Protocol group and the Paris-Little Entente alignment. For he, unlike his predecessor Barthou, saw French security not in an alliance with the Soviet Union, but in friendship with Italy and a *modus vivendi* with Germany.[9] For this reason he counselled moderation in Belgrade. He was anxious, however, to satisfy public opinion and to see the weakening of Italy's Danubian partners. He hoped that a diminishing of Italy's power along the Danube would tend to increase the chances of closer co-operation between Paris and Rome.[10] For these reasons he was ready to support Yugoslav demands on Hungary, as long as these were sufficiently moderate not to offend Mussolini.

Eden, who was at the helm in the British Foreign Office at the time, was also anxious to prevail upon Belgrade to ease the pressure on Hungary.[11] He wanted the balance between the Paris and the Rome group of states to remain undisturbed. In fact, it was his compromise formula which was accepted in the League Council on the tenth of December. This resolution rather vaguely asserted that "certain Hungarian authorities may have assumed, at any rate through negligence, certain responsibilities relative to acts having a connection with the preparation of the crime of Marseille." It also requested the Government of Hungary to punish those involved in the affair.[12]

It may seem that the Hungarian political leadership escaped the crisis without heavy losses after all. Yet this would be a false impression. Aside from the war-scare, the financial side-effects, the sufferings of the Hungarians temporarily driven away from their homes by the Yugoslavs, and the tensions in Budapest's relation with Berlin, the affair had other unfortunate repercussions. Hungarian aspirations for peaceful revision of the Trianon arrangements had little if any chance of fulfillment after such a crisis. Peaceful revision, if it ever had a chance, could only have come about if peace and the feeling of security prevailed in the Danube region, and if the great powers of Europe were sympathetic toward the idea. Now, at the end of 1934, these conditions seemed more remote than ever. The "affair", wrote the author of the memorandum to Horthy, "incredibly damaged our revisionist aspirations . . .," and it discredited Hungary with the great powers. "Great efforts" only, he continued, can restore a "peaceful atmosphere."[13] Indeed, the affair reduced the chances of a timely and reasonable settlement of issues between Hungary and the countries of the Little Entente which could have cleared the way for a Danubian solution to the threat posed by the rising power of Nazi Germany.

2. Restoration instead of Anschluss?

The plans for Habsburg restoration in Austria, and later possibly even in Hungary, had as their ultimate goal the prevention of German expansion along the Danube. Although restoration of the Habsburgs might at first sight appear to have been a strictly Austrian issue, it was really a problem affecting all the small countries of the Danube Basin. Its attainment was impossible without the consent, or at least the acquiescence of the governments of the succession states, particularly those of Yugoslavia and Czechoslovakia. Thus the restoration issue became an all-Danubian problem, even though Austria remained the focal point of the controversy.

During the 1930's it was widely accepted both in Austria and elsewhere in Europe that the ultimate fate of that young republic would be either union with Germany or a return to a monarchical form of government probably under Habsburg aegis.[14] Indeed, throughout this period, legitimism, as the movement working for restoration was called, was strong in Austria. Periodically plans and plots for the re-establishment of Habsburg power were rumoured to be in the making. In part the idea of restoration was plain traditionalism, a romantic attachment to the glories of an age bygone. The dynamic force behind legitimism, however, was the desire to keep Austria out of Hitler's reach. "The hatred of Germans," wrote a Hungarian agent from Vienna in a report to the Foreign Office, "is driving together the priests, Jews, Reds and Legitimists."[15] Schuschnigg himself had been reported to have said during 1937 that "legitimism is the best defence against Nazism."[16] At one time, Austrian legitimist organizations could boast of 1,300,000 members. Many municipalities elected Otto Habsburg, the claimant to the throne, to honorary posts in their city governments.[17] Some public figures, like Mayor Schmitz of Vienna, openly advocated restoration.[18] The officer corps of the country was also strongly legitimist in outlook.[19] The majority of Austria's population, however, seems to have been opposed to the idea, or at least remained neutral on this issue, and the younger generation everywhere and even the older groups in some provinces were against restoration.[20]

The Austrian Government, recognizing the dangers implicit in restoration, probably did not seriously contemplate such action. In spite of this, Schuschnigg often made ambiguous statements on the subject.[21] It seems that the Austrian leader chose to keep legitimist sentiments alive to offer his people an alternative to the Nazi idea.

Austria's neighbours adopted various attitudes to the prospect of restoration in Vienna. Neurath is said to have told Schuschnigg that it was "unbearable" for Germany to see Austria re-establish the monarchy.[22] Göring, too, informed the Yugoslavs that restoration in Austria would be a *casus belli*; would mean the "end of Austria."[23] Yugoslavia seems to have been opposed to the re-appearance of the Habsburgs in Vienna even more desperately than officials in Germany. Regent Paul, the country's ruler, was known to have been ready to take military action in case of restoration.[24] In the council of the Little Entente too, it was the Yugoslav Government which urged the toughest line concerning this matter.[25] This attitude was the result of Belgrade's fear of pro-Habsburg Croatian separatism. "Yugoslavia knows," wrote von Papen at the time, "that the Croats long only for the moment of a restoration."[26]

The Czech opposition to Habsburg restoration was not as clear-cut and outspoken as either the German or the Yugoslav. In 1935 Schuschnigg asked the Prague government to promise not to oppose restoration in Austria, in case it became necessary to reinforce that country's independence by such a step. His overture was not accepted at the time.[27] During the following years, however, Prague, out of consideration for Vienna's good will, ceased to voice its opposition to restoration. Indeed, at the time of Hodza's visit to Vienna in the spring of 1937, it was rumoured that the Czech Prime Minister himself had secretly proposed the creation of a triple-monarchy of Austria-Czechoslovakia-Hungary under Habsburg aegis.[28] Although this was most likely nothing but a rumour, had the Czech statesman been sure that restoration could save Vienna and Prague from Hitler's rule, in all probability, he would have accepted the idea.[29] By that time, however, it must have been obvious in Prague also that the ascent of Otto to the throne would have been too much of a provocation to Nazi Germany.

The issue of Habsburg restoration in Austria had deep repercussions on Hungarian politics also. It must be kept in mind that Hungary at the time was a kingdom without a king, and many of her citizens regarded this situation as temporary. The supporters of a monarchical form of government in Hungary, however, were divided into two camps. One group supported the Habsburg claim to the throne, the other proposed that the country choose its king according to its own wishes. The proponents of the latter view were called the Free Electors. The division between the two camps was historic, dating back at least to the seventeenth century when Magyar magnates led a futile struggle of national liberation against the House of Habsburg and its Hungarian supporters. In the 1930's Free Elector sentiment predominated in the most influential circles of the country. Gombos had been an outspoken opponent of Habsburg restoration. The Regent, in spite of his attachment to the late emperor-king Francis Joseph, was a Free Elector. His personal interest also dictated against Habsburg restoration. In October 1933 in a speech Horthy defended the idea of not having a king in the Kingdom of Hungary, and reminded the nation that restoration was *casus belli.*[30]

As the years passed and the threat of Nazism grew, opinions changed in many quarters in Hungary. In October 1937, Hungarian legitimists, favouring eventual restoration in Austria and in Hungary, met at a great rally in Körmend. Many notable public figures, including Eckhardt, a former Free Elector, appeared at the rally.[31] At about the same time, the leader of the Hungarian Social-Democratic movement declared in a press statement that if it came to a choice, Hungarian socialists would sooner accept a constitutional monarchy than a dictatorship.[32]

The Hungarian Government, however, did not change its views, not even with regard to restoration in Austria. The explanation for this continued opposition might be found in the complex circumstances which surrounded the issue. Early in 1937, a secret report prepared by the Hungarian security service on legitimist activities in Hungary and Austria noted that pro-German elements, and even persons in the service of Germany had recently infiltrated some of the Austrian legitimist organizations. The author of the report concluded that Berlin might be planning to create a German satellite out of Austria under the nominal rule of Otto.[33]

Some Hungarian leaders, however, could have easily deducted from these developments that Berlin was not after restoration under German aegis, but probably wanted to promote restoration in order to use it as a pretext for intervention in Austria. This is perhaps why German agents, at one time at least, joined the legitimist movement. In either case, restoration was undesirable and dangerous. It is no wonder then that in February of 1937 Gabor Apor, the permanent secretary of the Foreign Office, asked Ciano to advise Chancellor Schuschnigg against restoration.[34] Hungarian policymakers realized that the return of the Habsburgs to the Austrian throne might result in unfortunate consequences, therefore they rejected this idea as one that would surely fail to prevent *Anschluss* and to stem the spread of Nazi influence along the Danube.

3. *Danubian Co-operation?*

Ever since the disintegration of the Dual Monarchy, plans were frequently brought forth to re-create at least a semblance of economic and political unity in the Danube region. The appearance of the threat of Nazi expansion tended to reinforce the belief in the need for stronger co-operation among the nations of this area.

The first major scheme of this nature to make its appearance on the international scene in the 1930's actually pre-dated the emergence of Nazi power in Germany. It was the *"Plan Tardieu"* of 1932. The plan called for the creation of an economic bloc in the Danube area composed of Austria, Hungary and the countries of the Little Entente. The Tardieu plan was to be based on mutual preferential tariffs, the abolition of import and export prohibitions and exchange restrictions, and on French financial assistance and loans. Suspecting the plan of being an instrument of French interests, Germany and Italy opposed the scheme. Nor could the French and British governments come to an agreement on how to improve the plan. The whole affair came to a premature end.[35]

Next came attempts at strengthening political stability in the area. These were the plans for a Danubian Pact advocated by the French Government throughout most of 1935. The essence of the Pact would have been that the signatories would have promised to refrain from attacking each other and from supporting the aggressor in a conflict. There were to be provisions for consultation and peaceful settlement of issues.[36]

The proposed pact was received in Budapest with suspicion. Kanya, in a statement to the Foreign Affairs Committee of Parliament early in 1936, stated his conditions for accepting the scheme. A future pact, expressed the Hungarian Foreign

Minister, should allow for the possibility of peaceful evolution in the Danube area, should consider the interest of the Hungarian minorities, and should contain no provision for mutual assistance. Above all, Hungary must be accepted as an "equal partner" at the discussions.[37] These conditions were probably more than what some of the other would-be signatories of the pact were willing to grant Hungary. All in all, efforts at the creation of the Danube Pact seem to have been dropped in 1936.

A great advocate of Danubian co-operation and the originator of several schemes for closer Danubian collaboration was Milan Hodza, the Czechoslovak politician.[38] He outlined the first "Hodza plan" to an Austrian newspaper, the *Neue Freie Presse* in December of 1934. The essential idea behind the plan was an economic *rapprochement* between Austria, Hungary and the Little Entente.[39] At the end of 1935 Hodza became Prime Minister of Czechoslovakia and began to work earnestly for the realization of his ideas. In January 1936 he launched his campaign for a "new Central Europe." Some of the basic features of the plan called for gradual diminution and eventual abolition of tariffs, a lowering and ending of trade restrictions, co-ordination of production and marketing in the area, improvement of communications, simplification of monetary transactions and the establishment of an Agricultural Bureau, in Vienna. The ultimate aim was a customs or even economic union.[40]

The international reaction to the Hodza plan was greatly varied. Both Germany and Italy opposed the scheme from the beginning.[41] The Yugoslavs, possibly fearing that an Austrian-Czech-Hungarian *rapprochement* might lead to restoration, at first opposed the idea, but on French pressure changed their views. They still insisted that any such bloc should not be anti-German.[42] Poland was also unfavourably disposed to the efforts of the Czechoslovak Prime Minister.[43] There was also economic opposition to the idea throughout the entire area. Hungarian and Austrian manufacturing firms, fearing the competition of the advanced and efficient Czech industries, and Czech and Slovak graingrowers, worried about the opening of their markets to Hungarian produce, put up an opposition to the plan which transcended international boundaries.[44]

Hodza's schemes, nevertheless, also found some support at the international level. Eden personally intervened to impress upon the Hungarian Government how anxious he was to see better relations between Hungary and the Little Entente. Lest it might damage British-Italian relations, however, Eden refused to play the role of the mediator.[45] But the greatest enthusiasm for the plan was shown by the Austrian leader Schuschnigg. It was toward the end of 1937 that he, on his visit to Budapest in October, urged reconciliation with the Little Entente and praised Hodza.[46]

The initial reaction of the Gombos government to the Hodza proposals of early 1936 was cool to say the least. The issue was dicussed between the Austrian and Hungarian political leaders at a meeting in Budapest in March.[47] Kanya expressed the view that the idea of political *rapprochement* with the Little Entente was premature, except perhaps in the case of Yugoslavia. He stressed that there should be no political agreement with Czechoslovakia. Calling attention to the official German viewpoint he concluded that neither the Tardieu plan, nor the idea of linking the Rome and Little Entente economic blocs, had the least chance. The Rome Protocol countries must beware of any Danubian alignments and they must avoid any measures which might appear to be anti-German. Kanya voiced no opposition to increased economic co-operation in the Danube region, but remarked that in his view this was possible only on the basis of bilateral agreements.[48]

The Hungarian policymakers' response to the idea of Danubian co-operation, or *rapprochement* with the Little Entente was, in spite of all this, far from being entirely negative. In October Kanya told the Parliamentary Committee on Foreign Affairs that he would place no obstacles in the path of economic and perhaps in future times even political co-operation among the Danube countries.[49] Although in view of the Foreign Minister's statement to Schuschnigg in March about political agreement with Prague, this declaration was not sincere; the Hungarian Government kept the door open to negotiations for a settlement with the Little Entente. It even showed readiness for an agreement, provided the price was right. The price for which Budapest was willing to step on the path of far-reaching political reconciliation with the capitals of the neighbouring countries seems to have been beyond what the latter were willing to offer.

Throughout 1936 and 1937 the Hungarian Government's conditions for coming to terms with the Little Entente were made public in declarations by Kanya and Daranyi, the new Prime Minister. After the spring of 1936, Kanya insisted that the recognition of Hungary's equal rights to armaments was a precondition to any negotiations with the Little Entente.[50] To dispel the possible suspicions of Berlin and Rome, he emphasized that a solution which might be arrived at must not be injurious to the interests of "our Friends".[51] In a speech at Szeged on April 17, 1937, Daranyi added one more demand to the list. In declaring Hungary's readiness to come to terms with the Little Entente "on the basis of complete equality of rights," he stated that in any agreement the "protection of Hungarian minorities must be legally guaranteed."[52]

On the Little Entente side different ideas prevailed. The diplomats in Prague, Belgrade and Bucharest were willing to concede to Hungary the principle of equality of rights in armaments, but not without asking them in return that a "strictly defined guarantee of security chould be offered" to them by the Hungarian Government.[53] To Kanya such a "cheap" bargain held no attraction. He wanted to use the offer of non-aggression to exact a higher price, a formal guarantee of the rights of the Hungarian minorities.

Negotiations between the two sides reached a peak during August and September of 1937. They took place at Sinaia, where Hungary was invited to send an observer to the Conference of the Little Entente states, and subsequently at Geneva. In the course of the discussions various proposals and counterproposals were exchanged. The Hungarian Government offered to make a declaration of no resort to force in its relations with the Little Entente in return for the acknowledgement of its equal rights to armaments and a promise from the other side of improvement in the position of Hungarian minorities.[54] The governments of the Little Entente, however, showed the greatest reluctance to have the minority issue included in any agreement. Antonescu, the Rumanian Foreign Minister, argued that the Rumanian public did not permit him to adopt far-reaching commitments with regard to Hungarian minorities in his country. Kanya argued back that in view of public opinion in Hungary he could not accept an agreement which did not contain a statement on the minority problem.[55] And thus the discussions were protracted without positive results. The situation was made worse by an occasional lack of understanding within the ranks of the Little Entente itself.[56] In the end it was the rock of the minority question on which the negotiations finally broke.[57] And this issue was still the bone of contention six months later when the discussions were resumed in earnest.

Viewed from a historic distance it seems that during the late summer of 1937 the international atmosphere in the Danube region was favourable to a general *rapprochement*. Hungary's leaders desired a normalization of their country's relations with its neighbours. The heads of the Little Entente states, Hodza, Tatarescu, and Stojadinovic agreed on the desirability of closer collaboration with Hungary.[58] Yet the opportunity slipped by without the countries of the Danube Valley improving their mutual relations. Soon there was an election crisis followed by a change of government in Rumania. As a result, according to Hodza, the idea of "Hungarian *rapprochement* was dropped in Little Entente councils."[59] Although the Goga regime did not last long in Rumania, and *Anschluss* gave stimulus to new negotiations, with Austria gone and Czechoslovakia threatened, the opportunity missed in 1937 was not to return in 1938.

It would be a mistake, however, to attribute too much significance to the failure of the negotiations of August and September 1937. Although the atmosphere surrounding the discussions of Sinaia and Geneva was favourable to a settlement of issues, there was never at this time a chance for a far-reaching agreement between Hungary and the Little Entente. Suspicions on both sides were too great to be bridged abruptly and permanently. Most Hungarian leaders had no desire to go beyond a normalization of relations. Only a few of them accepted the type of solution advocated by Hodza.[60]

4. The Vienna-Prague-Budapest Triangle?

From early 1936 up until the eve of *Anschluss* frequent suggestions were made, in international circles of Central Europe concerned with the threat of expanding German influence, of some form of alignment among Austria, Czechoslovakia and Hungary. These schemes were different from the plans for Danubian unity only in that they left outside, temporarily at least, the countries less directly threatened by the German danger. Suggestions for such a solution came from very much the same quarters as the ones for all-Danubian co-operation, namely from the Czech, Austrian and French governments.[61]

The first serious feeler came from Benes, the Czechoslovak President, in September of 1936. Benes had a discussion with Janos Eszterhazy, the leader of the United Hungarian Party in Czechoslovakia. The Czech President informed Eszterhazy that Prague was ready for serious discussions with Budapest provided the latter made no excessive preconditions. He warned that the Hungarians could not expect the annulment of the 1919 treaties, after all no one could expect "me to erase my lifetime's work." He offered to drop the "Soviet link" of his foreign policy in case of a successful *rapprochement* with Hungary and Poland. To show his good intentions he promised to redress the complaints of the Hungarian minority in Czechoslovakia and offered a cabinet post to Eszterhazy. He also disclosed that Hodza had already contacted Eckhardt, the leader of the opposition in Hungary, about these matters.[62]

The interview, which Eszterhazy described to the authorities in Budapest in great detail, was followed during the next few months by similar, though less extensive overtures through regular diplomatic channels. Kanya's response was cold. He pointed out that a Czech agreement with Hungary was incompatible with the spirit of the Little Entente.[63] The whole affair seems to have come to an impasse with a stormy interview between Kanya and the Czech Minister to Hungary in February of 1937, when the two men accused each other of harbouring evil plans against their respective countries.[64] For the rest of the year, it seems, the Czechs insisted that Hungary negotiate with the Little Entente as a whole.

Early in 1938, however, the Prague government renewed its efforts to reach an understanding with Budapest. In February it informed the Hungarian Government that in view of the political crisis in Rumania and the resulting slowdown in the discussions between Hungary and the Little Entente, the Czech Government would be ready to improve relations with Hungary on a bilateral basis.[65] Probably as a response to this new feeler, the Hungarian Government sent a special envoy to Prague for discussions. In the course of the ensuing talks Benes told the Hungarian envoy that the Vienna-Prague-Budapest triangle, supported by the Western great powers was the best assurance against Germany. He expressed his hope for better relations with Hungary and promised to terminate the situation which emerged in 1930 when Czechoslovakia closed most of her markets to Hungarian produce. Benes, as well as Hodza and Krofta, however, stated that there could be no territorial concessions to Hungary at that time, that the minority problem must not be subject to an international agreement and that Prague would continue to adhere to the Little Entente alliance.[66] It is ironic that the report on this latest overture for the "triangle" arrived in Budapest on March 12, at a time when the German army was marching toward Vienna.

The idea of the "triangle" and *rapprochement* with Prague did have at least a few adherents in Hungary. The most notable of these were Endre Bajcsy-Zsilinszky, a politician and later a leader of the resistance movement against the Germans, and Echkardt, the opposition leader whom the Czechs allegedly contacted already in 1936.[67] "The security" wrote Eckhardt in his recollections, "of all the Danubian and Balkan States was built upon the power of resistance of the triangle, Vienna-Prague-Budapest. Should any of these three pillars crumble, the rest were bound to go down with it."[68]

Official Hungarian reaction to the idea, however, was different. Not that the idea was unfamiliar to Kanya. In fact, at the time of the Marseille crisis when a German-Yugoslav alignment seemed to be in the making, the Hungarian Foreign Minister threatened Berlin with the creation of an Austrian-Czechoslovak-Hungarian bloc if Germany ever decided to drop Hungary in favour of Yugoslavia.[69] Kanya, however, never considered this idea seriously. He informed the Austrian Government about this and even voiced his opposition to the idea of *rapprochement* between Vienna and Prague.[70] In a speech given after *Anschluss* he referred to this scheme of saving Austria as a "naive illusion."[71]

Kanya, and no doubt the other Hungarian policymakers as well, realized that such an alignment would have been undesirable and dangerous. It would have been inconsistent with the revisionist sentiments of the citizenry. The obvious unpopularity of such a policy in many quarters could have been exploited by rightist groups to the disadvantage of the government. More important still, the idea of linking the country's fate to that of Austria and Czechoslovakia, states which were doomed to destruction by Germany's leaders, was alien to the mind of a political realist like Kanya. The Foreign Minister realized that Hungary could not afford to incur the animosity of the German Government. He probably believed that is was easier to retain some independence in Hungarian foreign policy with a Germany that considered Hungary a friend than with one which regarded Hungary as one of her enemies. Therefore, if the Hungarian Government's freedom of action in its foreign relations was to be safeguarded from the effects of the emergence of an all-powerful Germany on the European scene, some means had to be found which did not run the risk of bringing upon the government and country the suspicion and wrath of the leaders in Berlin. Obviously the schemes aimed at restoration, a Danubian bloc, and an Austrian-Czechoslovak-Hungarian alignment were not suitable answers to the question how to preserve the policy of the "free hand" in an age of increasing German preponderance. The search for a solution, however, continued during the crisis-ridden year of 1938; the hope of containing the spread of German influence in the Danube region, at least to some extent, was not given up.

PART IV

THE DANUBE — VISTULA AXIS

1. Anschluss and its Consequences

Just like the efforts of the previous year to forestall German expansion, the efforts of early 1938 were aimed primarily at preventing, delaying or at least anticipating the consequences of the German annexation of Austria. No responsible person in Hungary could look forward to *Anschluss* without deep concern. "We would rather see," said Kanya in a message intended for Colonel Beck, the Polish Foreign Minister, "the maintenance of Austria's independence than become neighbours to an empire of eighty millions. Knowing, however, the very determined intentions of the German National Socialist Government, in principle we must be prepared that the union of the two states will sooner or later materialize."[1] As has been seen, Kanya, and Horthy also,[2] realized that there was little Hungary could do, without incurring grave risks, to influence the German leaders' "very determined intentions" with regard to this matter.[3] Yet they made some efforts to try to delay the coming of *Anschluss*.

To avoid the impression that the Rome accord was no longer functioning, Kanya categorically denied to the Germans the existence of frictions in Italian-Austrian-Hungarian relations.[4] The Budapest government also insisted that the appearance of the Rome bloc's unity be maintained. The Austrian and Hungarian statesmen co-operated in overcoming the reluctance of Ciano and arranging a conference of the Protocol states in January 1938 in Budapest.[5] Last but not least, the Germans were even warned, though not through diplomatic channels, of the possible consequences of further German expansion on Hungary's policy of friendship toward Germany.

In the spring issue of one of the country's leading foreign language journals, Ottlik reviewed the country's foreign policy in an article. He concluded that friendship to Germany had been the basis for Hungarian policy in recent years. He warned, however, that should Germany take Austria or Bohemia, "Hungary's position would of course become totally different."[6]

It was evident, however, to the leaders of Austria's partners in the Rome bloc, that Vienna could not be saved once Hitler decided to act. Kanya, like Ciano, doubted not only the ability of Austria to resist a German intervention successfully, but also the will of the Austrian population to put up any effective opposition to *Anschluss* at all.[7] As a result, both foreign ministers anticipated Austria's annexation and formulated their plans for the future accordingly.

Ciano's thoughts for the future were revealed to Villani, the Hungarian Minister to Rome. The Italian Foreign Minister declared that Czechoslovakia's fate was sealed and that nothing could prevent *Anschluss*. He explained that Italy needed Germany's friendship. He added, however, that this friendship could only be prevented from becoming domination if Italy united with the states nearby her. Next, he suggested the creation of a Rome-Belgrade-Budapest Warsaw "horizontal axis", an alignment equal in strength to the *Reich,* friendly to Germany but independent from her.[8] Ciano's proposal seems to have impressed Kanya, for a few days later he instructed the Hungarian Minister to Poland, to sound out Beck urgently on the idea of the Italian-Yugoslav-Hungarian-Polish line.[9]

While the leaders of Austria's Rome Protocol partners were contemplating plans for the time when Vienna would be ruled from Berlin, events were rapidly coming to a conclusion in the relations of the two German states. Soon Austria disappeared from the map of Europe as an independent country. Although the coming of this development was a foregone conclusion in many quarters in Hungary, the abruptness of *Anschluss* profoundly disturbed the nation. Many citizens were struck with panic. Rumours were circulating that Budapest was next on Hitler's list. The transfer of Austria's share of the country's trade and economic enterprise to Germany caused many businessmen to despair. The Jews, who occupied a prominent place in the nation's economic life, were particularly frightened. But legitimists, liberals and socialists had also cause for alarm. There were many, however, who rejoiced over Hitler's success: rightists, anti-Semites and members of the German minority.[10] Those who were shocked by *Anschluss* recalled past German attempts to dominate Hungary. One member of the Hungarian diplomatic service remarked in a pessimistic tone that in the past the threat came from "*gemütlich* Vienna" but in the future German supremacy might be exercised from Berlin "with brutal Prussian methods."[11]

The country's leaders considered it to be their most immediate task to dispel the fears caused by *Anschluss* and to calm aroused emotions. Speeches to this end were made by Horthy, Kanya, Daranyi, and later by the latter's successor as Prime Minister, Bela Imredy.[12] Of these declarations, that of Kanya dealt with Hungary's new external situation in greatest detail. Like the others, Kanya stressed the value to Hungary of Germany's friendship and denied the existence of danger from that quarter. Then he emphasized the country's good relations with Italy, expressed his hope for "still closer peaceful co-operation" in the future with Poland, and re-stated his desire "to normalize our relations with the states of the Little Entente."[13] At about the same time he sent a circular to Hungarian legations abroad instructing their staffs to talk along similar lines, and emphasize Hungary's desire to maintain a policy of the free hand in their conversations.[14]

There can be little doubt that Kanya was sincere when he stated that the maintenance of an independent foreign policy was the aim of the Hungarian Government. How he hoped to achieve this increasingly difficult task became evident during and immediately after the *Anschluss* crisis. Basically he was hoping to counterbalance Germany's growing influence through cultivating the old friendship with Italy, lessening the tensions in his country's relations with the states of the Little Entente, particularly Yugoslavia and Rumania, gaining the understanding of Great Britain, and attaining very close co-operation with Poland. The scheme never developed into a rigid dogma in Kanya's mind. Unlike Ciano's "horizontal axis" and Colonel Beck's *"intermarum"*, it had no name. It was more than a simple "paper alliance". In fact, it was not an alliance but a policy which, to some extent, simultaneously aimed at serving the cause of Hungarian revisionism and that of curbing the growth of German influence in Eastern Europe.

2. *Hungary, Poland, and the Rise of the Danube-Vistula Alignment.*

Friendship and co-operation with Poland was one of the major cornerstones of Hungarian foreign policy during 1938. By that year the two countries had many common interests. The governments of both desired to retain their independence from the ever more powerful German *Reich*. As a consequence, they were both anxious to curb the spread of German influence. The Polish and Hungarian regimes shared a common aversion to communism and Soviet Russia. At the same time there were many persons in both countries who wanted to settle accounts with Prague, for what the Czechs had done to Hungary in 1919, and to Poland in 1920 during the Russo-Polish war.[15]

In addition, Hungary and Poland were linked by sentimental ties going back many centuries in the two nation's history. The memories of historical figures common to both countries, such as Stephen Bathory and Joseph Bem, and of struggles and tragedies affecting both peoples made for a deep-rooted tradition of Polish-Hungarian friendship.[16] True, in 1919 the two countries had parted ways temporarily. In the 1920's Poland was a *"status quo"* power, while Hungary became a "revisionist" state. Relations between the two were cordial, but until 1938 they were cool.

From 1933 on efforts were made, particularly on the part of the Hungarian Government, to improve the relations of the two countries. In 1933 Kallay, and in the fall of 1934 Gombos paid official visits to Poland. Neither visit resulted in agreements of political nature. Kallay's journey to Warsaw had no such aim, and Gombos' coincided with the outbreak of the Marseille crisis, which made the atmosphere unsuitable for serious discussions.[17]

In 1935 Hory was appointed Minister to Warsaw. He eventually turned out to be the staunchest advocate of close co-operation between Hungary and Poland.[18] In April 1936 a Polish delegation visited Budapest. In the course of the ensuing discussions it was agreed that both countries aimed at disrupting the cohesion of the Czechoslovak state.[19] The rest of 1936 and all of 1937 were devoted to efforts on the part of Hungarian diplomacy to strengthen the ties already established with Poland.[20]

Thus far there were apparently no anti-German overtones in the increasingly friendly relations of the Polish and Hungarian regimes. At first glance their new-found friendship seems to have been aimed at promoting the disintegration of Czechoslovakia. From the evidence it appears that in this scheming against Prague not the Hungarians, who had by far the greater grievance against the Czechoslovak state, but the Poles led the way. Is it possible that Beck and his associates were fed with a blind feeling of revenge over Teschen, and this alone guided their policy with regard to Czechoslovakia? Very unlikely. There was more to the Polish designs on Czechoslovakia than the desire to regain a few towns and mines for Poland. Beck's policy was probably motivated by considerations of the security of the Polish state; and the security of Poland, a country wedged in between two dangerous great powers, demanded that the territory south of Poland be kept out of the control of either of these powers at all cost. By the end of 1937 it was evident to Polish policymakers that the German leaders were determined to destroy Czechoslovakia. The destruction of this country by Germany threatened Poland with encirclement through the establishment of Nazi control over Slovakia and Ruthenia. It was this possible turn of developments the Polish leaders were trying to anticipate by seeking the close friendship and confidence of Hungary, and by egging Hungarian revisionist designs on the eastern half of Czechoslovakia.[21]

Believing that the time for action was rapidly getting closer, the Polish leaders decided, in December 1937, to bring the slowly improving relations between the two countries to some positive conclusion. Horthy was invited to pay a visit to Poland. Even before the visit materialized, a Polish official told Hory that soon the Sudeten, and therefore the Slovak and Hungarian questions of Czechoslovakia would have to be settled bringing about the disintegration of that "artificial state."[22] Hory, anxious to convert Kanya to Beck's ideas, outlined the Polish leader's "different" policies in a report to Budapest toward the end of January. The policy of Poland, explained Hory, was the preservation of the *status quo* in her relations with Germany and the U.S.S.R., good relations with Scandinavia, and a cultivation of the French link, for appearance's sake. Polish policy also aimed at the building up of a link south of the Carpathians, the attainment of a common frontier with Hungary, and the creation of the Warsaw-Budapest-Belgrade line "to stem German expansion."[23]

In the first half of February, Regent Horthy, Kanya and their retinue arrived in Poland for a visit. Their reception was extremely friendly. The political discussions, however, which accompanied the ceremonies, seem to have disappointed the Polish hosts. Kanya gave no demonstration of the Hungarian desire to struggle for the historic common Polish-Hungarian border.[24] During a meeting of Kanya and Beck the problem of the German danger was brought up, but the Hungarian Foreign Minister apparently avoided its discussion. Only an agreement to exchange information on Germany was made.[25] In fact, the Hungarians seem to have tried to convince the Poles of the need for a friendly accomodation with the Germans.[26]

The modest start that was made in Polish-Hungarian political collaboration during the February visit was widened during the spring of 1938. *Anschluss* seems to have removed any hesitations on Kanya's part about still more intimate relations with Poland. Beck, of course, kept pressing for some positive measures. At the end of March, he suggested that the Polish and Hungarian minorities co-operate with each other in their relations with the Czech leaders. He also sounded Budapest out on the possibility of military discussions.[27] By this time apparently, the Hungarian Government had told the Poles that it desired the return of Slovakia and Subcarpathia to Hungary and thereby the attainment of the common boundary with Poland. Kanya also informed Warsaw that the linguistically Slovak and Ruthene areas would be given autonomy within the Hungarian Kingdom.[28] The Polish leaders welcomed the news. They, however, expressed concern over the idea of giving autonomy to the Carpatho-Ukraine.[29]

At the end of June the Polish leaders had still another opportunity for a round of intimate talks with a representative of the Hungarian Government. The occasion was the visit of Colonel Andorka, a member of the Hungarian General Staff, to Warsaw. Andorka came to pave the way for staff talks suggested by Beck at the end of March. Now, however, it was the Polish leadership which deemed such discussions "premature". Instead, the Poles talked of politics. Kobylanski, Beck's spokesman on foreign affairs, outlined plans for the building of a North-South "reinsurance belt" stretching from Oslo to Ankara, including even the state which would be left after the Sudeten, Polish, Slovak, Hungarian and Ruthenian questions of Czechoslovakia were settled.[30]

Summing up the development of Polish-Hungarian relations up to the summer of 1938, it can be stated that gradually and cautiously, the two governments came to adopt a common approach to the major international problems affecting their countries. With one notable reservation, of which more shall be said later, Hungary's policymakers accepted the idea of collaboration with Poland in the dismemberment of Czechoslovakia for the purpose of regaining Slovakia and Ruthenia. They also welcomed the plans for building an alignment of East-Central European states, a Danube-Vistula axis, to curb the spread of German influence in this area.

By the summer of 1938, the policy of the Hungarian Government with regard to the problem of containing the expansion of German influence became more than the seeking of closer association with Poland and, to a lesser extent, Yugoslavia.

Kanya, and probably most of the other persons associated with the making of Hungarian foreign policy, realized that such a bloc would be useless unless it was buttressed by the support of one or more great powers. They knew that German influence could not be rendered less effective unless the influence of other powerful nations was brought in to counterbalance it. Although it was evidently difficult, in the circumstances prevailing in Europe during 1938, to get the leaders of any great power interested in the problems of Eastern Europe, the Hungarian Government proceeded to attempt to do precisely this.

Of the world's great powers the isolationist and distant United States was not available to play a role in this part of the globe. Soviet Russia was considered both in Warsaw and in Budapest to be a dangerous power whose involvement in European problems would have undesirable consequences. France, the other "end" of the Moscow-Prague-Paris line, was also regarded by the Hungarian leaders as unsuitable. There remained Italy and Great Britain.

Prior to 1938 Italy had been the power whose influence was often brought into the power-balance of the Danubian area. In 1934 this worked effectively in containing German power. After that date Italian strength was felt less and less in the affairs of the Danube region. The question after the Austrian *Anschluss* was: would it still be possible to use Italy's influence as a counterweight to that of Germany now that the former indisputably became the junior partner within the Rome-Berlin Axis? This question could not be answered in 1938. Italy was still a power factor in Europe, although perhaps not as important as many Hungarian politicians of the day believed. Everything depended on the attitudes of her leaders. And they, particularly Ciano, time and again reaffirmed their country's continued interest in Danubian Europe. Already before *Anschluss*, as has been seen, the Italian Foreign Minister outlined his plans for the building of the "horizontal axis" to curb German expansion. On March 15th he told Villani that the Italo-Hungarian friendship created by the Rome Pact had to be deepened, and that in the interest of the creation of the "horizontal axis" Hungary should improve her relations with Belgrade.[31] The two returned to the same topic on March 25. To Villani's question, what to put in place of the Rome Protocols, Ciano hinted at the inclusion of Yugoslavia, but cautioned against hurry lest the Germans take suspicion.[32]

The active interest of Warsaw and Rome in Danubian affairs, the apparent willingness of both to make some efforts to counterweigh German influence in Eastern Europe, and the improving relations among the three countries during the first half of 1938,[33] seems to have kept alive Kanya's interest in the idea of the Warsaw-Budapest-Belgrade-Rome bloc. By the summer, however, the Foreign Minister realized that this alignment had little chance of success unless relations between Hungary and Yugoslavia improved, the common border with Poland became a reality, and the members of the proposed bloc remained on good terms with Germany. Kanya hoped to discuss this matter on the occasion of his visit to Italy in mid-July.[34] To his disappointment the "horizontal axis" was not brought up by the Italians during the talks, and he found it advisable not to mention it.[35] Although the Italian leadership continued to exhibit its interest in Danubian affairs, and occasionally it even made attempts to counterbalance German ambitions, this meeting with Ciano and Mussolini served as still another warning to the Hungarian Government that it was dangerous to count on Italian support when it came to matters involving Germany. However, there are situations in international relations, just as in everyday affairs, when men are forced to rely even on "unreliable" friends.

If the idea of pursuing a foreign policy which in part depended on the support of Ciano and Mussolini may seem naive, the hope of interesting the British Government in playing a role in the affairs of Danubian Europe in 1938 might appear foolish. Yet it was precisely this that Hungary's politicians attempted to do. To the Hungarian advocates of the "British orientation" such efforts probably did not appear unrealistic. In their view Britain was a great power whose might even Hitler would have to respect. She was, moreover, interested in preventing the spread of German influence.

The policy of trying to gain London's support for Hungarian aspirations manifested itself in various ways. There was a general tendency to avoid acts which might be regarded as unfriendly in Britain. For example, the refusal of the Hungarian Government to withdraw from the League in the face of repeated Italian requests, was probably out of consideration for the "British viewpoint".[36] There were many attempts at catering to British public opinion. The journal *Hu garian Quarterly* was the instrument of these efforts.[37] The change of leadership in the government in May 1938 was in some respect also a move in this direction. Daranyi implicated himself in dealings with a right radical organization and resigned in the midst of the resulting scandal.[38] Next, Horthy appointed Bela Imredy as Prime Minister. At the time Imredy was regarded to be a man of good English connections and few German sympathies.[39] In one of his first speeches as the leader of the government he remarked that England's greater interest in the problems of Central Europe was "noted with pleasure".[40]

To many politicians in Hungary the policy of seeking the support of Britain seemed not at all contradictory to that of maintaining friendship with Italy. One of Horthy's advisers reasoned at the end of 1934 that Italy, because of her geographical and strategical position, would be forced to side with Great Britain in case of a European conflict. The failure to realize Italy's special position *vis-à-vis* British naval power, argued this person, had been the greatest blunder of the Central Powers in the First World War.[41] Many Hungarian diplomats believed, probably correctly, that even after *Anschluss* the British Foreign Office, and particularly Chamberlain, sought the friendship of Italy in order to counterbalance German power in Europe. Those concerned about the rise of Nazi German power would have welcomed a serious Anglo-Italian *rapprochement*. In May of 1937 Kanya had even made an attempt to convert Ciano to the idea of Italian friendship with Britain. He told his Italian colleague that during his recent visit to London he became convinced that Eden really wanted friendship with Rome. Then Kanya went on describing England's military might.[42]

Of course, the policies of collaboration with Poland, *de-*

tante with Yugoslavia and Rumania, friendship with Italy and Britain were not envisaged in Budapest as being simply and solely instruments for the containment of Nazi influence. These policies were also serving the cause of Hungarian revisionism, even if only *vis-á-vis* Czechoslovakia. It appears, however, that in the minds of some Hungarians the idea of revision, especially in that direction, was connected with the problem of Germany's containment. These persons might have believed that once Hungary recovered at least some of her lost territories, she would be in a better position to oppose German aspirations in the Danube region. This type of reasoning was revealed by Jungerth-Arnothy, the Hungarian Minister to Moscow, in a conversation with a Soviet official. Jungerth-Arnothy explained that the Hungarian Government was aware that "German expansion toward the southeast might bring not just advantages but serious disadvantages" to Hungary. He also hinted that if the country could be strengthened through revision it would oppose this expansion more vigorously and more effectively. "... for a satiated strong Hungary", he said, "will resist the German expansionist ambitions in the Danube valley."[43]

The problem of revision, however, was a painful and complex one. It could not be solved by simple bilateral agreement. Benes, for example, could not be expected "to erase" his life's work. To attain revision, pressure or force was needed. Of the two the first was by far the less risky, and therefore the more attractive instrument for the purpose. However, the collaboration of Poland, the support of Italy, the sympathy of Britain and the neutrality of Yugoslavia and Rumania, even if attained, which was in itself questionable, would not have been enough to bring sufficient pressure on the Prague government to yield. Germany could not be left out of the picture. There was no reason, however, not to take advantage of German pressure on the Czechs. The only problem was that the leaders in Berlin might choose to resolve the whole issue not by using the threat of force, but by using force itself.

The idea of revision through military means in collaboration with Germany, however, was quite unattractive, though not entirely alien, to the minds of Hungary's political leaders.[44] First of all, in view of the state of Hungarian rearmament, it was risky, to say the least. Secondly, even if the war was localized, it might have lead to a situation in which Germany was aggrandized out of all proportions, while Britain, Yugoslavia and Rumania were antagonized, and Hungary was left completely at the mercy of her mighty comrade-in-arms. Lastly, if the military conflict was not localized, the country might be involved in a war on Germany's side, the possible outcome of which might be defeat and a "new Trianon". The Hungarian leaders had good reason to be wary when it came to solving the whole Czechoslovak question by other than "diplomatic" means.

3. Confrontation with Hitler; the Bled Agreement and the Kiel Visit.

Developments came to a climax in Hungary's external relations at the end of August. On the 22nd of the month Regent Horthy and his wife, accompanied by the country's chief political and military leaders, arrived in Kiel, Germany. Ostensibly they came to participate in a naval ceremony, but in reality for a round of talks with the German leaders over foreign policy issues, particularly the problem of co-ordinating German and Hungarian plans against Czechoslovakia. Meanwhile, in Bled, Yugoslavia, negotiations were taking place between representatives of Hungary and the Little Entente powers. The discussions in Bled resulted in the signing of a controversial agreement between the governments of Hungary and those of the Little Entente states. At the same time, the talks in Germany with the Nazi leaders brought about a crisis in Hungarian-German diplomatic relations.

In order to explain these climactic events in Hungarian foreign affairs, it is necessary to trace the two main threads of developments leading to the crisis of late August: the evolution of relations between Berlin and Budapest over the question of plans against Czechoslovakia, and the history of the negotiations between Hungary and the Little Entente in 1938.

In discussions between Germans and Hungarians in the 1930's no secret was made of the desire, shared on the whole by both sides, to see the demise and disintegration of Czechoslovakia. By 1936, moreover, the government in Budapest could have little doubt that the coming of some German move against this state was only a matter of time.[45] Designs against the Czechs were probably one of the topics of discussion at the meeting between Hitler and Horthy at Berchtesgarden in August of 1936.[46] During a round of discussions between the German leaders and Daranyi and Kanya, on the occasion of the latters' visit to Germany in November 1937, the issue was mentioned a few times, always briefly and in the most general terms. Göring reminded the two Hungarians of Hitler's statement that Hungary's present generation could not hope to achieve more than to regain the "Magyar areas" which had been awarded to Czechoslovakia in 1919. The Prussian Minister-President also asserted that, with timely concessions and astute manoeuvering, Hungary should be able to secure the neutrality of Yugoslavia and Rumania for the event of Czechoslovakia's dismemberment, which, according to Göring, could only come at the time of a major war in Europe. Apparently, in reply to such Nazi suggestions, the Hungarian Foreign Minister made a noteworthy statement to Hitler himself regarding Hungary's policy to treaty revision. "At the conclusion of the conversation," states the German record of one of the meetings, "Kanya again stated emphatically that, contrary to various rumours, Hungary had no intention whatever of achieving her revisionist aims by force of arms and thereby possibly unleashing a European war. He asked the *Führer* to take cognizance of this."[47]

Throughout this period it never came to the holding of discussions between the German and Hungarian general staffs on the future of Czechoslovakia, in spite of the fact that hints at the desirability of doing this were probably made as early as the November discussions.[48] As time passed, however, the Hungarian Government's concern increased over a possible military conflict which could result from a solution of the Sudeten problem. As a result, on April 5, 1938, Kanya instructed Szojay in Berlin to enquire from Ribbentrop about the holding of such staff conversations in case a peaceful solution of the Czechoslovak question would not prove possible and hostilities broke out. The feeler got an evasive answer from the Germans.[49] During the summer it was re peated by a member of the Hungarian General Staff to a high-ranking German officer. Again the Hungarians were turned down.[50]

The leaders of the *Reich,* with the possible exception of a few generals who desired to forestall Germany's involvement in a war, were certainly not against the idea of conducting staff talks, even though the still largely disarmed Hungary was indeed not an indispensable ally.[51] They were only against making premature agreements. They left the discussion of the political and military details of the plans against Czechoslovakia for the time of the Regent's visit to Kiel.[52] Hitler did not plan to move until the fall, thus he and his associates felt no need to make agreements with the Hungarians before late August.

It is difficult to pinpoint the aim of Hungarian diplomacy in its contacts and negotiations with the Little Entente governments during 1938. Undoubtedly Kanya and his associates aspired to weaken the unity of the Little Entente as much as possible. At the same time they, or at least some of them, were eager to gain at least some friends in Eastern Europe so as to counterbalance the increasing political weight of the Third *Reich* in the affairs of that region. They probably understood that, for example, Hungarian hostility toward Rumania and Yugoslavia might force the governments of those countries to seek more vigorous support not so much from their old benefactor France, but from another potential and more powerful source, the German *Reich* itself. Then there was the desire for a common border with the Polish "brothers", a desire which was closely linked with the designs on Czechoslovakia and the attempts to drive a wedge into Little Entente unity. Lastly, in going through the primary evidence available on this subject the reader is impressed by the strong concern of the Hungarian leaders and diplomats for the lot of the Hungarian minorities in the neighbouring countries, particularly Rumania.[53]

The story of Hungary's relations with the Little Entente as a whole has been traced up to the fall of 1937. The specific problem of Hungarian *detente* and subsequent *rapprochement* with Yugoslavia in the period 1935-38, however, has not been dealt with. Since Yugoslav-Hungarian relations in this period are closely related with the aspirations of Hungarian diplomacy to split the Little Entente, and at the same time to participate in the construction of an East European alignment to restrict the spread of German influence, it is necessary to examine them briefly.

The atmosphere of hostility in the relations of the governments at Belgrade and Budapest created by the Marseille affair gradually disintegrated in the first half of 1935. On July 17th of that year Kanya, on the prompting of Vukacevic, the Yugoslav *Chargé d'Affaires* to Hungary, agreed to create a *modus vivendi* between the two countries. This was followed by a tourist agreement. At the same time pressure was put on the press of both countries to conform with the *detente*. On February 28, 1936 the Hungarians expressed their wish to Stoyadinovich to attain "good neighbourly relations" between the two nations. The Yugoslav leader responded by speaking favourably of the two countries' relations in a public address. Kanya reciprocated in a speech in Parliament at the end of May. This *rapprochement*, however, was still plagued by border incidents, excesses on the part of Yugoslav local authorities in dealing with the sometimes restless Hungarian minority, and by popular antipathies of Serbs and Magyars in general.[54]

For a variety of reasons, the Yugoslav-Hungarian *rapprochement* was welcomed and even encouraged by practically every European power interested in the Danubian area.

The Germans were actively pressing for better relations between Budapest and Belgrade all through 1936-1938.[55] At first they might have aimed at lifting Yugoslavia out of the French orbit; later they hoped to embolden the Hungarians in their attitude toward Czechoslovakia by assuring them of Yugoslavia's friendship and neutrality.

Ever since the signing of the Pact of Friendship between Italy and Yugoslavia on March 26, 1937, Ciano too, became a staunch advocate of closer Hungarian-Yugoslav relations.[56] Ciano's motives for this were at least in part anti-German. Following Stoyadinovic's visit to Italy in December 1937, the Italian Foreign Minister wrote this in his diary: Nothing new has been put on paper. But there is not much more between the two countries than the Belgrade Pact. The conversations of the last few days have even laid the foundations of a possible alliance. An alliance which might be aimed in various directions. Possibly northwards even, one day."[57] Evidently Ciano's mind was already gravitating toward the idea of the "horizontal axis". For similar reasons Beck of Poland was also an active promoter of the Belgrade-Budapest friendship.[58]

The gradual and cautious *rapprochement* between Yugoslavia and Hungary was accompanied as it has been already seen, by periodic negotiations between representatives of Hungary and the Little Entente states. In the fall of 1937 these talks came to an impasse, but conditions became conducive to their resumption with the demise of the Goga regime in Rumania in February of 1938. Already in December of 1937 Masirevich, the Hungarian Minister to Britain, asked Sir Orme Sargent that London exert its influence in the capitals of the Little Entente for the renewal of serious negotiations "so that a peaceful atmosphere could develop" in the Danube area.[59]

From the middle of March to the end of August numerous notes were exchanged between Hungary and the Little Entente. At the same time many official declarations were made on the issues involved, in Budapest and the other capitals of the Danubian region. In a speech made on June 1st, Kanya explained that Hungarian aims in the negotiations were the improvement of the position of the Hungarian minorities in the neighbouring states, the recognition of an equality of rights for Hungary, and a declaration on the part of the four countries involved of an agreement in the spirit of the Kellogg-Briand Pact. Of these, Kanya stressed, the minority problem was of "decisive importance".[60] It was precisely on this issue that the Little Entente governments were reluctant to come to an agreement. The Rumanians, it seems, were even ready to make unilateral concessions to their Hungarian minority, rather than be partners to a formal agreement on the issue.[61] By June 12th all outstanding questions except that of the minorities were settled.[62]

Evidently the Little Entente leaders were suspicious of Kanya's designs in connection with the proposed minorities agreement. They had every reason to be wary. For Kanya, while he desired to attain an agreement which would reduce the chances of the outbreak of a general conflagration in Danubian Europe, wanted not a permanent settlement of the minority problems, but one which would enable him to keep the issue very much alive, to turn it on and off so to speak, at his own discretion, whenever and wherever he felt it necessary. At the end of June he explained his intentions to Bardossy, the Hungarian diplomat then in charge of the negotiations with the Little Entente leaders. "After an agreement is reached on the minorities" Kanya stated, "I must be able to say" that this issue was "central" to the agreement and on this separate negotiations with the individual governments of the Little Entente states would follow.[63]

Kanya knew perfectly well that no Hungarian Government could afford to accede to a settlement of the minority issue which appeared as being final. That would have been tantamount to abandoning the cause of the Hungarians beyond the country's borders, and accepting the judgement of Trianon. To expect, however, that after signing an agreement the members of the Little Entente would oblige themselves to further negotiations on the issue, was certainly too much on his part. This was pointed out to him by Bardossy, who ventured to disagree with his chief. Bardossy argued that the Rumanians at least, would regard such an attempt as a trap, and, as a result, the negotiations might be jeopardized.[64] Kanya rejected this argument apparently believing that if the text of the agreement would be ambiguous enough Rumanian suspicions could be overcome and he could still have his way.[65]

Events in Hungarian-Little Entente negotiations came to a rapid conclusion during the second half of August. On the 21st, the day the Hungarian delegation departed for Germany, the Council of the Little Entente met in Bled, Yugoslavia. Hungary had been invited to send an observer to this meeting. On the same day, Baron Bakach-Bessenyey, the Hungarian negotiator, sent a message from Bled stating that the Little Entente leaders were willing to accept the agreement proposed by the Hungarians except for minor modifications. Pointing out the desire of the Little Entente leadership for an immediate answer, the Hungarian diplomat asked for authorization to initial this modified version of the agreement plan.[66] Apor, in whose hands the direction of the country's foreign policy remained with all top Hungarian politicians being virtually out of reach in Kiel or on German warships at sea, forwarded the message to Kanya, suggesting acceptance.[67] Whether or not Apor succeeded in contacting his chief, remains a question.[68] In any case, Apor gave instructions to Bakach-Bessenyey in Bled to accept the latest Little Entente version of the agreement.[69] In the early hours of the 23rd the document was signed, and it was published the same day by both sides.[70] The agreement consisted of two parts and concerned three matters: Hungary's right to armaments, the relations among the states concerned, and the minority issue. Part one was an agreement between Hungary and the Little Entente containing a declaration of Hungary's right to equality in the matter of armaments and a promise that the powers concerned would refrain from the use of force in their mutual relations. Part two was a supplementary protocol in which Hungary on the one hand, and Rumania and Yugoslavia on the other, promised to settle between them outstanding issues blocking the development of mutual good relations.[71] The agreement immediately gave rise to different interpretations. Briefly, the Hungarian position, as explained by Kanya, was that the agreement was one and indivisible, and that it would take effect only if and when the Czech Government agreed to accede to the contents of the supplementary protocol, i.e. when it promised to settle the issue of the Hungarian minority in Czechoslovakia.[72] The Czechoslovaks, on the other hand, claimed that what had been reached at Bled in fact were two separate agreements, the first of which, the problem of armaments and the mutual promise of no-resort to force, was now in effect since these issues were settled. According to this view the so called second agreement concerning the minority issue was unrelated to the first one.[73] The fact itself that the agreement lent itself to such interpretation caused much controversy and even sensation. The press of France and Britain acclaimed the news of the agreement. The Nazi leaders, however, were furious. They made no secret of their feelings when they met the Hungarian delegation in discussions at Kiel.

Horthy and his entourage left for Germany on the 21st of the month. Several hours after their departure, Apor sent a coded telegram to the Hungarian Legation in Berlin. The urgent message was apparently forwarded to Kanya by a legation official who managed to catch the train carrying the delegation at a railway station. Apor's telegram contained what seems to have been the latest report on the political and military situation in Germany from a "reliable source", probably a member of the German General Staff itself. This report asserted that Hitler was bent on a war against the Czechs. He cared not for the advice of his generals, and did not fear British and French intervention. He was planning to move by the end of September in spite of the fact that military preparations were inadequate for protracted hostilities, and public opinion in the *Reich* was against war.[74]

The message must have made a strong impression on Kanya and his colleagues, although it hardly caused surprise since reports of this nature, though never as dramatic as this one, had been trickling in from Germany in the past.[75]

After a day of ceremonies and a voyage on the sea, the Hungarians got down to serious talk with their hosts. The chief problem discussed at a meeting of Imredy, Kanya and Ribbentrop was the Bled *communique,* which had been signed during the early hours of the day (August 23). The German Foreign Minister assailed Kanya stating that the Bled accord apparently renounced the use of force as well as Hungary's revisionist aspirations, and made it more difficult for Yugoslavia and Rumania not to assist the Czechs in case of an outbreak of hostilities.[76] Kanya denied that the Bled agreement had such connotations, and tried to impress upon Ribbentrop that the only feasible interpretation of that document was the Hungarian one. The German Foreign Minister refused to see the logic of Kanya's arguments. The old diplomat became impatient with his German colleague and began to talk with an aristocratic contempt which Ribbentrop did not fail to notice, and for that matter, ever to forgive.[77] Reminding his guests that "he who does not assist departs with empty hands," Ribbentrop asked what Hungary would do now, in the light of the Bled accord, in case of a German-Czech armed conflict. While refusing to admit that they were against the idea of armed Hungarian participation, Imredy and Kanya gave an answer that was conditional to say the least. "Yugoslavia must remain neutral" they said, "if Hungary were to march . . ." and they explained that their country's rearmament "would require another year or two to complete."[78]

On the same day Hitler met Horthy for a conversation which appears to have been even more vehement and disappointing from the Nazi point of view than the former. Hitler apparently asked for a promise of Hungarian participation in a combined attack on Czechoslovakia, hinting that all areas taken by Hungary would become hers. Hitler, however, failed to obtain the Regent's promise even after he offered to supply Hungary with armaments. "I adhered to my refusal" wrote Horthy in his memoirs, "and even warned him against the risk of major war . . ."[79] Apparently, on being told that Britain would not only intervene but would defeat Germany in war, Hitler nearly flew into a rage and told Horthy to "Shut up". Upon this the Regent terminated the conversation.[80]

The *Führer* remained furious for the rest of the day. "Hitler," writes Guderian, the commander of Germany's new panzer divisions, who had a conversation with the German leader during a reception given later on that day, "was disappointed by the political results of Horthy's visit. He had doubtless hoped to persuade the Regent to sign a military pact, but in this he was not successful. Hitler made his disappointment fairly obvious both during the speech he made, and by his behaviour after dinner."[81]

Not getting along with Kanya and Horthy, the Germans tried to get somewhere with the other members of the Hungarian delegation. On the 23rd Hitler also talked to Imredy. He told the Hungarian Prime Minister that he "demanded nothing from Hungary" but reminded Imredy that "wer mittafeln wolle, müsse allerdings auch mitkochen."[82]

The obvious excitement and fury of the German leaders apparently caused the Hungarians to have some second thoughts.[83]

After all they could not afford to offend the Germans by haughtily rejecting everything the Nazi leaders asked of the Hungarian regime. While still refusing to commit themselves to a military venture, they adopted a somewhat more conciliatory tone during the second round of talks, held this time in Berlin, on the 25th. On this occasion Ribbentrop was still complaining about the international reaction to the Bled accord. He pointed out that the British, French and Czech press regarded the Bled events as the sign of a rift between Hungary and Germany. Kanya argued that the Bled agreement was not disadvantageous to the *Reich*, since it would never be signed by the Czechs, because the Prague government could never fulfil the minorities provisions of the document. To calm the excited German leaders, however, Kanya stated during this conversation that it would be possible to complete Hungary's rearmament by October 1.[84]

While Kanya had gone a long way to recant his stand taken two days ago, Horthy refused to do so. His second talk with Hitler "not only failed to dispel the tension created by our first talk" testifies the Regent in his memoirs, but "it aggravated it". For the *Führer*, apparently suspecting that his own generals were behind this whole matter of Hungarian reluctance, reproached Horthy for discussing problems with Field Marshal Brauchitsch.[85] After such a start there was no chance of reconciliation between the two men on this occasion. Indicative of the unchanged attitude of Horthy to this problem of war against the Czechs is the fact that four days later, on the 29th, he was still advising Göring, this time in Budapest, to postpone the quarrel with Czechoslovakia "till spring or later."[86]

On the last day of the visit Ribbentrop had still another talk with Imredy and Kanya. Once again Kanya made efforts to mollify the German Foreign Minister, and promised a clarification of Hungary's attitude on the Bled agreement in the Hungarian press. Discussing the issue of Czechoslovakia, however, Imredy expressed the view that France would not remain neutral in case of a German-Czech conflict.[87]

The visit was topped by still another incident that did much to solidify the ill feelings of the Germans toward the Hungarian leaders created by the discussions at Kiel. Up until the end of August neither side revealed publicly that a serious confrontation had taken place between the German and Hungarian political leaders during the visit, although this had been suspected in many quarters in Europe.[88] On August 26, in fact, Imredy had made a public statement to the effect that agreement between the two countries was so complete "that it needs no formal confirmation."[89] A few days later, however, he made some unguarded remarks to a correspondent of the *London Daily Telegraph* on the events of the Kiel visit. The article carried by the London paper was in turn published in the Budapest daily *Az Est,* this time written in a tone which made it sound like a "studied provocation" to Germany.[90] It carried headlines like "The Hungarian State as an obstacle to National Socialist expansion."[91] The Berlin government protested in no uncertain language. Imredy became frightened, suspended the paper and fell into what has been described as a "panic of indecision".[92] His behaviour after this incident was an indication of the trend in Hungarian policymaking in the immediate future.

At Kiel Hungarian diplomacy made a stand against Hitler's ambitions. Hungary's leaders insisted on following an independent foreign policy in spite of the pressure exerted on them by the German Government. By doing so they probably hindered, temporarily it least, the further expansion of German influence and power. They might have been instrumental in delaying the outbreak of war. At Kiel, it seems, a skirmish was won in the struggle of Hungarian diplomacy to curb the growth of Nazi power in the Danube region. The developments of the subsequent few weeks proved, however, that what had been achieved at the end of August was a Pyrrhic victory. For the events at Kiel left the Nazi chieftains with a feeling of resentment against Hungary's leaders. They suspected the Budapest regime not only of indecision but also of deliberate machinations aimed at frustrating German ambitions. During the next two months the leaders in Berlin made it their objective to drive home the lesson in the minds of the Hungarian policymakers that it was futile and worthless for them to oppose the will of the German leadership.

During this time the Hungarian Government experienced, perhaps for the first time, the full weight of the pressure that could be exerted by German diplomacy. Under this the will to resist, so audaciously demonstrated at Kiel, weakened and almost disintegrated.

4. The Signs of Failure; Munich and its Aftermath.

In spite of the fact that the crisis of the autumn of 1938 ended in the return of southern Slovakia to Hungary, the three months which followed the Kiel visit brought only disappointments to the country and demonstrated the weakness of her foreign policies. In the course of the protracted international crisis, the policy of co-operation with Poland combined with a reliance on Italian and British support for the purpose of buttressing Hungary's international position *vis-à-vis* Germany proved almost completely futile. When the storm was over, the expectations attached to this policy stood unfulfilled. German influence in East Central Europe was stronger than ever before. The Hungarian Government's reputation had suffered in the public opinion of Western Europe because of its complicity in the weakening of Czechoslovakia. At the same time the country's leadership was discredited in Warsaw for its timidity in handling the question of Ruthenia. On top of all this, the common border with Poland did not become a reality. The policy of a Hungarian-Polish alignment, a Danube-Vistula or "horizontal" axis revealed its bankruptcy.

The discussions which had begun at Kiel between Hungarian and German leaders over the fate of Czechoslovakia continued intermittently throughout the fall. To dispel any suspicions which the Nazi leaders might have had about the Hungarian Government's reluctance to help Germany if it came to a conflict between the *Reich* and the Czechs, Imredy promised, soon after his return from Kiel, to place an airfield in Hungary temporarily at the disposal of German warplanes.[93] To arrange the details of this and possibly to make other similar military agreements, General Halder received Lajos Keresztes-Fischer, the Hungarian Chief-of-Staff, on the 6th of September in Berlin. Nothing of importance seems to have been discussed on this occasion, the Hungarian negotiator was not even informed on the timing of the proposed German move against the Czechs.[94] It seems that, for some time at least, the Nazi leaders gave up counting on Hungarian military participation in the war against Czechoslovakia.[95]

This did not mean that Hitler and his associates would not urge Budapest to take tougher measures against Prague. In the middle of the month Göring virtually demanded that Hungary's press, and Hungarian irredentists in Slovakia take a more active role in the crisis.[96] On the 20th Hitler used even firmer language. He told Imredy and Kanya, who, along with Kereszter-Fischer, once again came to Berlin for discussions, that now was Hungary's last opportunity to "join in", and reproached the two men for Hungary's "undecided attitude" in the crisis. To excuse himself and his government, Imredy complained of the "speed" of events, the unpreparedness of Hungary, and the "weakness" of the pro-Axis forces in Yugoslavia.[97] On the eve of the Munich conference the German leaders were once again demanding outright Hungarian military participation. Göring warned that if Hungary did not take part in military action she might be left out of a solution entirely.[98] Ribbentrop was suggesting a simultaneous attack on Czechoslovakia by the two countries' armed forces. Kanya answered that in view of Yugoslavia's uncertain attitude this was impossible.[99]

What may partly explain the persistent determination of some Hungarian leaders to resist the German pressure, at least up to the middle of September, was the belief that Hungarian aspirations to regain the Magyar regions of Slovakia, or even most of "Upper Hungary", might be realized through international arbitration. First of all, the statesmen in Budapest held it to be inconceivable that Berlin would side against Hungary if it came to deciding the future of eastern Czechoslovakia at the conference tables. When, early in the summer of 1938, the warning came from the Italian politician Gajda, the manager of the government inspired *Giornale d'Italia*, that Hitler desired a weak Hungary, and would retain Slovakia under German tutelage after the demise of the Czech state, Kanya responded by calling the rumour "baseless".[100] Secondly, the Hungarian Government had a vague promise from London of British support for the claims of the Hungarian minority in Czechoslovakia. On the third of August, Vansittart had told the Hungarian Minister to London that it was the view of the Birtish Foreign Office that any concessions made by Prague to the German minority would be automatically applicable to the Hungarians also.[101] Thirdly, Budapest counted on the unfailing support of the Warsaw government not only in settling the problem of the Magyar minority in Czechoslovakia, but also in pressing the Slovaks toward a Hungarian rather than a Czech or German solution.[102]

From the middle of September on it became more and more evident that the hopes for the realization of Hungarian ambitions in eastern Czechoslovakia through a peaceful international settlement were not much more than pleasant daydreams. The "rude awakening" began on the 13th, when news came from London that the British Foreign Office was in favour of a plebiscite in the Sudeten area, but not in Slovakia.[103] The bad news was confirmed by Ciano a week later. He informed Budapest that the British were not willing to sponsor the interests of the Magyar and Polish minorities.[104] Meanwhile rumours were being circulated that, in order to drive a wedge between Warsaw and Budapest, the Czech leaders decided to accept the Polish demands, but continued to reject those of Hungary.[105]

The realization that Hungarian claims might not receive

attention during a settlement of the international crisis aroused the fears and indignation of politicians in Budapest. Time and again the Hungarian Government protested this discriminatory treatment of the minority issues in Czechoslovakia, and demanded that concessions granted to the Sudeten Germans should be extended to all the nationalities of the Czechoslovak state. Such protests were sent not only to London, Paris and Prague, but even to Berlin.[106] All this, however, was in vain. The Munich conference did no more than relegate the problem of Hungarian claims to direct negotiations between the Czech and Hungarian governments, and state that if no agreement was reached in three months, the issue would be taken up by the next meeting of the four-power conference.[107]

At the time of the Munich agreement other similarly bad news arrived to the Ministry of Foreign Affairs in Budapest. From a "reliable source" came the information that Hitler did not want to strengthen Hungary. Soon the news came from Ciano that Berlin was not sympathetic to the idea of a common Polish-Hungarian border and would not support it.[108] Other reports asserted that the German Government wanted to be on the best terms with the new Czech and Slovak regimes, that it probably already reached an agreement with the latter, and that the Germans were opposed to the "Polish-Hungarian corridor" because they feared the establishment of a "counterbloc".[109]

These developments undoubtedly disappointed and alarmed the Hungarian leaders. Early in October it seemed that the crisis was over and Hungary had yet to receive anything. The prospects for a favourable settlement of the dispute with Czecho-Slovakia[110] through direct negotiations with Prague were very slim. The Czechs and Slovaks, faced now by a much weaker antagonist than Germany or Poland, could not be expected to yield easily.[111] More important still, they now received limited backing from an unexpected corner: Berlin. Apparently Hitler, who had every expectation to turn the enfeebled and humiliated Czechs and Slovaks into his own vassals, had no interest in giving to Budapest any valuable territory he could hope to control more directly through

Prague.[112] Under these circumstances it was not surprising that, when the Hungarian and Czecho-Slovak negotiators met on the 9th of October, the latter offered token concessions only.[113] These, of course, failed to satisfy the Hungarian leaders who demanded the return to Hungary of the Magyar-populated districts of Slovakia as well as all of Ruthenia. After four tense days the discussions were broken off.[114]

At this point the position of the Budapest government became desperate. The country's leaders faced the prospect of being totally discredited in the eyes of the public at home which expected them to attain the return of at least some Magyar-populated regions as a result of the settlement of the Czechoslovak question. Even more disturbing seems to have been the failure to regain Ruthenia and thereby to achieve the common border with Poland.

The fact was that the Hungarian leaders desired this area more than they wanted many of the territories inhabited by Magyars. After the Munich conference, they even made preparations for some drastic measures to assure the success of their aspirations in Ruthenia. Taking perhaps the advice of Ciano to create a *"fait accompli"* if Hungary's minimum demands were not satisfied,[115] the Imredy government took steps to precipitate an uprising of separatist elements in this part of Czecho-Slovakia first through the use of agitation and, if this failed, by sabotage and the intervention of military irregulars recruited and armed in Hungary. Imredy appointed Miklos Kozma to direct this secret operation.

Kozma, a politician, soldier and an ardent nationalist, was determined to regain Ruthenia by any means. In his diary he wrote that Hungary needed not only the return of "Magyar territories, but also Ruthenia, and through Ruthenia the common Hungarian-Polish border." In Kozma's estimate the importance of this area to Hungary was "immeasurable". "It might not be popular what I say," he continued in his diary, "(but) in its political value Ruthenia is more than any one or more of the disputed (visszakövetelt) Magyar cities."[116] He was ready to make any sacrifice for the achievement of his aim. On October 9, Kozma saw Imredy and begged for permission that the irregulars assembled for action in

95

Ruthenia be equipped with a few artillery pieces 'stolen" from the army. He told the Prime Minister that he, Kozma, cared not if it later became necessary for the government to deprive him of his rank, position and personal freedom because of his part in this illicit venture against the Carpatho-Ukraine. "For the sake of the Hungarian future," Kozma stated, "I hold the immediate solution of the Ruthenian question so paramount that I am willing to risk everything for this, if necessary, even the firing squad."[117]

During the second week of October the preparations for action in Ruthenia began in earnest. The leaders of at least one of the Ruthenian separatist movements were contacted, properly instructed and supplied with money.[118] Kozma's irregulars took up positions near the border. In Poland, arrangements were made for similar units to move into Ruthenia from the North, once the "uprising" got under way.[119] The Italian Government was consulted for possible military aid. Mussolini promised airplanes and ammunition.[120] The gradual infiltration of the Ruthenian border by Kozma's irregulars began in the 11th. The Czechs, however, captured scores of them and succeeded in sealing the border completely.[121]

With the failure of the direct negotiations with Czecho-Slovakia and now the setback in the plans for a separatist rising in Ruthenia, the Hungarian Government was left with two choices: one, to continue its efforts to attain a negotiated settlement of the question; two, to escalate the military action against Ruthenia and thereby to create a *fait accompli*. At first, the first of these alternatives was probed.

The Munich Agreement contained a clause stating that if a solution of the problem of Hungarian minorities within Czechoslovakia could not be settled through direct negotiations between the parties concerned, the participants of the Munich Conference would deal with the question. According to this, the way to handle the issue would have been to convene a new meeting of the "Big Four". Before calling for this, however, the Hungarian Government carefully reconnoitred international opinion regarding the idea.

Mussolini immediately endorsed the Hungarian suggestion for calling a meeting of the four great powers. Hitler, however, warned against it.[122] From Berlin also came a report by Sztojay to the effect that the French Ambassador there advised the Hungarian Government not to call for a four-power conference.[123] In view of all this the Hungarian leaders, in consultation with Ciano,[124] asked for arbitration in the dispute by the two Axis powers and Poland. Their decision was communicated to the British Government on the 25th of the month. On the next day the Czech Minister to the United Kingdom announced that his government "would be in favour of arbitration by Germany and Italy."[125] Apparently the leaders in Prague accepted Hitler's assurances that Germany opposed the return of more territory to Hungary than could be justified on strict ethnic grounds.[126]

Now it was the German Government which, for a time, refused to accept the idea of Axis arbitration. Ribbentrop even made a suggestion for the calling of the four-power conference. The Germans, no doubt, waited to pressure both parties to the quarrel into making higher and higher bids for Berlin's support.

On the 28th of October Ribbentrop finally agreed to the idea of German-Italian arbitration in the dispute between Hungary and Czecho-Slovakia.[127] During the next few days Ciano and the German Foreign Minister made preparations for reaching an agreement on a new boundary between Hungary and her northern neighbour. In their discussions, the former gave his wholehearted support to the Hungarian claims, while the latter worked to restrict Slovak and especially Ruthenian losses to a reasonable minimum. The results of the arbitration were announced on the second of November in Vienna.

By the Vienna Award Hungary regained large Magyar-populated areas from Czecho-Slovakia. Nothing, however, came of the expectations of obtaining all of Ruthenia. The common border with Poland remained a dream which was as far from realization as it had been before the Czechoslovak crisis of 1938.

The Hungarian Government, to be sure, did not acquiesce in the decision reached in Vienna regarding the Carpatho-Ukraine. Throughout much of November it continued its diplomatic efforts to attain a new settlement in this region more in line with its original plans of a common frontier with Poland. It also continued, in collaboration with the Polish Government, to prepare for a separatist rising in Ruthenia. Apparently, the new scheme was that local pro-Hungarian elements were to issue a call for Hungarian intervention in the name of the Ruthenian National Council. At that moment Kozma's irregulars, along with large units of the regular army, were to march into the Carpatho-Ukraine. A few Polish "insurgents" were to enter from the North to create a diversion.[128] Squadrons of the Italian air force, promised earlier by Mussolini, were to provide air cover for the operation.

Once again everything went wrong from the beginning. To be sure, the appeal for intervention came although, as Professor Macartney put it, "probably not from the most authorative quarters."[129] The Hungarian military command, however, refused to march on the appointed date — claiming that the troops needed a day of rest before the attack.[130] As a result of this delay, the German leaders, who hitherto had not quite realized the proportions and seriousness of the planned venture, became fully aware of the nature of Hungary's intentions. Ribbentrop immediately contacted Mussolini, and told him *inter alia* that the *"Führer* was of the opinion that a Hungarian occupation of the Carpatho-Ukraine would discredit the Axis Powers" who had been the arbitrators of the dispute between Hungary and her northern neighbour.[131] The Italian Government, realizing the very determined opposition of Berlin to Hungary's ambition in Ruthenia, reversed its earlier position of support for the operation. The orders for the Italian air force to send planes to Hungary were cancelled. Finally, on November 21, the day the attack was to take place, a joint German-Italian *démarche* was presented in Budapest protesting Hungary's planned move.[132] On the very same day the whole affair was called off.[133]

The failure further discredited the government both at home and in Poland. Although the preparations for the operation had been kept secret, enough leaked out for anyone to suspect that in the second half of November a major move had been afoot to attain the common border, but was abandoned prematurely. The authorities in Budapest were accused of having lacked resolution. They were blamed for bucking under to German pressure. Revisionists and advocates of the Danube-Vistula axis alike, if it is possible to make a clear-cut distinction between them, were deeply disappointed.

After this affair the faith in the workability, indeed in the attainability of an effective Polish-Hungarian alignment seriously declined in Hungary. In the relations of the two countries, moreover, a cooling-off period set in at the end of November. No one would claim, of course, that had things taken a different turn, that is, had the common border become a reality, a powerful bloc would have developed in Eastern Europe — a bloc which would have been strong enough to pose an effective barrier to a German military drive to the East. The attainment of a direct link with Poland, however, could have served as a psychological factor especially in Hungary. It could have reassured the faith of many Magyars in the feasibility of a policy of resisting the expansion of Nazi political and economic influence in the Danube Basin. This in turn would have reinforced the country's determination to maintain an independent course in its internal and external policies. It is noteworthy that Lord Halifax of the British Foreign Office realized all this at the time. He stated in a letter at the end of October that the attainment of the common Polish-Hungarian border "might strengthen Poland and Hungary in their desire to retain sufficient independence to avoid becoming the vassals of Germany."[134]

Indeed, the failure to achieve this long-dreamt-of objective caused the Hungarian Government to abandon, for a while at least, the idea of conducting an independent foreign policy.

PART V

THE TELEKI ERA

1. The Fall of Imredy and the Reassertion of an Independent Course.

After the Ruthenian fiasco the Hungarian Government grudgingly but obediently towed the German line in the field of foreign and, to some extent, even in internal politics for almost three months. This turn of developments did not come about overnight. Ever since Kiel, the Imredy administration had been giving in more and more to the threats and promises made from Berlin. During the early phase of the international crisis there had been strong concern in Budapest that if the Hungarian Government categorically rejected the German demands for the stepping up of pressure against the Czechs, the Nazi leadership might be completely alienated, and Hungary would be dropped by Berlin in favour of some other country more willing to tow the German chariot. At the same time, the fact that during the Italian-German discussions prior to the Vienna Award Ribbentrop had opposed Hungarian ambitions, especially in regard to Ruthenia, tended to drive home the lesson in Budapest that a policy of opposing the expansion of German influence was not only futile but also dangerous. Thus, in the fall of 1938, the need began to be felt in Hungarian leading circles that the confidence and friendship of Berlin, which seemed to have been almost completely lost as a result of the Kiel visit, had to be regained.

This realization of the need to mollify the German leadership was combined with a general disappointment in the idea of depending on the Western democratic powers, particularly Britain, for a policy of resisting the expansion of German influence in Eastern Europe. Prime Minister Imredy, in particular, abandoned even the last traces of that "British orientation" which he had been noted for up until the end of August at least.[1]

These factors were instrumental in bringing about a gradual change in the direction of Hungarian foreign policy. At first this transition took the form of promises made by the Imredy administration to the German Government. These were made either to mollify the Nazi leaders, or to gain Berlin's support or approval for some Hungarian scheme or ambition. The Germans, incidentally, were most adept at this game of blackmail, for they always exaggerated their dissatisfaction with Hungary, and never granted favours without substantial concessions in return. As a result, by the end of the crisis, Imredy and his associates bargained away everything but their shirts.

During the middle of October, when things looked bleak for the Hungarian leadership, ex-Prime Minister Daranyi, acting as his government's emissary to Hitler, made hints to the *Führer* about his country's withdrawal from the League of Nations. He also seems to have indicated the possibility of the removal from the cabinet of Kanya, the man whom Hitler attacked with particular vehemence.[2] Hard on the heels of the Ruthenian fiasco the government promised to the leadership of the *Reich* Hungary's adhesion to the anti-Comintern pact,[3] and the attainment of closer economic cooperation between Hungary and the Axis powers.[4] More important still, Kanya was ousted from office during a cabinet reshuffle in the last days of November. Ever since Kiel, the veteran chief of the Ministry of Foreign Affairs had been a thorn in the eyes of Ribbentrop and Hitler. Now, with the help of the subservient Imredy, the German leaders at last succeeded in dislodging the old man from the Hungarian Government.[5] The next Minister of Foreign Affairs was Istvan Csaky. Although he had been Kanya's *protégé*, Csaky believed in the "German orientation". "There is nothing else we can do" he is supposed to have remarked once to Hory.[6] In addition to such changes in the composition of the government, Imredy embarked upon a radical legislative programme which included, *inter alia*, a new Jewish restriction bill.

During the winter the Hungarian Government took steps

to implement its promise to adhere to the anti-Comintern pact, and to withdraw from the League of Nations. In fact, Csaky's first public statement contained a call for Hungary's joining of the anti-Comintern front. The necessity of this move was again emphasized a few weeks later in discussions between Hungarian and Italian leaders on the occasion of Ciano's visit to Budapest.[7] Hungary's adherence to this primarily anti-Soviet organization was announced on the 13th of January. The actual signing of the documents did not take place until a few weeks later. The immediate result of the whole affair was that the Soviet Union broke off diplomatic relations with Hungary.[8]

During the winter promises were again made by the Imredy government to both Berlin and Rome concerning Hungary's withdrawal from the League of Nations. This was mentioned in the discussions with Ciano,[9] and it came up for discussion between Hitler and Csaky on the occasion of the latter's visit to Berlin in mid-January 1939. Indeed, during his encounter with Hitler, Csaky must have felt the absolute necessity of such a move to regain the confidence of the German leaders, because the *Führer* was still voicing his displeasure with Hungarian foreign policies during the Czechoslovak crisis, and denounced Kanya as an "enemy of Germany". Although not admitting that Hungary could have acted otherwise in September and October, Csaky went far to assure the Nazi leaders of his country's future loyalty and co-operation. To offer them an evidence of this, he promised to withdraw Hungary from the League by May.[10]

In attempting to find an explanation for the pro-German turn in Hungarian foreign policy during the early winter of 1938-39, it would be misleading to believe that the proponents of that policy possessed much enthusiasm for the new Nazi order in Europe. Neither Imredy nor Csaky had much faith in Hitler's "New Order", nor did they have much confidence in Germany's leadership. Their subservience stemmed from a pessimistic, and it must be admitted, not entirely unrealistic, appraisal of the country's power position *vis-á-vis* Nazi Germany. They saw no feasible alternative to a pro-German course. They resigned themselves to the idea that German power was supreme, and to oppose it was unreasonable and unnecessary. Unlike some others who were at the helm of the country's government before and after them, they lacked somehow that moral strength and courage which enables men to fight for their convictions, even if this fight involves risks and sacrifices. Thus Imredy's and Csaky's policy was not so much the product of a desire for marching together with the Nazi leaders toward the creation of a new order in Europe, although such considerations were not entirely absent, but was the product of these men's fear of German power. This was detected by Ciano on his visit to Hungary in December. The Italian Foreign Minister observed that the Hungarians were anxious to adhere to the Axis in spite of "an atmosphere of open hostility to Germany." "They are afraid of Germany," wrote Ciano in his diary, "Csaky does not conceal his anxiety, nor does Imredy."[11]

The Imredy government's pro-German course, particularly its internal programme, the Jewish law, the proposed land reforms, the rise in taxes resulting from increased military expenditures, the failure to curb right-radical propaganda and the growing demagoguery of the administration itself met with considerable disapproval and outright opposition in certain political circles of the country. Numerous liberal and conservative politicians, the former because they believed that the radical politics of the Imredy group might do serious harm to the country's internal order and even its international position, the latter, to use the words of Professor Macartney, "nominally in defence of the Constitution, but really out of dislike of the proposed land reform" began "intriguing against Imredy."[12]

One way in which the opponents of the radical programme hoped to achieve their end was to convince the Regent that it was necessary to drop Imredy at the first opportunity. An attempt to this end was made as early as the end of October, in the form of an appeal addressed to Horthy by Hugo Payr, a long-standing member of the government party and a distinguished parliamentarian. In his letter, Payr outlined the danger of growing right-wing radicalism in the country. Then he pointed out the failure of the Imredy administration to meet this threat head-on, to curb extremist activities effectively. Payr next accused Imredy of harbouring plans of abolishing Parliament and establishing a dictatorship before any of the neo-Nazi groups could succeed in doing so. "This would be the beginning of the end! . . ." continued the letter, "for the first dictator will necessarily lead to the dictatorship of (the Nazi leader) Szalasi . . ." Payr's appeal concluded that Imredy's policy of out-bidding the right extremists by radical appeals and gestures was ineffective and totally unnecessary. He suggested that instead of a policy of trying to steal the show from the neo-Nazis, the rightist danger could be averted by "smart social measures and political know-how" and "a strict and courageous administrator."[13] Apparently Payr's attempt to undermine Imredy's position did not have the intended result, for when Imredy resigned in the midst of the political crisis which followed the Ruthenian fiasco, the Regent refused to accept his resignation.[14]

The opposition to the Premier's radical political programme and the intriguing against his person, however, continued unabated. Imredy's once powerful party was by now divided, for during the crisis a group of 63 conservative M.P.s quit the government party, and began acting as an independent faction within the Lower House. The Dissidents, as the group was called, found a leader in Bethlen. Led by this old and respected magnate, Imredy's opponents made another move during the middle of January. They addressed themselves again to the Regent in a long memorandum, signed this time by Bethlen, two leading figures of the left-of-centre Smallholders' Party, and eight other prominent Dissidents. The appeal outlined the dangerous situation which developed in the country since the Munich crisis, and proceeded to suggest measures to solve the nation's problems. The authors of the document stated that the Imredy government, under the weight of Germany's ever growing influnce, and pressures from below that were "similarly inspired", was trying "to outrace the (Nazi) revolution." They accused Imredy of "radicalizing the country," a trend which threatened the peace and stibility of the country and the feasibility of an independent Hungarian foreign policy. To avert this, the memorandum suggested that the incumbent administration should be pressured into solving the controversial Jewish question and land question to the general public's satisfaction, and when the furor over these issues abated, Parliament should be dissolved. By solving these two outstanding problems before the new elections rather than after, the letter argued, much dangerous ammunition would be taken out of the hands of radical hot-heads and agitators. After the dissolution of Parliament, a new, strong government party would have to be organized, based on "serious principles". A newly elected government backed by such a party would then be able to eliminate the danger of fascist revolution.

The authors of the document next pointed out that considerations of external relations also demanded the proposed changes in party alignments and political tendencies. They admitted the necessity of seeking the friendship of the mighty German *Reich*. They argued, however, that this must not be a one-sided affair; it must not mean the abandoning of an independent foreign policy. They also warned that the establishment of a one-party system on the German or Italian pattern would weaken, rather than strengthen the government's position *vis-à-vis* its "huge foreign partners." In such a state independence of political thought and freedom of speech would disappear and the government would have nothing to fall back on in case of external pressure.

Finally, the authors of the memorandum implored Horthy to withdraw his confidence from Imredy in view of the dangers of his policies and to turn to them for advice concerning the composition of the next government.[15]

This, however, was not the only document submitted to Horthy in those days of January. Bethlen also handed the Regent a paper attesting that Imredy was of part-Jewish descent. This information was passed on to Bethlen by the liberal politician Rassay and the Legitimist leader Count Sigray. This pair of inquisitive persons, no doubt inspired by their dislike of the Prime Minister and his programme, decided, during the summer of 1938, to enquire into the family tree of Imredy. Their inverstigation revealed that one of the great-grandmothers of the Prime Minister had Jewish parents.

During the international crisis of the fall of 1938 Rassay and Sigray remained silent about their findings, but in January of next year they decided to use their document to start the avalanche which would bury Imredy. Apparently they gave the proof of the Prime Minister's Jewish ancestry to Bethlen, who in turn handed it over to Horthy.[16]

At last, the intrigues against Imredy bore their desired fruit. Horthy decided to act this time, in a manner suggested by Bethlen and his associates. After the Land Reform Bill and the Jewish Restriction Bill were prepared for passage in Parliament, (the latter became law only after Imredy's fall) and after a secret investigation by the Ministry of the Interior confirmed the findings of Rassay and Sigray, Horthy summoned the Prime Minister. During their interview the Regent reproached Imredy for his handling of the proposed legislation on the land and Jewish questions, and showed him the documents attesting to his Jewish ancestry. Realizing that the Regent had no confidence in him any longer, and that the discovery of his Jewish descent had made his position as a political leader ludicrous, Imredy resigned.[17] The next day (Feb. 15), Horthy asked Pál Teleki to form a new government. The new Prime Minister, in conformity with the plans submitted to Horthy by Bethlen and his group, proceeded to allow the passage of the Jewish Restriction Bill, called for new elections, reorganized the government party, and dissolved the neo-Nazi Hungarist Party, arresting many of its leaders and outlawing its organs. All this was done with such decisive swiftness that it seems impossible that it had not been planned well in advance.

The figure of Teleki was an anomaly on the stage of European politics in 1939. In a world increasingly dominated by opportunists, demagogues, militarists and professional revolutionaries, he stood almost alone as a scholar, a devoted Christian and a man of high moral principles. Today it can hardly be doubted that few European statesmen of the time possessed a greater aversion to Nazism than did Teleki.[18]

Being a university professor, Teleki was scholarly in his approach to problems. His speeches often turned into long lectures on history, economics and geography. It seems that he was more at home in the academic world than in the boisterous politics of his day. Although he was a count, Teleki's views on social issues were more enlightened than those of most Hungarian aristocrats.

Teleki's personal traits would have made him an ideal political leader in a setting more peaceful than that of 1939-1941. These traits, however, did not always enable him to be an effective national leader in times of crisis. The grave responsibilities and enormous pressures of his office often drove Teleki into fits of pessimism bordering on depression. His despondency usually intensified as the stormclouds became darker over the horizon. Teleki, moreover, was not surrounded by men who would give him valuable assistance in the formulation and execution of his policies, especially in the realm of external affairs. The Regent did not share the Prime Minister's foresight. Teleki often had to restrain Horthy when the latter got carried away in his moments of enthusiasm. Nor did Teleki's aspirations receive much support from Csaky, the essentially pro-German Foreign Minister, who was retained in the cabinet in order to avoid creating the impression that the new administration would drastically alter the course of Hungary's external policy. Yet, by gradually assuming a more important role in the making of foreign policy than his immediate predecessors had done, the Prime Minister succeeded in reducing Csaky's influence on Hungarian diplomacy.

While some members of the country's leadership did not offer constant or wholehearted support to Teleki, others often openly resisted his efforts. One of his strongest adversaries proved to be Henrik Werth, the Chief of the Hungarian General Staff. The fact was that, by the end of 1939, Werth became an advocate of an exclusively German oriented foreign policy. Although the details of his conflict of view with Teleki have not yet been documented completely, it is evident that the Chief-of-Staff tried to exert his influence to impose his ideas on the government. His efforts almost led to open clashes with Teleki, whose concepts on the country's foreign policy were different.

Being a geographer by profession, Teleki had a definite

inclination toward geographic determinism. He believed that in geopolitics the overall physical features of the land constituted a more important force than the ties of nationality. These beliefs made him into a staunch revisionist at heart. He was convinced that the return of Ruthenia and most of Transylvania was essential for the security and prosperity of Hungary. It was in these regions that the rivers of the *Alföld* originated, and it was with these areas that the communities of the Hungarian Plain traditionally conducted much of their commerce. It is not surprising that under Teleki the regaining of some of these territories continued to remain one of the major objectives of the country's foreign policy.

This, however, did not mean that the new administration endorsed a policy of intimate co-operation with Germany and an increasing reliance on Nazi support for the attainment of of Hungarian aspirations. Teleki abhorred the idea of total Nazi victory in Europe. After the outbreak of World War II he always maintained the hope that ultimately the Western powers would win the conflict. Although his government was not reluctant to take advantage of the opportunities created by the war for the strengthening of Hungary's position, Teleki did not desire to attain his aims through collaboration with the Third *Reich*. He knew that advantages gained through the use of such methods would never be accepted by the West and, therefore, would not benefit his country in the long run. As a result, he strove to safeguard Hungary's free hand in dealing with external affairs, while he continued the long-standing policy of avoiding involvement in a confrontation between the opposing camps of the European great powers.

Teleki was a Transylvanian. His ancestors had been prominent statesmen of that land. They were famous for the *finesse* with which they had maintained Transylvanian independence by balancing the power of the Turks against that of the Habsburgs. Teleki believed that with his Transylvanian acumen for balance-of-power politics he could preserve the strength, neutrality and independence of Hungary by "keeping in", as Professor Macartney has expressed it, "with both sides" of the divided European political world.[19]

108

Under Teleki then, there came a return to the foreign policy lines of Kanya's days. Renewed emphasis was placed on courting the favour of the British Foreign Office. The idea of close co-operation with Poland was revived, although in view of Beck's resentment of Hungary's uncertain attitudes during the Ruthenian crisis, and the increasing Nazi pressure on Poland, the value of this policy of friendship with Warsaw had an ever diminishing value. This was soon realized in Budapest, but not before another significant development took place which had serious repercussions in Hungary's relations with both Poland and Germany. This event was the return of Ruthenia to Hungary at the time of Hitler's occupation of the rump Czech state on March 15.

After the fall of 1938, when expectations for a common Polish-Hungarian border had been dashed, leaders in Budapest did not give up their hopes for the regaining of Subcarpathia in the near future. As has been mentioned, Teleki believed in the necessity of acquiring that area and continued his predecessor's manoeuvres designed to attain this end with equal determination but with more luck.

Already in February Csaky made an overture to Berlin aimed at finding out the German leaders' present attitude toward the idea of Ruthenia's annexation by Hungary.[20] The affirmative answer only came on the eve of Hitler's occupation of Bohemia in mid-March, 1939. The German Government not only reversed its opposition to Hungarian ambitions in Subcarpathia, but even urged prompt and bold action.[21] The German permission to march was kept a strict secret, so that the impression in Budapest and Warsaw was that the occupation of Ruthenia was carried out against the wishes of Berlin.[22]

2. The Last Months of Peace.

On the 15th of March Hungary's mobile units, equipped mainly with bicycles, began marching into Ruthenia. Easily overcoming any opposition offered to them, they soon reached the Polish border. The news of the quick success of the operation was greeted with wild enthusiasm not only in Budapest but also in Warsaw. The course of the next several weeks, however, proved that there was little cause for celabration in Hungary and Poland in March 1939. For in the wake of the crisis, Slovakia, worried about possible Hungarian designs against her, signed an agreement with Germany. Hitler guaranteed Slovakia's borders and that country became a virtual satellite of the *Reich*. As a result, the strategical value of the newly attained Hungarain-Polish common boundary declined considerably. Thus, the acquisition of Ruthenia did little, if anything, to strengthen Hungary's position *vis-á-vis* Germany.

When Hitler allowed the Hungarians to move into Ruthenia he apparently did not have in mind to yield that territory without some strings attached. The conditions under which Subcarpathia was to go to Hungary had been laid down prior to March 15. According to these, the economic agreements between the *Reich* and Ruthenia were to remain in effect after the occupation of the region by Hungary.[23] On this ground, a few weeks later the Berlin government began demanding concessions in the exploration and exploitation of the natural resources of the area, claiming that this bad been promised in March. After a few acrimonious exchanges the Germans were finally told that such far-going concessions were never promised to them, and that Hungary would insist on conducting the search for resources in Subcarpathia by herself, but would not bar Germany from participating in the exploitation of any finds.[24]

Far more significant than this minor friction with Berlin over economics was the fact that in Ruthenia Hungary acquired an area which, after the disappearance of Poland a few months later, became contiguous with the Soviet Union, and which area was the scene of some of the incidents that were to involve the country in the fatal Russian campaign some two years later. In view of all this the regaining of Ruthenia, which in part at least was intended as a measure to strengthen the country's international position *vis-á-vis* Germany, in the long run turned out to be more harmful than beneficial. All this, however, was not apparent in March of 1939. At this time many still valued the friendship with Poland as an insurance against Germany's growing weight in East Central Europe. Such illusions, however, did not have to wait long to be shattered.

During the second half of April, Teleki and Csaky visited Rome and Berlin. In the course of their discussions with the Italian leaders it was emphasized that within the Rome-Berlin Axis there was a special Italo-Hungarian community of interest, and that it was the desire of both countries' governments to attain a balance within this political alignment between Germany on one hand, and Italy and Hungary on the other. Csaky, anxious to buttress his country's position against German preponderance in the Danube region, told Ciano and Mussolini that "a strong Italy is almost a precondition to Hungary's existence." Noting the Italians' desire for continued peace in Europe, Teleki and Csaky attempted to convince them that a German-Polish conflict would inevitably involve Italy in war. This way the Hungarians were hoping to ease the lot of their Polish friends faced by the Nazi threat. Perhaps they still believed that Mussolini's opinion carried some weight with Hitler. Csaky also managed to secure the Duce's assurance that he would not tolerate the violation of Hungary's independence by the domineering Germans.[25] Mussolini, of course, had no intention of making good his promise, if it ever came to a showdown between Berlin and Budapest.[26] In spite of this, Hungary's link with Italy still had some value in reinforcing her government's position vis-à-vis Berlin, much more value indeed than the link with Poland. Teleki and Csaky must have become fully aware of this fact during their stay in Berlin at the end of April.

In the course of the discussions in Berlin, the German leaders, probably because they desired to increase Poland's isolation by forcing the Hungarians to abandon their policy of friendship with Warsaw, impressed upon Csaky and Teleki that German-Polish relations were very bad and that continued Polish "intransigence" would lead to conflict. Ribbentrop testified at his trial in Nuremberg that "... the Hungarians were somewhat worried with regard to the German policy (toward Poland) ... the Führer had told me ... to use particularly clear and strong language on these subjects ..."[27]

111

Apparently, Ribbentrop accomplished his task with considerable success. Even though the Hungarian leaders showed great reluctance to curb their protestations of friendship with Warsaw during the following months,[28] and refused to entertain ideas of participating in military action against Poland,[29] these discussions had delivered the *coup de grace* to the idea of the Danube-Vistula axis.

After the end of April there could have been no doubt in the minds of Hungary's leaders that sooner or later the time would come for an armed showdown between Germany and Poland. Ribbentrop's and Hitler's statements on the state of German-Polish relations were confirmed by reports from Hory. In one of these, which was written on the eve of the Berlin talks, the Hungarian Minister to Poland summed up the situation with remarkable political foresight. Hory stated that in view of Hitler's aspirations and the nature of the Nazi system, a German-Polish conflict was inevitable. He predicted that the war could not be localized and because of American superiority, Germany would be defeated after some initial successes. Hungary would probably become involved in the struggle, which would be a tragedy, for Germany would exploit the country to her own interest. "Hungary", wrote Hory with sincere grief, "has tied its fate to the Axis."[30]

Throughout the summer the attention of Hungary's leaders was in large part devoted to keeping an anxious eye on German-Polish relations. Their aim was to avoid offending the Nazis and, at the same time, to ensure that the country would not become involved in any way on either side in the coming conflict. This policy was opposed by the Poles who resented Hungary's conforming with the Axis at the expense of her traditional friendship with Poland;[31] while it displeased the Germans who were expecting the Budapest government to display a tougher attitude toward the Poles. Moreover, the desire to insure Hungarian non-involvement led to a notable incident in the relations of Hungary and the *Reich*.

On July 24 Teleki addressed two letters to Hitler which clarified the position of the Hungarian Government concerning any future German-Polish conflict. The first letter explained that "... in the event of a general conflict Hungary will make her policy conform to the policy of the Axis ..." without prejudicing the country's national sovereignty. The second letter went as follows: "In order to prevent any possible misinterpretation of my letter of July 24, I have the honour to repeat ... that ... Hungary could not, on moral grounds, be in a position to take armed action against Poland."[32] The official reaction to the letters in Berlin was highly unfavourable.[33] At a discussion between Hitler and Csaky on August 8 in Obersalzberg, the German leader stated that he was shocked by the second letter and warned that should Germany lose the coming conflict, not only would Hungary's dreams of revision end, but Czechoslovakia would be strengthened and the Czecho-Yugoslav common boundary would become a reality. It can be suspected that Hitler was putting on an act when he pretended to be outraged by the incident in order to scare Csaky into a more submissive mood. The Foreign Minister was apparently both frightened and resentful as a result of Hitler's tirade. He proposed to withdraw the letters.[34] Several days later he told Ciano in Rome that he worried about a "friendly German occupation", suggested the putting of the Duke of Aosta on the throne of Hungary to strengthen ties with Italy, and made no secret how "95% of Hungarians" hated Germans.[35]

In the meantime reports on German war preparations and on improving Nazi-Soviet relations kept coming in.[36] No German demands for Hungarian participation in any form were made before the beginning of the hostilities. German policy in this regard, however, underwent considerable change in the midst of the military operations against Poland.

3. Neutrality in Nazi Germany's Shadow.

On the first of September Hitler's armies invaded Poland. The struggle that ensued was not a war for Danzig and the "corridor". It was a war for Nazi supremacy in East Central Europe. In his younger days Hitler dreamed of conquering *Lebensraum*, or living-space, for Germany in the East. In 1934 the Nazi leader explained to an acquaintance of his, Hermann Rauschning, that to attain this objective Germany had to establish an Eastern Alliance with the small states of East Central Europe. According to Hitler this was to be "an alliance, but not of equal partners ... an alliance of vassal states."[37] When, in the spring of 1939, the Polish Government rejected German overtures for collaboration, and accepted an offer of a British guarantee to Poland, the Nazi leader saw his plans threatened. He decided to crush the uncooperative Poles at the next favourable occasion. He hoped to localize the war by causing the British and French governments to lose their nerve in the critical hour. The move that was designed to attain this result was the sudden announcement of the Nazi-Soviet Nonagression Pact of August 23rd, three days before the invasion of Poland was originally planned. The world was stunned by this unexpected news. The British Government, however, confirmed its determination to stand by Poland. On the 26th Hitler called the invasion off. Next he made offers to settle the issue through negotiations. He was not after another Munich conference, but aimed to drive a wedge between London and Warsaw. He outlined his plan to his generals: "... we demand Danzig, corridor through [the] corridor, and plebiscite ... England will perhaps accept, Poland probably not. [We drive a] wedge between them."[38]

Thus, Hitler was aiming to create an Anglo-Polish misunderstanding which would have allowed Germany to deal with Poland alone. His plan did not come off as he expected, for the British and French governments honoured their pledge to Poland and declared war on Germany. The ensuing conflict, however, was not really an all-out European military struggle. A state of war existed, but after the capitulation of Poland, the fronts remained inactive.

Hungarians in general resigned themselves to the bitter fate of their Polish friends. They threw the border open to refugees. Some 100,000 Poles fled to Hungary,[39] where they were well received, much to the disgust of the German leaders. A few Magyar irregulars even joined the Poles in their struggle,[40] otherwise nothing was done, as indeed nothing could be done to save Poland from defeat. The Polish soldiers who escaped to Hungary were allowed to leave the country and to travel to France, in spite of frequent protests from Berlin.[41] Many of them eventually joined the Polish army in exile.

The Hungarian Government was in no position to offer more effective assistance to its Polish friends. To get involved in a war against Germany would have been senseless in view of Hungary's military unpreparedness and geographic situation. The country's leaders realized this. Unlike the Poles, they had no illusions about their army's strength. Nor did they feel to be immediately threatened by Germany. There were no outstanding issues between the *Reich* and Hungary, no territorial claims, no English "alliances" and the like, as in the case of Poland. In view of this, most Hungarian political leaders believed it to be safe to assume that, as long as minor economic and political concessions were made to the Germans, there would be no conflict with the Nazis. On the basis of this assumption there was good reason to prefer a policy of seeking Hitler's favour to one which risked incurring his anger. While the latter undoubtedly would have led to immediate disaster, the former, if conducted shrewdly, even offered prospects of incidental benefits such as the possibility of further territorial revision. Of course, some of the country's leaders were aware of the dangers implicit in a pro-Axis policy. Therefore these men, foremost among them Teleki, were resolved to pursue this policy with definite reservations in mind. They were willing to follow the German line only to the extent that it did not endanger the country's sovereignty, compromise national honour, unduly discredit the government in the eyes of the British leaders, and as long as it did not involve Hungary in the European war on Germany's side. How difficult, if not impossible, it was to conduct such a policy became evident already during the fall of 1939.

German-Hungarian relations during the September crisis were particularly tense. Berlin put heavy pressure on Hungarian authorities even before the invasion of Poland began. Alleged pro-Polish statements and moves on the part of Hungarian politicians and the press were denounced by the Nazis already on the 31st of August.[42] The German Government, moreover, suspended the shipment of war material to Hungary. The excuse was Hungary's uncertain attitude,[43] but the real motive undoubtedly was to influence the actions of her government by making the resumption of arms shipments subject to the satisfactory conduct of Hungarian diplomacy during the crisis. Already on the first of September Ribbentrop warned Csaky not to make a declaration of neutrality.[44] This was, however, only a modest indication of things to come. Four days later came the ominous message from the *Reich's* Foreign Minister enquiring if Hungary had any territorial ambitions in Poland and asking Csaky to come to Germany for secret discussions.[45] When the two met a few days later, Ribbentrop advised the Hungarian Government to refrain from any hostile action against Rumania. Csaky assured Ribbentrop that his country had no designs on that country.[46] Hardly had the Hungarian Foreign Minister returned from his trip when his German colleague confronted him with a much more serious demand: a request for transit rights on a railway line through Hungary for German troops destined for Poland. The word was given over the telephone, with less than 24 hours allowed for a reply.

That same evening the country's highest civilian and military leaders met in council. They decided to decline the request arguing that to yield would be incompatible with national honour and would bring an Anglo-French declaration of war against Hungary. At the meeting of the Ministerial Council next morning this decision was unanimously endorsed. It was communicated to Ribbentrop by telephone.[47] The reply was in conformity with Mussolini's advice which called for polite refusal.[48] The German leaders were obviously not pleased with the answer. Next, they encouraged the Slovaks to make a similar demand for their own troops. Csaky rejected this one as well, but indicated his willingness to allow the transport of war materials through Hungarian territory.[49] The Nazi leaders, realizing the uselessness of their efforts, desisted from making new demands for transit rights to Poland.[50] Concerning the incident Ciano wrote in his diary at the time that the Germans will not forget this and Hungary will have to pay for this someday.[51] The whole affair was a clear indication that the Hungarian policy of trying to please Hitler without commitments on the part of the country was

116

a difficult one indeed, one which, at times, seemed to have little if any prospect for lasting success.

An examination of German-Hungarian economic relations at this time will only confirm the above observation. During the first months of the war the country's economic subservience to German interests considerably increased. As in the field of politics, Berlin confronted Budapest with incessant demands in the realm of economics also. The Hungarians were once again requested to yield on the question of exploration and exploitation of the natural resources of Ruthenia as it had allegedly been promised in March by Teleki. They were asked to give special consideration to Slovakia's food needs within the context of Hungarian-Slovak trade. A demand was made for a change in the exchange policy of the National Bank of Hungary which, in the view of the Germans, discriminated against the *Reichsmark*.[52] The Hungarian Government found it impossible not to yield at least to some of these demands.[53] Not to do so would have brought on the threat of another embargo on the shipment of German arms and that of other exports to Hungary.

While in the matters of trade the concessions made to Germany's interests continued, German influence was growing stronger and stronger in the economic life of the nation also. A contemporary foreign ministry memorandum on German penetration of Hungarian economic life concluded that the *Reich's* influence was "extensive and wide-spread". According to the author of the document, the origin of this was the one-time Austrian capital investment in Hungarian enterprises. As a result of the establishment of Nazi control over the activities of former Austrian firms, this influence assumed political significance. The memorandum pointed out that the *Osterreichische Creditanstalt Wiener Bankverein* held a significant share in the stock of several leading Hungarian industrial enterprises. It also listed some 100 manufacturing and transport firms in Hungary whose control was exclusively in German hands, and close to 50 companies in which Germans shared control with Hungarians. The author of the study warned that in such a state of affairs Germany possessed the means to influence Hungary's economic life.[54]

The nation's press also showed signs of yielding to German pressure. The official government press was writing in a pro-German tone by the end of the year. Some liberal and Social-Democratic newspapers still refused to conform. Teleki, moreover, made sure that the country's public did not become exposed to a completely one-sided pro-German press. Soon after the outbreak of the war, he secretly took steps to organize a publication which was to shoulder the task of disseminating Teleki's own views on international issues, views that the Prime Minister did not dare to air publicly out of fear of German retaliation. For this purpose he summoned a couple of reliable journalists and informed them of their task. Teleki told his audience that sooner or later, perhaps only after the passing of years, Germany would lose the war. She would lose it because the moral and material superiority was on the Allied side. Against such superiority only temporary successes were possible, but not final victory. Teleki stated that he, as the Prime Minister of Hungary, was in no position to do anything but to conduct a policy friendly to Germany. He did not know how the situation would evolve, but as German pressure upon Hungary increased, he might be forced to take the country into the war on Germany's side. Teleki then stated that he needed a forum in which he could express his own views. The public had to be informed that while Hungary was a state friendly to Germany, the material and moral superiority in the struggle was not on the side of the Nazis but on that of the Allies.[55]

As a result of this interview the daily paper *Magyarország* became Teleki's own unofficial press organ. Its staff, which included men who previously worked with the Hungarian press of Prague, assumed full responsibility for publication and editorial policy.[56]

The greatest worry of the Teleki government during the winter of 1939-40 was neither the extent of German economic penetration of Hungary, nor the problem of the press, but the question where Hitler would make his next military move. Poland had been subjugated without heavy losses to the Germans. The western front was inactive. The enormous German war-machine was idle. Everyone knew that it was being prepared for new conquests in the spring.

For the statesmen of Hungary, most signs seemed to point to the fact that the *Führer's* next major move would come in south-eastern Europe, more precisely, in Rumania. In January, a German general informed the Hungarians that if a future conflict between Soviet Russia and Rumania over disputed territories were to spread into the Balkans, Germany would take steps to secure the oil-fields of Ploesti in south-central Rumania.[57] Soon the Hungarian Government learned that strategic highways were being built for the Germans in eastern Slovakia. Next came the news of German troop concentrations in this same region.[58]

These developments caused considerable alarm in Budapest. The prospect of a German move for the occupation of the Rumanian oil-fields threatened Hungary with a German demand that troop movements across the country be permitted. Compliance with the Nazis' wishes would have discredited the government in the West, particularly in London, while a denial of the request could have led to a military occupation of Hungary by the *Wehrmacht*.

It was under these circumstances that Teleki, apparently in consultation with his most intimate friends and advisers, made secret preparations for the establishment of a Hungarian government in exile. This government, which was to be established in the United States, would have shouldered the task of representing a Hungary which had fallen under Hitler's influence as a result of developments in south-eastern Europe. The plan for a government in exile was not a novel idea in Hungarian circles in January of 1940. Apparently, it was first mentioned during the crisis-ridden month of September 1938. At that time, Janos Pelenyi the Hungarian Minister to Washington, suggested the idea to Csaky. In April 1939, Pelenyi repeated his proposal, this time to Teleki.[59] When the Minister to Washington next met the Prime Minister, Teleki had the following to say: "The memorandum has my closest attention and if the situation envisaged should arrive I myself will dash abroad, provided that I can still get to a plane."[60]

Late in the winter of 1939-40 the situation, it seemed, had become serious enough to warrant some definitive action in connection with the proposed Hungarian government in the West. Consequently Teleki, acting in consultation with Horthy, made arrangements for the transfer of five million dollars in government funds and securities to America for safekeeping. The instructions regarding the handling of the funds were brought to Pelenyi by a secret emissary, Andor Teleki, the Prime Minister's nephew. The Hungarian Minister to London, Gyorgy Barcza, was told at the time to turn to his colleague in Washington "should a certain situation arise."[61]

In the letter delivered by Andor Teleki, Pelenyi was instructed to safeguard the funds and, when the hour for the establishment of a government in exile came, place them at the disposal of the leaders "of a possible Hungarian emigration." According to the document, Regent Horthy, ex-Premier Count Gyula Karolyi and Prime Minister Teleki, were "authorized singly and individually to take over the funds and to dispose of them for the defence of our national freedom." Provisions were made for other individuals to control the funds jointly, in case neither Horthy, nor Karolyi, nor Teleki could succeed in fleeing to the West.[62] Pelenyi was also informed that should the danger to Hungary and her regime pass, he would be notified. He then should place the money at the disposal of the National Bank of Hungary.

Still another move in connection with this plan for preparing the establishment of a powerful Hungarian "emigration" in the West, was Eckhardt's departure to the United States. Over the past few years, this diplomat and politician had built up a reputation as a liberal reformer and an opponent to Rightist extremism. Evidently, Teleki believed that it would be valuable to have a person like him in the West. At the end of January 1940, Eckhardt resigned as the leader of the Smallholders' Party. After several weeks of preparation, he left for the United States. It was announced that he was going on a lecture tour.[63]

Apart from the revelations of Pelenyi, and a few details in connection with Eckhardt's activities, not much is known of Teleki's plans and preparations for a Hungarian government in exile. The historians of present-day Hungary are most reluctant to disclose any facts in connection with this. A recently published 368 page monograph on the Teleki administration's foreign policies, for example, completely disregards this incident of Hungarian diplomatic history.[64] This, in a way, is typical of communist historical scholarship.

Teleki, however, did not satisfy himself with making preparations for a government in exile. He also turned to the Italian leaders. At the end of March he paid a visit to Ciano and Mussolini. In Rome, however, Teleki did not find the comfort and aid he had probably expected. He got no answer to the question what Hungary should do if the Germans demanded the right of transit for their troops through the country.[65] He also suggested that Hungary and Italy should stay out of war. Much to Teleki's disappointment, Mussolini stated that Italy would intervene in the conflict on the side of Germany at an opportune moment. Throughout the discussions Teleki made no secret of his dislike and fear of Nazi Germany.[66]

Hard on the heels of Teleki's visit to Rome further disturbing news arrived in Budapest. In Moscow, Molotov, the Soviet Foreign Minister, declared his government's intention to settle its territorial disputes with Rumania. From Berlin Sztojay sent an alarming report that the Germans, in anticipation of a Russian attack on Rumania, were contemplating the military occupation of that country's oil-fields. For this purpose Berlin would demand the right of transit through Hungary. The denial of this request, according to Sztojay, would result in war between Hungary and the Third *Reich*.[67]

The Hungarian Government's response to this new threat was hesitant at first. Soon after the arrival of the news the Ministerial Council met to iron out the details of a policy of countering the danger of an impending German military thrust toward the South-East. The Council, however, could not reach a definitive decision.[68] Next, the issue was discussed at a smaller meeting in which only Horthy, Teleki, Csaky, the Minister of Defence Karoly Bartha, and General Werth participated. Here it was tentatively agreed upon that Hungary would comply with a German demand for the right of transit and limited Hungarian collaboration in the venture only if a Soviet advance into Rumania actually took place. Under such circumstances, the leaders of Hungary apparently believed, their action could somehow be justified as a move to forestall the penetration of the Balkans by communist Russia.[69]

To prepare for the possible emergence of a situation in which Hungary found herself in no position to go along with the Germans, Teleki once again turned for help to the Italian Government. On the 8th of April he informed the leaders in Rome of the situation. At the time Ciano commented on the Hungarian Prime Minister's message in these sentences:

For the Hungarians there arises the problem either of letting the Germans pass, or opposing them with force. In either case Hungarian liberty would come to an end. Acceptance would spare the devastation and ruin, while fighting, though more painful for the moment, would prepare for a future rebirth.[70]

Teleki had some definite questions for the Italian leaders: 1. whether they were willing to help Hungary in case of German aggression, 2. whether the Italian Government would consider participating in a scheme to secure the areas threatened by Russia and Germany, 3. whether Rome would intervene in Berlin to demand that a reorganization in the Balkans should not be undertaken without Italy and Hungary being consulted, and 4. what precise steps the Italian leaders envisaged for helping Hungary if Italy's interests in this part of Europe ever had to be defended by armed force.[71]

To these desperate questions Mussolini's answer was simple. He told the Hungarians that he stood "firmly with Germany", and that he was getting ready to enter the war on Hitler's side.[72]

As a result of the Italian Government's negative response to the Hungarian overture, Teleki was once again left to his own devices. Although in Rome he was assured that Germany did not plan to march toward the Balkans, the Prime Minister still wanted to gain better insight into the German plans for this region of Europe. For this purpose he wrote a letter to Hitler suggesting discussions among the governments of Germany, Italy and Hungary on the problems of the Danube

Valley and the Balkans. Teleki proposed that issues which went beyond the realm of diplomacy also be included among the subjects to be considered by any such three-power conference.

By sending this letter the Prime Minister hoped to gain admittance to the councils of Hitler. The price Hungary would have to pay for this privilege was evident to Teleki. If the government offered to discuss questions of a military nature with the Germans, then it obviously could not refuse participation in the solution of such problems. Participation in Hungary's case meant at least permission to the German army to pass through Hungarian territory. Teleki's decision to abandon the idea of resisting a German plan which called for transit through Hungary was clearly revealed in a conversation he had at the time with O'Malley, the British Minister in Budapest. To the question whether the Hungarian Government would allow the Germans to march through the country against Rumania, the Prime Minister replied that, under the circumstances, it would be too much to expect Hungary not to do so.[74] Thus, eight months after the outbreak of the war, Hungary came one step closer to abandoning its neutrality.

To be sure, the Hungarian fears of a German move toward the South-East soon proved to be premature. Hitler's next big offensive came on the Western front. On May 14, four days after the attack on Holland, Belgium and France began, the *Führer* answered Teleki's letter. He stated that in view of the life and death struggle in the West, Germany did not want to see peace in the Balkans disturbed under any circumstances. He turned down the Hungarian proposal for three-power discussions.[75]

At this point it became clear in Hungary that as long as the *Reich* obtained its foodstuffs and raw materials from south-eastern Europe, this region would be safe from German military attack, at least for the time the Western front was active.[76]

The crisis of the spring of 1940, however, did not pass without important consequences. First of all, the promise of no opposition to the transit of German troops, intimated by Teleki's letter to Hitler, was a concession which Hungary "was never", to use the words of Professor Macartney, "thereafter able to retract, even is she wished."[77] Secondly, the prospect of Rumania's demise and dismemberment aroused revisionist sentiments in the country and heightened expectations of a new territorial settlement in the East. Both of these developments had important repercussions which became evident during the summer and fall of 1940.

4. Crisis over Transylvania and the Second Vienna Award.

Ever since the beginning of the war it was widely believed in Hungary that in the course of the struggle, or after it was over, the map of East Central Europe would be redrawn. It was also held that the task of the country's government would be to strive to attain the best possible terms for Hungary in this process of revising the national boundaries in this area. There was no agreement, however, on how the most advantageous settlement was to be attained. Those who believed in German victory, like Sztojay,[78] the still influential ex-Premier Imredy, and many high-ranking military officers, among them General Werth himself, advised closer co-operation with the Third Reich. Others, however, had different views. One of these was Bethlen who, in March 1940, submitted his suggestions for future Hungarian policies with regard to the expected reorganization of Danubian Europe.

Bethlen's proposals took the form of a very long memorandum. Its basic assumptions were quite remarkable: 1. that Hungary's aims could be attained only at the end of the war; 2. that Hungary would remain neutral in the conflict between Germany and the Allies; 3. that in all probability Germany would lose the war.

Starting from these tenets, Bethlen continued by analyzing in great detail all the possible situations which could emerge in East Central Europe after the defeat of Germany.[79] He argued that a change in the Trianon status quo would become a possibility at the time of the peace settlement. Apparently he believed that the victorious great powers could be persuaded to return some of the former Hungarian possessions in exchange for Hungary's participation in a federation or al-

124

liance designed to counterbalance and contain Germany. If, however, no such arrangement was to be made, then Bethlen saw no other way of attaining Hungary's aims than by confronting the peace conference with a military *fait accompli* in Transylvania. He argued that the future peace of Europe and the security of Eastern Europe could then be assured through a loose confederation composed of Poland, Hungary, independent Transylvania and Rumania.[80]

Bethlen's proposal that Hungary should wait till the end of the war for a revision of the Trianon settlement, was not adopted by the government. Developments during the early summer of 1940 induced the country's leaders to press for an immediate solution of the Transylvanian question.

Perhaps the deepest wound that the judgement of Trianon had inflicted upon Hungarians was the decision to take away Transylvania from the ancient Kingdom of St. Stephen. While many in the country readily reconciled themselves to the loss of Croatia, only a few did not dream about regaining the land which for centuries had been the cradle of Hungarian strength and culture. Even fewer realized that any attempt to regain that land would only endanger Hungary's international position. Hory, for example, predicted already in April 1939 that out of the Hungarian-Rumanian animosity only Germany would benefit.[81] Other Hungarians, Teleki among them, were not entirely unaware of this danger, yet they apparently believed that, given the favourable moment, the issue could be solved in a manner satisfactory to Hungary without compromising the country's and its government's position. Consequently, the Hungarian Government insisted on keeping the issue very much alive.

It might be recalled that, already at the time of the Polish crisis of August-September 1939, Teleki had written to Mussolini begging him to speak in behalf of Hungary for a settlement of the Transylvanian problem at the four-power conference which the Italian leader had hoped to convene.[82] Nor was the issue forgotten during the winter of 1939-40. In December General Werth presented a memorandum to the government calling for a military solution of the question.[83] The Supreme Defence Council of the country met, and considered his proposal. Its decision in the matter was communicated to the Italian Government at the earliest opportunity.

Early in January 1940, Csaky told Ciano in Venice that Hungary desired the return of at least half of Transylvania. The Hungarian Foreign Minister also stated that if Rumania turned bolshevik, or threatened the lives of Hungarians in Transylvania, or yielded territory to Russia and Bulgaria without making similar concessions to Hungary, his government would take matters into its own hands and would deal with Rumania in a radical manner.[84]

It seems that apart from consulting the Italians on the matter, the Teleki government also sounded out the other great powers concerned, including Britain. As a result, the original enthusiasm for taking action against Rumania was soon tuned down considerably. The new Hungarian position was published in *The Times*. It stipulated that "Hungary, while by no means abandoning her territorial claims on Rumania, will make no attempts to force a settlement of these claims during the war except in the case of two eventualities — (1) If Russia should attack Rumania successfully and thus threaten to overrun the Balkans; and (2) if Rumania should offer Dobruja to Bulgaria." In any case, the Hungarian Government promised that even if it did occupy Transylvania as a result of a Rumanian collapse under a Russian attack, "the question would, at the end of the war, be submitted to the peace conference for a permanent decision."[85]

The next development in the Transylvanian issue came in April, at the time of Teleki's suggestion of three-power talks between Germany, Italy and Hungary on issues affecting them in South-Eastern Europe. The suggestion alarmed Hitler. Tension in the Danubian realm was not in the interest of Germany. It threatened with the prospect of bringing Russia into the Balkans and the destruction of the extremely important Rumanian oil-fields. Thus, the *Führer* had every reason to shudder at the thought of Hungarian machinations against Rumania. He even expressed the view to General Halder, the commander of Germany's armed forces, that the Hungarians were possibly emboldened in their designs by the

British who had an interest in seeing the Rumanian oil-wells go up in flames.[86]

Up till June, however, the Transylvanian question was not a serious international issue. True, some of the Hungarian Government's declarations on its claims in that region were quite militant. Yet they were only designed to keep the issue alive or to find out the attitudes of other powers to the problem. Toward the end of June, however, events took place which turned the Transylvanian question into the key issue of the day. These events were the moves made by the Soviet Union for the recovery of Bessarabia from Rumania.

By the early summer Rumania's international position had seriously deteriorated. Her old allies and benefactors, France and Britain, were no longer in a position to help. Her traditional enemies, Hungary and Bulgaria, openly voiced their demand for the return of some of the territories Rumania had gained from them after the First World War. Her greatest potential enemy, Russia, had been in league with Nazi Germany ever since the destruction of Poland in the fall of 1939. At that time, moreover, there had been a secret agreement between these two powers according to which Eastern Europe had been divided into a German and a Russian sphere of influence. The eastern provinces of Rumania had been assigned to the latter one.

It is little wonder under the circumstances that the leaders of the U.S.S.R. made use of Rumania's weakened position to recover Bessarabia, one of the many regions which the Rumanians had gained in the wake of World War I.[87] On the 26th of June, the Soviet Government confronted Bucharest with a 24 hour ultimatum calling for the cession of this area to the Soviet Union.

With Rumania faced with such a predicament, the chance of a lifetime seemed to have arrived for Hungary. All the more so since from Moscow came Stalin's message that the time had come for Hungarians to "move" if they ever wanted a solution of the Transylvanian question.[88] As a result, the Hungarian diplomatic machine swung into action. Once again the German and Italian governments were informed that Hungary would not tolerate a discriminatory treatment of the

Transylvanian problem by Rumania, that is, she would consider it a serious affront if the Rumanian Government agreed to settle its territorial dispute with the Soviet Union but not with Hungary.[89]

Meanwhile, fundamental developments took place in Rumania. The leaders of that country realized that they could expect no help in the crisis from Britain, which formerly had guaranteed Rumania's independence. They, therefore, turned to Hitler for aid. They assured him of continued supplies of crude oil for the German warmachine, and the loyalty of the country to the Rome-Berlin Axis. In return they asked the *Führer* to restrain the Hungarians and Bulgarians. The Germans advised the Rumanian Government to yield to the Russian demands. Soon the Red Army occupied Bessarabia. At the same time, Rumania denounced the British guarantee. Her King reorganized the country's government. The new administration's first move was to request Hitler for German troops and a formal guarantee to Rumania. Thus, within a few days following the Soviet ultimatum,Rumania threw herself into the arms of Hitler.[90]

During this time the Hungarian politicians did their utmost to exploit the situation created by the Soviet move against Rumania. On the 28th of the month Csaky made an effort to find out what Germany's attitude would be to a Hungarian attempt to re-occupy Transylvania by force. He told the Germans that internal order in Rumania would collapse in the course of a Russian invasion of Bessarabia. To prevent the spread of anarchy quick Hungarian action seemed necessary. The Foreign Minister then gave assurance of continued supplies of Hungarian foodstuffs for Germany even during a possible Hungarian-Rumanian war. In addition Csaky promised to shelve any other major Hungarian revisionist demands for a long time to come.[91]

An answer to the feeler was slow to come. Not wasting precious time, Hungary began massing her army on the Rumanian border. Upon learning this, Berlin reacted immediately. In the small hours of the morning of July 2, Erdmannsdorff, the German Minister to Hungary, paid a visit to Csaky, and warned against the use of force in the settling of the dispute over Transylvania. The warning was repeated on the 4th.[92]

The Germans then, had complied with the request of the Rumanians. The next day instructions went out to the German Minister to Bucharest to inform the Rumanian King that the German Government had "urgently advised Hungary to keep the peace."[93]

There remained one ray of hope for the Hungarians. The German notes of the 2nd and 4th contained a promise that the Government of the *Reich* would examine the problem of revision in the Balkans. It is quite possible that the Hungarian leaders had aimed to exact such a promise all along. Subsequent developments seem to indicate this.

The next significant development came a few days later when Hitler invited Teleki and Csaky for discussions in Munich. Ciano was also asked to attend. The meeting took place on July 10. Teleki opened the talks by presenting a letter from Horthy to the *Führer*. In it, the Regent argued that it was in the interest of Germany and Europe that Transylvania should be in Hungarian hands.[94] Next, the Hungarian Prime Minister, in his usual academic style, elaborated upon the ethnographic, economic and historic justice of Hungary's claims. Following this the *Führer* startled his Hungarian guests by bluntly asking them whether in their opinion Hungary could defeat Rumania single-handedly. After some hesitation, Csaky answered in the affirmative. He also admitted that "One favourable moment at which Rumania might have been successfully attacked had ... already passed by. This was the moment shortly before the Russians marched into Bessarabia ..."[95] Next, Hitler argued at length against a solution of the issue through the use of force. He even warned that "Germany could not be indifferent to what happened to the Rumanian oil-wells." Finally he assured his guests "that Germany was sympathetic to their demands" and suggested that they achieve their aims "through negotiations". In reply, Teleki stated that in his opinion the negotiations with Rumania would not lead to positive results unless both Germany and Italy participated in them. He asked Ciano whether the Italian Government was ready to take part in the talks.

The Italian Foreign Minister answered that this would have to be discussed with the German leaders.[96]

At Munich, the Hungarian leaders had committed themselves to the idea of negotiations with Rumania over Transylvania. Originally they had hoped that the discussions on the issue might take the form of a four-power conference with Germany and Italy participating as well. Hitler and Ciano, however, gave no indication of their intention to take part in such an arrangement. Since there was little chance that the Rumanians would yield when confronted by the Hungarians alone, the Munich discussions represented a failure for Hungarian diplomacy.

Returning home from the meeting with Hitler and Ciano, the Hungarian leaders were in no position to acknowledge publicly the setback their plans had suffered. Therefore, they created the impression that an agreement had been attained in Munich among Berlin, Rome and Budapest over the Transylvanian issue. Had they done otherwise, they would have further strengthened the Rumanians in their determination not to yield any part of Transylvania to Hungary. Unfortunately, these statements by the government caused the rise of undue expectations on the part of the Hungarian public. Large portions of the country's population, not satisfied with the prospect of regaining the predominantly Magyar areas of Transylvania, began voicing the slogan "everything back".[97]

A few days after the Munich talks the Hungarian Government dispatched a note to Bucharest requesting the start of negotiations. Hitler also sent a long letter to King Carol of Rumania urging him to settle the dispute with Hungary.

The Rumanians did not seem to have been greatly impressed by the Hungarian and German notes. The former they disregarded completely, and Hitler's letter was answered only at the end of July.[98] King Carol and his ministers were not inclined to yield to the Hungarian demands. Only a while before the crisis a high-ranking Rumanian official had informed the British Government that "territorial integrity was the bedrock of (his) Government's whole foreign policy."[99] Although Rumania hed yielded large areas to the Soviet

Union, she continued to maintain this policy of "territorial integrity" vis-á-vis Budapest. Hungary, after all, was only a small power. The Rumanian leaders, moreover, probably suspected that Hitler would not allow the Hungarians to attack their country. They knew that a war in that part of Europe would cut off the German army's vital oil supply. Thus, they apparently believed that their country could escape the crisis without great losses, if only its government appeased Hitler by economic and political concessions. They thought that they could avoid a new territorial settlement in Transylvania by accepting some border adjustments. At the end of July, for example, the Rumanian statesmen informed the Führer that they were willing to offer to Hungary about 11.4% of the area awarded to Rumania from the lands of the Holy Crown of St. Stephen by the Treaty of Trianon. They also asked him to play the role of arbitrator in the dispute, in case direct negotiations with Hungary did not bring about a settlement. At the time the German leader rejected the request.[100]

During the second week of August preparations began, at last, for the holding of the Hungarian-Rumanian discussions. To represent Hungary, Hory was recalled from virtual political exile which had begun when Poland had been crushed in the previous fall.[101] On the 12th, the veteran diplomat called on Teleki and Csaky to receive his instructions. At the meeting the Prime Minister began by saying that it was not the intention of his government to demand the return of the southern counties of Transylvania. For the Magyar inhabitants there, Hungary would ask for full minority rights only, including that of transfer to Hungarian territory. Teleki also stated that if necessary, he would be willing to leave more than these southern counties to Rumania. The land of the Magyar-speaking Szeklers in eastern Transylvania, however, would have to return to Hungary, as well as the lines of communication between this region and the mother country. Hory was told that a mass transfer of the Szeklers to a more westerly area was unthinkable, since no one could force these people to abandon the land where their forefathers had lived for the past thousand years.[102]

131

The Hungarian-Rumanian discussions took place between August 16 and 24 in Turnu-Severin, in south-western Rumania. As might have been expected, the Rumanians proved most reluctant to make any concessions. They insisted on solving the whole problem through a complex scheme for the exchange of populations. At the same time, they also tried to drag out the discussions as long as possible. On the first day already, the Rumanian delegates asked for a two day adjournment to study the Hungarian proposal. When the conference met again on the 19th, they began by disputing the credentials of the Hungarian delegation. Hory finally had to ask for new letters of accreditation from his government.[103]

Since the Hungarian demands presented at the beginning of the discussions were flatly rejected by the other side, Hory wired to Budapest proposing that the negotiations be broken off. The Hungarian Government, however, did not accept his suggestion. Instead, it recalled Hory for consultation. Back in Budapest, Hory met with Teleki and Csaky, and made a verbal report to the Ministerial Council. At the meeting of the Cabinet Hory gained the impression that a majority of the Ministers present were inclined to risk a military showdown with Rumania if that country showed no inclination "to accept a meaningful compromise."[104]

Upon returning to Turnu-Severin, Hory presented a memorandum to the conference which called upon the Rumanian Government to declare forthwith "whether or not it would be willing to indicate those areas which it is ready to return to Hungary."[105] The Rumanians, not budging an inch from their original scheme of solving the issue by a population exchange followed possibly by border adjustments, refused to comply with the Hungarian request.[106] Thereupon Hory, who realized that the further exchange of memoranda and the consequent prolongation of the negotiations would only serve the purpose of the Rumanians, asked for a suspension of the discussions and returned to Budapest.

During these days the Hungarian Government was in a desperate position. The negotiations with Rumania offered no hope for a satisfactory settlement. According to the rules of traditional diplomacy, the next step in the dispute should

132

have been the application of the *ultima ratio,* the resort to arms. By this time, however, the invasion of Rumania involved too many risks. Teleki saw no way out of the situation. "We have drifted into an impossible situation," he wrote at the time, "or rather I drew the country and nation into it." He saw no chance of attaining a favourable agreement with the Rumanians. He feared that a disadvantageous one would lead to internal turmoil in Hungary. He blamed himself for accepting Hitler's idea of direct negotiations with the Rumanians. The *Führer,* according to Teleki, "should have been persuaded to postpone his intervention... I failed to do so and this was a fatal mistake..."[107]

There was, however, still one remote possibility of escaping the predicament the Hungarian Government found itself in when the failure of the negotiations in Turnu-Severin became obvious. This was the hope that Hitler, in his fear of a conflict in the Balkans, would intervene and impose a settlement in the dispute. Not that the statesmen in Budapest especially cherished the idea of a German "dictum". In the above described memorandum, for example, Teleki called it a „nightmare". Yet it was still more acceptable than the prospect of an impossible settlement with Rumania, which would have aroused profound resentment in Hungary, or an armed conflict over Transylvania which could have led to undesirable consequences.

Thus, the Hungarian Government once again mobilized part of its army on the Rumanian border, and made hints to the Germans that Hungary was about to launch an invasion of Transylvania.[108]

Budapest's sabre-rattling had its desired effect. On August 24, the day of the breakdown of the negotiations in Turnu-Severin, Erdmannsdorff warned his government in Berlin that Hungary would soon resort to force against Rumania unless Germany and Italy intervened in the dispute.[109] In subsequent days this conviction only intensified in German circles.

At this juncture Hitler, alarmed by the prospect of a conflagration in the Balkans, resolved to settle the whole issue once and for all. On the 26th he gave orders for two armoured divisions to be dispatched to a position in occupied Poland from which they could quickly reach the oil-fields of Rumania.[110] This, however, was a precautionary measure only, for the *Führer* envisaged a "diplomatic" settlement. Accordingly, the next day he invited the Foreign Ministers of Hungary and Rumania to a conference in Vienna on the 29th.[111]

Prior to the meeting in Vienna, Hitler saw Ciano in Berchtesgaden. Here the Italian Foreign Minister gained the impression that the German leader was not much concerned with the details of the settlement in Transylvania. "The only thing," wrote Ciano in his diary "(Hitler) has at heart is that peace be preserved there, and that Rumanian oil continue to flow into his reservoirs."[112]

When the Hungarian and Rumanian delegations arrived in Vienna to confer with Ribbentrop and Ciano, the stage was all set for another arbitration award. The proposed new border between Hungary and Rumania had already been decided upon. It was worked out by Ribbentrop, altered by Hitler, and adjusted in detail only during the actual arbitration.[113] Meanwhile, additional orders had gone out to the *Wehrmacht* to stand by ready to roll into Hungary and Rumania just in case those countries refused to accept Hitler's dictum and decided to settle their quarrel in a way disagreeable to the Nazi leader.[114]

Before their arrival in Vienna, the Hungarian leaders were apparently not aware that they were called upon to witness another arbitration meted out by Ribbentrop and Ciano. At a meeting of the Cabinet prior to the departure of the Hungarian delegation, Teleki described the forthcoming event as a conference of the Foreign Ministers of the four powers concerned in the dispute. The Prime Minister, who was to accompany Csaky as an observer, told his Ministers that at the Vienna discussions the Hungarian delegation would insist on the return of the city of Kolozsvar and the land of the Szeklers to Hungary.[115]

When Teleki and Csaky arrived in the once proud capital of the Austro-Hungarian Empire, they were immediately summoned for a talk with Ribbentrop and Ciano. At the meeting Ribbentrop bluntly informed the Hungarians that Germany would not tolerate any interference in the flow of Rumanian oil. He stated that the *Reich's overridi g* aim at the moment was the defeat of Britain, and Hitler expected his friends to lay aside their own particular interests in order that this supreme goal may be realized. Next, the German Foreign Minister reminded his audience of the ungrateful acts the Hungarian leadership had committed against Germany: the failure to co-operate against Czechoslovakia, the refusal to allow German troops to march against Poland through Hungarian territory, and so on. Ciano described this part of the discussion in his diary: "... Ribbentrop assails the Hungarians. Courtesy is not his forte. He accuses Hungary of having engaged in anti-German policy on more than one occasion. His words are rather threatening."[116] The purpose of the German Foreign Minister's menacing outbursts was obvious. He wanted to cow the Hungarian leaders into accepting the idea of German-Italian arbitration without preconditions.

Ribbentrop's words apparently frightened Csaky. In his reply, the Hungarian Foreign Minister did not dare to insist on the conditions the Cabinet had agreed upon the previous day. Teleki was more adamant. However, after he realized that Ciano supported the German viewpoint, the Prime Minister also began to soften up. As a last resort, it seems, the Hungarians asked to have the issue solved through discussions among the four countries' Foreign Ministers. Ribbentrop, however, insisted on arbitration. The meeting ended with Csaky and Teleki asking for a chance to consult their colleagues in Budapest.[117]

Immediately following the talks Csaky telephoned home. He explained the developments, conveyed his impression that the Szekler areas would revert to Hungary even though no definite promises had been made to this effect. Finally, he asked that the government accept the idea of German-Italian arbitration. The same afternoon the Cabinet met and endorsed Csaky's suggestion.[118]

Although the Rumanians had, on several previous occasions, expressed their desire to see a German arbitration in the Transylvanian dispute, they now found the idea of being confronted with a *Diktat,* against which there was no appeal, quite dreadful. They were told in Vienna that a solution based on a population exchange would not suffice, and that they would have to brace themselves for a territorial settlement. In compensation, they were promised that Germany and Italy would guarantee the remaining territory of Rumania. After an all-night session, the Rumanian Crown Council finally decided to authorize its delegation to accept the proposed arbitration by the Axis powers.[119]

The terms of the award were announced in the Golden Chamber of the Belvedere Palace on the afternoon of August 30. Close to half of Transylvania was returned to Hungary.[120] When the map with the new boundary line marked on it was unfolded, Manoilescu, the Rumanian Foreign Minister, promptly fainted.[121]

Before discussing the consequences of the Second Vienna Award, an incident should be mentioned. This incident throws much light both on Teleki's policies and on the political situation prevalent in the Hungary of the time.

The text of the award contained a statement to the effect that the governments of Rumania and Hungary had requested an arbitration of their dispute by Germany and Italy. The assertion was of course true to the extent that Bucharest had several times asked for such a measure and, after Ribbentrop had a chance to "soften" the Hungarians on the day before the Award, they too agreed to an arbitration. But never before had the Hungarian Government, or any member thereof, made a request for Axis arbitration. In fact, Teleki's policy was not to ask for such a solution. In a memorandum submitted to Horthy, the Prime Minister himself stated in this connection that "we don't ask for arbitration, because our interests desire that the Rumanians should ask . . ."[122] Teleki's scheme during the last phase of the crisis was to convince the leaders in Bucharest, Berlin and Rome that a threat of war existed along the lower Danube unless Hungary's territorial claims were settled. This, the Prime Minister hoped, would induce the Rumanians to ask Berlin and Rome for arbitration, or the Axis governments to offer their intervention voluntarily. He expected his scheme to work because not one of these three states wanted peace to be disturbed at the time in Danubian Europe. The Rumanians probably feared a Russian attack as well; the Germans dreaded an interruption in the flow of Rumanian oil to their country; the Italians worried about the possible establishment of absolute German control over this area in the wake of a war. Thus Teleki was ready to accept Transylvania as a "gift", as long as the record showed that his country had not solicited that gift from anyone, especially Germany. This way he hoped that Hungary would be obliged to pay less to prove her gratitude to Hitler, than if she had begged for the arbitration herself. She would, moreover, have a much better chance of retaining the areas received after the conclusion of the hostilities even if Germany lost the war. After all, the Hungarians could say at the peace conference that "it was the Rumanians and not *we* who asked for the arbitration." Teleki's risky scheme, however, did not work out exactly as he wished.

First of all, the Prime Minister was double-crossed. A few days before the announcement of the Award, General Werth had informed the Germans that Hungary wanted arbitration. Teleki considered the Chief-of-Staff's gross indiscretion disastrous, and told the Regent that if similar incidents were to be avoided in the future the military would have to be prevented from meddling in the affairs of the government. Teleki, unlike many of his compatriots who could hardly contain their joy over the Award, seems to have sensed that the events of the last days of August had done little to benefit his country in the long run. This is why he so bitterly reproached the country's militarists and, above all, himself.[123] He was concerned about the settlement, but he dreaded even more the possible consequences of the whole affair. That his despondency and fears were not groundless was proven soon by developments.

5. The Consequences of the Award; Accession to the Tripartite Pact.

When the initial excitement over the events of August 30 subsided, it became evident that the Second Vienna Award satisfied no one. The Rumanians were bitterly resentful for having had to yield such a large portion of their country's area and population. Nor were the Hungarians pleased. The settlement, which still left some 400,000 Magyars in Rumania, but at the same time transferred close to one million Rumanians to Hungary,[124] soon became criticized in many quarters. While it provided a wide "corridor" between central Hungary and the Szekler counties, the main railway connection between the two areas still passed through Rumanian territory. Nor did the takeover of the administration of such a large and complex area pass without stress and strain. Weeks before the settlement had taken place, Hitler had remarked, rather slyly, that "no matter how the dispute would be settled one side will always wail, in the case of Transylvania probably both."[125]

The *Führer* proved to be a good prognosticator.

Indeed, if anyone had reason to be satisfied with the settlement it was Hitler himself. For the dislocations and internal strain brought about by the Award created a situation in which political conditions became quite conducive to the strengthening of the Third *Reich's* influence in both Rumania and Hungary. In fact, during the rest of 1940, the chief aim of Nazi diplomacy in Danubian Europe seems to have been the exploitation of the situation which emerged there in the wake of the arbitration of August 30. In Rumania, the Vienna Award was followed by significant developments. King Carol fell from power and fled the country. A new government assumed office under the leadership of Marshal Antonescu. From this time on Rumania adhered, even more closely than before, to a policy of appeasement toward Germany. Apparently, the country's new leaders believed that only through the cultivation of Hitler's friendship could they hope to regain some of the areas they had lost in the summer of 1940. The Germans were not reluctant to encourage this belief.

The developments in Rumania had undesirable repercussions upon relations between Berlin and Budapest. From this time on, the Government of Hungary often found that it had to outbid the Rumanians when it came to soliciting any favours from Germany. Thus, following the Award, the race

138

between Bucharest and Budapest for Hitler's graces intensified. The *Führer,* moreover, made sure that both of these capitals had ample motives for cultivating the friendship of Germany. While to the Rumanians he held out the hope that with his help they could recover some of their recently lost territories,[126] only a few days after the Award, Hitler made a hint to Sztojay that in spite of the Axis guarantee to Rumania, he did not consider the new border in Transylvania as final. The Hungarian Minister to Berlin concluded from the *Führer's* words that if the Government of Hungary made more concrete gestures of friendship toward the Reich and refrained from obstructing its ambitions, a further revision of the Trianon settlement would become possible.[127] Thus, by feeding the territorial ambitions and mutual jealousies of the East European nations, the *Führer* hoped to gain an even stronger grip on this area.

Indeed, during the fall of 1940, the expansion of Nazi political and economic influence toward the South-East proceeded at an accelerated rate. This is revealed by the internal developments which took place at the time both in Rumania and in Hungary.

When the new government was formed in Bucharest after the ouster of King Carol, Marshal Antonescu found it necessary to make a deal with the Iron Guard, an organization of Rumanian fascists. In Hungary, possibly as a result of German intervention,[128] Szalasi, the Nazi leader, was freed from prison. Hard on the heels of his release, he suceeded in uniting, under his personal leadership, several of the country's neo-Nazi parties and organizations. The merger was accompanied by a vociferous propaganda campaign aimed at toppling Teleki, and replacing him with someone who would follow a strictly pro-German policy. Within the ruling party there were elements who also desired to see the Prime Minister's political demise. Imredy and his followers, as well as others, hoped to undermine Teleki's position within the party. Through this they hoped to engineer his defeat, in order to force the Regent to appoint someone more agreeable to the Germans in his place.[129]

Although the efforts to oust Teleki failed, mainly because

his opponents could not muster enough votes to defeat him either on the floor of the party convention or in Parliament, the existence of an increasingly vociferous and active opposition to the government did not fail to exert an influence on the country's internal as well as her external policies. Momentarily, at least, Teleki even suceeded in strengthening his hand against the political Right. At last he had an opportunity to force Imredy and his clique to resign from the government party. The Prime Minister also persuaded the Regent to effect some measures that would curb the powers of the country's military.[130] These victories for Teleki, however, could not be attained without some concessions on his part also. Early in October, when he outlined his administration's future legislative programme, the Prime Minister made reference to a new and foolproof Jewish restriction bill and an acceleration of the "social transformation" in the country.[131] The greatest concessions which followed in the wake of the Vienna Award, however, came not in the field of domestic legislation, but in the realm of the country's direct or indirect relations with the Third *Reich* itself.

Already on August 30, only a few hours after the announcement of the Award, the Germans asked the Hungarian leaders to sign a minority agreement with them. Through this protocol Hungary's German-speaking citizens were granted extensive rights and privileges. They were guaranteed, for example, the ways and means of preserving their cultural identity, or *Volkstum*. They received the right to profess the Nazi ideology and to move to Germany if they so desired. Who qualified as a German was to be determined by an organization of Germans in Hungary.[132] According to Professor Borsody, some of the privileges granted to the country's German minority were incompatible with Hungarian sovereignty.[133] The communist historian Juhasz remarks that "this agreement was the first big bill which Germany had presented" for the revision in Transylvania.[134]

The next payment for the Award was made in the field of economics. In October, the Hungarian Government agreed not only to increase exports of industrial crops, livestock and fodder to Germany, but also to take over part of the

140

export quota of Transylvanian lumber which the Rumanians had promised to Berlin prior to the settlement of the dispute.[135]

The minority protocol and trade agreements were followed by a concession in the military field. It might be recalled that in July the Rumanians, in their fear of an attack on their country by its neighbours, made an appeal to Berlin for the stationing of some German units on garrison duty in Rumania. Probably to gain the goodwill of Hitler, Marshal Antonescu repeated the invitation soon after August 30. To the German military leadership, which was already contemplating a confrontation with Russia, the suggestion came at the most opportune moment. Berlin decided to comply with the Rumanian request, and asked Hungary to facilitate the transport of the military units across her territory. The Hungarian Government, which in April had already intimated that it would not oppose the transit of German troops to Rumania, now consented to the Nazis' demand.[137] Soon, the movement of German military personnel began across Hungary. The whole operation was shrouded in secrecy. Every night a few trains, loaded with troops and equipment, made the journey through the peaceful Hungarian countryside.[138]

The greatest single concession, however, which the Hungarian Government made in these months to Nazi Germany came in the realm of international relations. It was Hungary's accession to the Tripartite Pact on November 20, 1940.

The Tripartite Pact had been concluded among Germany, Italy and Japan at the end of September. It provided that the signatory powers should assist each other against any new belligerent. Since the Pact specifically stated that its stipulations did not apply to the Soviet Union, the primary aim of the alliance, at least as far as the two Axis Powers were concerned, was to deter the United States from coming to the aid of Britain.[139]

Soon after the Pact was signed, the Hungarian Government indicated to the German leaders its desire to adhere to it. The diplomatic move was the result of a freak misunderstanding. At the time of the signing of the document Ribbentrop made a speech in which he stated that his government invited all states friendly to Germany to adhere to the Pact also. In the *Deutsche Allgemeine Zeitung,* which carried the text of the speech, the German Foreign Minister was quoted as saying that Berlin expected these countries to sign the Pact. Upon reading this, Sztojay immediately called on his government to comply with the German request. It was in response to this news from Berlin that the Hungarian Government informed the Germans of its desire to sign the agreement.[140] Once this had been done, it was, of course, difficult to make a retreat, even though there was plenty of time to do so since the Germans were in no hurry to give an answer to the Hungarian feeler.[141]

Nor was there much determination in Hungarian Government circles to retreat from the move. Signing the Pact seemed to offer some advantages, while it apparently imposed no new commitments upon the country. The text of the agreement, to be sure, did not give a clear definition of the obligations of the signatories;[142] the Pact, however, was not an offensive alliance. This was apparently the reason why Horthy, for example, decided to come out in favour of his country's accession to it.[143] Others in the Cabinet probably found the idea of being allowed to join an agreement among great powers too attractive to resist. They believed that Hungary's signing of the Pact would be a much needed diplomatic success for her government. Teleki and those who stood closest to him might have had another reason for not restraining their colleagues' enthusiasm for the country's accession to the Pact. They probably hoped that by such essentially outward manifestations of their friendship to Germany they could placate both the Nazi leaders and the increasingly restless pro-German faction of Hungary's body politic. Thereby they hoped to forestall the emergence of a situation in which the Germans would lend vigorous support to a movement aimed at bringing about a change of government in Hungary.[144] In addition to this, the fear of the loss of Berlin's favour and the possibility of a consequent reversal of the recent Vienna Award might have been another factor which induced these men to opt for adhesion to the Tripartite Pact. Indeed, it was considered a distinct possibility at the time that, should Ger-

142

many win the war, only the signatories of the agreement would be invited to participate in the making of the post-war settlement.

The claim made by Horthy in his memoirs that the refusal of the German invitation to join the Pact might have brought about a German occupation of Hungary[145] is, no doubt, an exaggeration. Once, however, the documents were signed, there was to be no return. It should be remembered that in the spring of next year it was the *coup d'état* in Belgrade, signifying the reversal of Yugoslavia's decision to adhere to this pact, which brought upon that country a full-scale German invasion.

The actual signing of the Tripartite Pact did not take place until November 20, by which time the Nazi diplomatic machine made preparations for the accession of several other European countries to it. The Hungarians had the dubious honour of being allowed to sign first. They were followed a few days later by the Rumanians and the Slovaks.

It is difficult to say just what obligations Hungary accepted by joining the Tripartite Pact. As it has been mentioned, the original agreement among Germany, Japan and Italy was a defensive one. This, however, mattered little. On November 20, 1940, Hungary entered a league of aggressive powers. When it came to interpreting the stipulations of the Pact, moreover, it was always the Germans who did the interpretation rather than the Hungarians. Thus, the accession to the agreement did mean a commitment on Hungary's part, a political as well as a moral one. It mattered little that at the time the move was assailed in both houses of Parliament. No lesser persons spoke up against the decision to sign the Pact than Bethlen, Eckhardt, Bajcsy-Zsilinszky, Rassay and Peyer, the leader of the Social Democratic Party.

Summing up the developments of the three months following the Second Vienna Award, it can be stated that during this period German influence in Danubian Europe further intensified. Hungary, in particular, continued to gravitate closer and closer to the Axis orbit, in spite of the fact that the majority of the country's leading figures considered this undesirable. The reason for these developments are not difficult to point out. By the fall of the year Germany became the undisputed master of continental Europe west of the U.S.S.R. Her grip on the Hungarian economy was, by this time, very strong. The country was no longer capable of reversing the tide of Nazi economic influence without substantial outside support. Britain's "buy dearer than Germany" campaign was too late and too feeble to divert Hungarian and, as a matter of fact, South-East European trade away from the Third Reich.[146] Public faith in German defeat, never too strong, dwindled as a result of German victories on the western front during May and June.[147] The policy of the Hungarian Government aimed at revision, moreover, cost the country a great deal. Instead of strengthening her *vis-à-vis* the *Reich,* it created a political situation favourable only to the interests of Germany. In Transylvania Hungary's leaders were looking for an economic and military asset to their country. What they obtained was a political liability. Their policies of trying to resist the expansion of German influence and at the same time to seek revision had at last proved to be a failure.

Reflecting upon Hungary's foreign policies of the summer of 1940 from a historical distance of almost three decades one might even consider it unfortunate that Teleki did not resort to the *ultima ratio* in settling the Transylvanian question. For when the Prime Minister chose to seek a diplomatic rather than a military solution to the dispute, he passed up an excellent opportunity to turn his nation squarely against Germany. A resort to arms against Rumania would have created enough strain in Hungarian-German relations to put an end to all friendship, feigned and real, between the two countries. Such a step, however, might have had disastrous consequences. It might have resulted in a German, or even a combined German-Rumanian occupation of the country.[148] This, no doubt, would have ushered in the beginning of Nazi rule in Hungary. The regime of quislings, the total exploitation of the country's resources in support of Hitler's war effort, and the violent persecution of the Jews would have lasted for a much longer period than they actually did.[149]

The solution of the Transylvanian problem through the

Vienna Award prevented a crisis in German-Hungarian relations over the issue of revision. The Award, however, still served to contribute to the process of the gradual smothering of Hungary's freedom of action by the Third *Reich*. This soon became evident to Teleki. Consequently, during the last months of 1940, he made efforts to counter this tendency not only by strengthening his hand at home, but also by reinforcing his country's position on the international scene. He sought to do this by seeking closer ties with Hungary's one remaining neutral (and non-communist) neighbour: Yugoslavia. His attempt, however, led to new disaster, which he could not have foreseen in 1940.

6. *The Yugoslav Crisis: a Prelude to Tragedy.*

The idea of a Hungarian-Yugoslav neutral bloc originated from earlier plans for a larger Danubian-Balkan alignment designed to keep the spreading flames of war out of this area. Some of the proposals for creating such a grouping of non-belligerent countries even predated the opening of the conflict.[150] Most of them, however, came during the first six months of the war. Grigore Gafencu, the Rumanian Foreign Minister, was, for a time, the chief advocate of the scheme. Official circles in both London and Ankara were favourably disposed toward the idea. The whole plan was wrecked on the rock of Hungarian-Rumanian relations. The Government of Hungary would have probably considered entering such bloc, but not before its demands for revision in Transylvania were satisfied. The leaders in Bucharest, particularly Gafencu, wanted no territorial change.[151] Thus, neither side was willing to accept the other's price for participating in the scheme. The Hungarians excused themselves for their cool reception of the proposals for the bloc by saying that the great powers most concerned were not in favour of the idea: the Soviet Union was violently against it, Germany was also opposed to it, and the whole plan was deemed "premature" by Rome.[152]

The Second Vienna Award doomed all plans for the inclusion of Rumania in any alignment of non-belligerent states, especially one that included Hungary. Relations between Bucharest and Budapest after the settlement were as bad as, if not worse than they had been before it. Antonescu's invitation of German forces into Rumania, moreover, threatened with the prospect of turning that country into a German satellite. These developments left only two powers of major importance in the area as possible candidates for a non-belligerent Danubian bloc: Yugoslavia and Hungary.

If the abortive Balkan bloc was one of the predecessors of Hungarian-Yugoslav friendship, then the defunct Danube-Vistula axis must be considered to be the other one. Belgrade was to have been an important link in the Rome-Belgrade-Budapest-Warsaw line. This "counter-bloc", it might be recalled, had received its last rites already in November 1938, and died a slow death during the next summer. Hungary's leaders, however, continued to strive for good relations with Yugoslavia even after Poland had been crushed by Hitler's panzer divisions in the fall of 1939. Indeed, late in November of that year, Csaky declared on the floor of Parliament, that he took pleasure in seeing the improvement of Hungary's relations with her southern neighbour. The Foreign Minister also stated that a "strong Yugoslavia" was "directly" in his country's interest.[153] Two days later the Yugoslav Government expressed its satisfaction at the statement and promised to reciprocate it at the earliest opportunity.[154]

During the ten months following Csaky's attempt at *rapprochement,* relations between Hungary and Yugoslavia were on the whole, cordial. Early in October 1940, however, Budapest suddenly made another move to strengthen the existing ties between the two countries.[155]

The considerations behind the Hungarian attempt at attaining closer relations with Yugoslavia were manifold. Many influential people in the governing circles of Hungary were anxious to counterbalance by some means the gains Nazi diplomacy was making in Danubian Europe. In the Yugoslavs they might also have hoped to find much needed potential friends at the coming peace negotiations. Teleki's most important reason for seeking closer ties with Hungary's southern neighbour seems to have been the desire to maintain

146

good relations with England. Yugoslavia was the only remaining state in the Danubian region on friendly terms with Britain. By establishing a closer friendship with Belgrade, Teleki hoped to preserve the connection between Budapest and London. In his view, Yugoslavia became Hungary's only "open window" to the West. The Prime Minister wanted to make sure that this last link with the outside world was not severed.

Many contemporaries believed that the new found Hungarian-Yugoslav friendship was aimed directly against Germany.[157] This, however, was a misconception. What the leaders of Hungary envisaged was a bloc of two non-belligerent powers, friendly to but independent from the Third *Reich.* Nor was Yugoslavia's acceptance of the idea of closer relations with Hungary motivated by an outright hostility to Germany. The leaders in Belgrade simply believed that the establishment of closer ties between themselves and Germany's "Hungarian friends" would reduce the chances of a Nazi attack on their country. Both sides felt that united they had a better chance of staying out of the conflagration which was engulfing more and more of Europe. Nor were the leaders in Rome and Berlin, for the time being at least, unfavourably disposed toward the prospect of better relations between Hungary and Yugoslavia. After Italy's involvement in the war, Mussolini seems to have shelved, temporarily at least, his plans for the dismemberment of the South-Slav state. The Duce, moreover, was about to launch an attack on Greece. Yugoslav non-belligerence, or even benevolent neutrality, was a prerequisite for the success of Italian aggression. In the beginning, even Hitler took pleasure in seeing relations between Belgrade and Budapest improve. Like Mussolini, he also seems to have hoped that the Hungarians will exercise a moderating influence on the Yugoslavs and restrain them from interfering with German plans and ambitions. Yugoslavia's attitude to international developments assumed even greater significance at the time when the Italian fiasco in Greece created a very embarrassing situation for the Axis in the Balkans.

In view of the mutual desire of the Yugoslav and Hun-

garian governments for closer relations between their countries, and the desire for the same in Rome and Berlin, it is
not surprising that Belgrade and Budapest quickly came to
an agreement as to what legal form this new friendship
was going to take. At the end of November the Hungarians
made a suggestion for the signing of a loosely worded peace
pact between the two countries. The proposal was soon accepted by the Yugoslav Government. On December 10 Csaky
arrived in Belgrade for discussions. Two days later the Pact
of Peace and Friendship was signed between Hungary and
Yugoslavia.[158]

The brief agreement declared that "permanent peace and
eternal friendship shall exist" between the Hungarian and
Yugoslav kingdoms, and that the contracting parties agreed
to discuss in the future problems affecting their mutual relations. Nothing was said of the revision of the boundary between the two countries. Apparently the Hungarian Government had given up its earlier plans for the inclusion of this
issue in any agreement with Yugoslavia. The matter was
not even brought up in Belgrade during the final discussions.[159]

Although the agreement had been approved previously in
Berlin, German reaction to the news of the Pact was now
cool. Apparently, the Nazi leaders began to have second
thoughts about the matter. They now realized that the agreement betweeen Hungary and Yugoslavia could serve not only
the purpose of bringing the latter closer to the Axis orbit,
but it could lessen Hungary's dependence on Germany. One
German official even told Sztojay that Berlin was worried
about the possible development of some sort of a "community
of interests" between Hungary and the "English-oriented"
Yugoslavia.[160]

Hitler, however, did not give up hope for attaining Yugoslavia's entry into the Axis camp through diplomatic pressure, rather than the use of force. Accordingly, during the
rest of the winter of 1940-41, he made several efforts to
persuade the Yugoslavs to join the Tripartite Alliance. The
statesmen of Belgrade, however, refused to comply with the
Führer's wishes. By mid-March, it became urgent for Hitler

to "clarify" Yugoslavia's attitude. Operation Marita, a German attack on Greece through Bulgaria, was about to begin. Preparations were also under way in Germany for the great offensive against the U.S.S.R. It was imperative for Hitler to settle his affairs in the Balkans before undertaking the latter operation. On 22 March, therefore, he sent an ultimatum to Yugoslavia demanding the immediate accession of that state to the Tripartite Pact. The Yugoslav leaders soon left for Vienna in order to sign the documents. While they were gone, however, anti-German elements of the country's military engineered a *coup d'état* and deposed the incumbent government.[161]

Upon hearing the news from Belgrade, Hitler became enraged. The change in Yugoslavia not only upset German plans concerning the Balkans, but also threatened to interfere with the execution of the impending invasion of Soviet Russia. In his anger, the *Führer* resolved to crush the "unfaithful" Yugoslavs at once. Italy, Bulgaria and Hungary were to assist in the attack. In return for collaboration, these countries were promised that they could satisfy their territorial aspirations at Yugoslavia's expense.

In his memoirs, Field-Marshal Keitel, one of Hitler's top officers, recalled the way the Nazi leaders attempted to secure the co-operation of Budapest in the venture. "Hungary's attitude was ostensibly pro-British", wrote the German general, "but in view of Germany's assistance in securing the Vienna award ... (her Regent) was obliged to show his gratitude in some way." Possibly with such thoughts in mind, Hitler dispatched a message to Horthy, informing him that Hungary "would get back her precious Banat territory in reward; we would all see," continued Keitel, "how old Horthy would be behind us breathing fire and brimstone for that price."[162]

The Regent took the Germans' bait this time. He "became very enthusiastic at once," wrote Teleki to a close friend of his at the time, "and not less but more so after he had slept on it." Apparently, Horthy was bent on giving an affirmative answer immediately. Teleki, however, prevailed upon him to wait. The next day, in the midst of heated argument, the Regent wrote his reply. Although the Prime Minister again succeeded in persuading Horthy to delete the "dangerous passages" from the text of his answer,[163] the letter remained full of statements which vaguely implied an acceptance of Hitler's proposal. Horthy told the *Führer* that the territorial aspirations alluded to in his message awaited fulfillment. The Hungarian Head-of-State also agreed to the establishment of contacts between the German and Hungarian chiefs of staff.[164] The Germans took the reply as an acceptance of the idea of Hungarian co-operation in the attack on Yugoslavia.[165] General Paulus was told to go to Budapest in order to begin discussions with Werth.

On this day the Hungarian Ministerial Council met to deal with the crisis. At the meeting conflicting opinions were expressed. Some of the ministers, notably Bartha, Homan (Minister of Education), and Remenyi-Schneller (Minister of Finance) were for full co-operation with Germany, while the new Foreign Minister Bardossy (Csaky had died during the winter), and Teleki were trying to tie Hungary's participation to certain conditions. The latter insisted that Hungary should enter the conflict only if 1, Yugoslavia disintegrated as a state, that is, the Croats declared their independence; 2, the Yugoslav civilian and military authorities turned against their country's Magyar population; 3, a political vacuum developed in Magyar areas as a result of the German venture. The Cabinet accepted these conditions.[166] The final decision in the matter, however, was to be taken at the meeting of the Supreme Defence Council, which was to be summoned soon.

It should be mentioned at this point that in the course of the Ministerial Council's session Teleki had announced his intention to resign. The circumstances of the incident are still not quite clear. Communist editors have remained silent on the affair even though they have published excerpts from the minutes of this meeting of the Cabinet.[167] In the end, however, Teleki was persuaded not to go through with his plan.

During the next few days frantic diplomatic activity went on in Budapest. On 29 March the Yugoslavs were warned that unless they gave some tangible proof to Hitler of their intention to abide by the stipulations of the Tripartite Pact they would have to prepare for the worst. Hints were dropped to London and Washington that an Axis action against Yugoslavia might create a situation which would require a Hungarian occupation of that country's Magyar populated areas.[168] General Paulus also arrived in Budapest and began discussions with Werth. The Hungarian Chief-of-Staff, a veteran advocate of full co-operation with Germany, now did not hesitate to promise the deployment of five Hungarian army corps in the invasion of Yugoslavia.[169]

On the first of April the Supreme Defence Council of Hungary met. At this meeting, the conflict of opinion, which had already been evident during the session of the Cabinet three days earlier, only intensified. The council was split right down the middle. Werth demanded Hungary's unconditional participation in the invasion of Yugoslavia. He called for immediate mobilization. Werth was supported by Bartha, Homan and Remenyi-Schneller. Several of those present, however, were opposed. Bardossy argued, more forcibly than ever before during the crisis, for the necessity of tying Hungary's co-operation in the attack on Yugoslavia to definite conditions. He asked his audience to bear in mind that Hungary might have to account for her actions at a future peace conference.[170] Keresztes-Fischer, the Minister of the Interior, one of the most consistent advocates of a British orientation among Hungary's leaders of the day, also warned against the participation of the Hungarian army in the actual military operations against Yugoslavia. He suggested that Hungarian troops should occupy the Magyar populated areas of that country only in the wake of the German campaign. Two other ministers also spoke against the idea of unconditional co-operation with the Germans.[171]

At the end of the meeting, Teleki prevailed on the members of the Council to adopt the following conditions regarding Hungary's participation: 1. The country's army would move only when the Croats seceded from Yugoslavia in the wake of German advance. 2. Hungarian troops would operate in a small and separate theater of war and in no case would they cross into Croatia and Serbia proper. 3. Horthy would retain supreme command over the units participating in the operation. The meeting also endorsed the technical details of the plans worked out by Werth and Paulus with the proviso that the order for mobilization could only come from the Regent.[172]

These then were the conditions for Hungary's participation in the affair. There were many reasons why Teleki's policy of non-involvement in Germany's ventures was abandoned to this extent. First of all, Hungary's leaders were afraid that an outright refusal of Hitler's demand for passage through the country might lead to a permanent German military occupation of Hungary. In the fall of 1939 it was possible to deny the *Wehrmacht* the right of transit against Poland. This denial did not effect the timing and outcome of the German offensive. Poland could easily be conquered without an encircling attack from the South. In the spring of 1941 the situation was different. Yugoslavia could not be overrun quickly and effectively without a massive blow delivered against her from the North — from Hungarian territory. Secondly, Hungary's Regent and many members of her Government and General Staff believed that with Yugoslavia doomed anyway, the opportunity should not be missed for the recovery of some of the territories their country had lost in 1919. It was also feared at the time that if Hungary did not occupy at least part of the Bacska-Banat area, the Nazis would set up a German state there based on the local Swabian and Saxon population, whose numbers the Nazi propaganda machine had been vastly exaggerating for the past few years.[173] Lastly there might have been some justice in Hitler's words when he said that Hungary got involved because "... she was afraid of falling behind Rumania, which was allied with Germany."[174]

The next day, April 2, proved to be a fateful one. In the morning the news arrived from Belgrade that there was no hope for a last minute agreement between Hitler and the new Yugoslav regime.[175] At about noon, Teleki sat down to write a hurried letter to his friend Apor, Hungarian Minister to the Vatican at the time. In it, the Prime Minister briefly reviewed the developments of the past few days. He also outlined his own and his country's position. "The situation is very difficult because" wrote Teleki, "if we resist, (the Germans) will roll over us first and worst — if we do not enter the Bacska, the Germans will make themselves at home there and — will set up a German state . . ."[176]

Teleki never had a chance to finish his letter. In the afternoon came the message from London that the Foreign Office would regard a Hungarian permission allowing the *Wehrmacht* to carry out its attack from Hungarian territory a highly inimical act, and Hungary's involvement in the campaign against Yugoslavia a serious enough offence to warrant a British declaration of war. In the evening Teleki, no doubt already in a desperate mood, paid a visit to his wife who lay seriously ill in a sanatorium. During the visit he received some news over the telephone which upset him terribly. It seems that before retiring, the Prime Minister also had a word with one or two leaders of the Smallholders' Party.[177] The next morning, at the Prime Minister's private residence, Teleki was found lying lifeless with a bullethole in his head.

It is difficult to separate fact from fiction when one comes to the problem of Teleki's sudden death. The wild rumours which began circulating on the morning of the third of April, had, in the course of time, become rigid myths in the nation's memory.

All historians discount the story, which was popular in Hungary in the spring of 1941, that the Prime Minister was murdered by Nazi agents for his attempts to obstruct Hitler's plans. Although Teleki was a devout Catholic, the idea of self-destruction was not alien to him. Only a year before, at a time when a German demand for transit was thought to be imminent, the Prime Minister had already considered the idea of political suicide.[178] Nor did the investigation by the police or the autopsy reveal any evidence that foul play was involved in Teleki's death.

Precisely what caused the Prime Minister to end his life on that fateful day has been the object of considerable controversy. Several authors seem to imply that Teleki was betrayed by the country's military leaders, who allowed the entry of the Germans into Hungary before he had given his final consent. According to this theory, it was the news of this double-cross which put him in the mood for his act of desperation.[179] There were also rumours at the time that Teleki, in order to forestall a British declaration of war on Hungary, had made a last minute effort to persuade Horthy to resign his office.[180] Such a step by the Regent would have documented to the world that Hungary had become involved in Hitler's Yugoslav campaign against the will of her leaders. According to this version, it was the refusal of this suggestion which greatly intensified the Prime Minister's already strong feeling of hopelessness. Juhasz believes that it was the news, received over the telephone in the sanatorium, of an announcement by Hungarian authorities of "provocations" by the Yugoslavs against Hungary, which made up Teleki's mind to take his own life.[181] According to Professor Macartney, however, the immediate cause of Teleki's suicide was the message from London.[182]

Indeed, the pressures of the crisis, coming to a climax in the events of the second day of April: the bad news from Belgrade and London, the entry of German troops onto Hungarian soil, and the story of the alleged provocations in the South, (which must have appeared as a possible prelude to an immediate Hungarian military involvement), put an unbearable strain on the mind of a man who abhorred the idea of his country being engulfed by the flames of war. Added to this was the knowledge of the inevitability of a break with Britain, a country which Teleki respected and wished to see victorious in the great struggle. Only a month ago the Prime Minister defined the primary task of Hungarian leadership as the preservation of the country's strength till the end of the war, and the secondary one as the struggle against the influence of alien ideologies.[183] On April 2 Teleki realized that his aspirations had suffered an irreversible setback. In the forenoon of this day he wrote (in the letter to Apor), that he was "trying to find a way out and to save face." Finding no "way out" of the situation, Teleki took his own life. By his last act he desired to save the honour of his beloved country. Forces largely beyond his control[184] prevented this true patriot

154

from serving his nation successfully in life; therefore he resolved to compensate for this by serving it in his death.

After Teleki's suicide, events came to a rapid conclusion. On the 4th of the month, Bartha was sent to Hitler with another of Horthy's letters. In this the Regent explained the circumstances of Teleki's death. He also asked the *Führer* not to demand from Hungary a greater measure of participation in the Balkan campaign than was compatible with her national conscience. Horthy, and his special envoy Bartha, were now desperately trying to persuade the Germans not to require Hungary to move before Yugoslavia disintegrated under the German attack.[185] Reluctantly, the Nazi leaders agreed to this, and even to a reduction in the size of the Hungarian army which was to take part in the operation.

On April 6 the German war machine began its invasion of Yugoslavia. For a few days Hungarian troops refrained from crossing the border, in spite of the fact that Yugoslav warplanes, in their desperate attempt to defend their country, had attacked several air-fields in southern Hungary. The German leadership became impatient with the delay, and made demands for the immediate commencement of the Hungarian advance. It has been pointed out that there was absolutely no military reason for requesting the entry of Hungary's divisions into the conflict during those days, since organized Yugoslav resistance had already been crushed. The Nazi demands had a political reason. Hitler, who viewed the hesitations and reluctance of the Hungarian leaders throughout the whole affair with increasing suspicion, now wanted to see Hungary involved in the venture — before it was all over — just to have her government discredited in the eyes of Allied statesmen, and thereby ruin Budapest's last chance of maintaining contacts with the outside world.[186]

On April 10 a group of Croatian separatists, acting no doubt in collusion with German military authorities, declared Croatia's independence. The time had come for the Hungarians to make their move. On the next day, the Government of Hungary, claiming that the state with which they had signed the pact of friendship only four months ago no longer existed, ordered its troops to move into the Bacska, a region bounded by the Danube and Tisza rivers.

Thus, in April 1941 Hungary at last became involved in the war on the side of Nazi Germany. Horthy's delaying of the country's entry into the hostilities did not save the face of his regime. Not even Teleki's noble sacrifice could wash away the stigma which was attached to the country for having taken part, even if a small one, in the invasion of Yugoslavia.

What did Hungary get for all this? She regained the Bacska and two smaller areas where a considerable portion of the population was Magyar-speaking. She did not, however, get back the rich counties of the Banat, in spite of Hitler's earlier assurances. This area was occupied and run by the Germans themselves. Aside from the territorial adjustments Hungary received nothing. True, a face-to-face confrontation with Germany was once again avoided. On this occasion, however, it became evident that the price the country had to pay for every postponement of a showdown with the Nazis was becoming higher and higher every time. In April 1941, besides the damage to Hungary's national prestige, the crisis cost the country the rupture of diplomatic relations with Britain.

The Yugoslav affair, however, did not prove to be the final stage of Hungary's involvement in the Second World War. The Balkan campaign was soon over. Hungarian troops took part in very few actual combat operations.[187] Nor did the threatened British declaration of war come in the spring of 1941. At the time of the next crisis, however, the country was not to escape with such relative ease. For Hitler's next great military venture, the Russian campaign, proved to be the occasion of Hungary's final and irrevocable involvement in the world struggle.

PART VI.

WAR AGAINST RUSSIA: THE LEAP INTO THE ABYSS

1. Hungary and Operation Barbarossa.

When Hitler's air offensive against Britain had failed to attain its intended results during the summer of 1940, the *Führer* resolved to find another means of cowing the British Government into submission. Apparently, the German leader believed that England refused to accept his terms because her leaders expected that Russia and America might come to their rescue. Hitler wanted to extinguish all such hopes on the part of the British. He thought of accomplishing this task by smashing the Soviet Union in one enormous military campaign. The elimination of the U.S.S.R. as a power factor, Hitler hoped, would not only make Germany the uncontested master of Continental Europe, but would also enhance the position of Japan in the Far East, making it impossible for the United States to offer substantial military aid to the English. Britain could then be forced to her knees.[1] The Nazi leader, however, did not decide to go ahead with his plan till December. Thus, it was only in the middle of that month that he issued orders for the preparation of Operation Barbarossa, as the planned invasion of Russia was called.

From early 1941 on the Third *Reich* was feverishly preparing for the great offensive. From the historical evidence available today, it is clear beyond doubt that the civilian leaders of Hungary were not informed of the planned move against the U.S.S.R. until the last hour.[2] Halder wrote in his diary that the military directive concerning Hungary's relation to Operation Barbarossa stated that while Finland was to have an active role in the plan, and the Rumanians were to be asked to join in at the last minute, the Hungarians would only be asked to keep their defences up-to-date.[3] Keitel is even more emphatic on this point. "The Führer had strictly forbidden", he wrote in his *Memoirs,* "any kind of preliminary diplomatic discussions and even of staff level talks with Hungary and Czechoslovakia [sic], although the War Office had stressed their importance ... Hitler refused to yield on this point, despite the risks it involved; he was afraid that the operation's security would be compromised ..."[4] This is also corroborated by the evidence Paulus gave at Nuremberg. According to him, Hitler did not disclose his plans to the Hungarians because he considered them garrulous. Nor did he want "to give Hungary a chance of seizing the oil fields in the Russian oil district of Dragovitch."[5]

The Hungarian Government then, was not asked by the Germans to take part in the preparations for the attack on the U.S.S.R. In fact, from the sparse evidence available,[6] it can be seen that at the time German-Soviet relations were going from bad to worse, relations between Moscow and Budapest were actually improving. Diplomatic relations between Hungary and the Soviet Union, it may be recalled, had been suspended between February 1939, the time of Hungary's accession to the anti-Comintern Pact, and September of that year when that pact lost its effect in the wake of the Nazi-Soviet Nonaggression Pact.[7] For some time after that, relations remained cool. By 1941, however, Teleki and his successor Bardossy were striving to improve them to counteract Germany's predominant influence in Hungary. Just before the Yugoslav crisis, for example, the communist leader Rakosi was freed from prison and exchanged for some flags the Russians had taken from the Hungarian revolutionary army in 1849.[8]

These attempts to establish closer relations with Moscow were, of course, made on considerations of pragmatic power-politics. Hungary's aristocratic leaders certainly had no sympathies for Stalin's communism just as they had none for Hitler's New Order. Horthy, in fact, in his occasional letters to Hitler, continued to talk, in quite vague terms, of a crusade against bolshevism. It is difficult to know why the Regent kept harping on this subject. True, Horthy's hatred of communism was almost matched by his Russophobia. He probably had another motive, however, in mentioning the war against the Soviets to Hitler. Perhaps Horthy, like many of his European contemporaries, was hoping to see the war diverted from the West to the East. The Regent, however, never ventured to state what role if any, his country would play in such a crusade against bolshevik Russia.[9]

Indeed, the question which preoccupied the minds of leading politicians and military men in Hungary of the late spring of 1941 was precisely this problem of the attitude the country's government should adopt in case of a German-Russian military confrontation. Opinions on this issue were widely divergent.

One element of Hungarian leadership which adopted a fairly uniform approach to this question was the military. Hungary's top officers were in constant contact with their German counterparts over such issues as deliveries of war material and the reorganization of the Hungarian Army.[10] In the course of the numerous discussions between German and Magyar officers, the latter had a chance to gain an idea of the German leaders' determination to expand the war to the East, and to eliminate Russia in one mighty blow.

In May, Berlin advised the Hungarian military to strengthen their defences on the Russian border. The real reason for the need for such a measure was not given.[11] In General Werth's mind the German move confirmed what he had long suspected. Only two days after Hitler's order that Hungary should be asked to reinforce its fortifications along the eastern border, the Hungarian Chief-of-Staff submitted a memorandum to his government. In it Werth predicted the coming of a German invasion of Soviet Russia in which Hungary would inevitably become involved because of her geographical location. The General suggested that to meet this contingency the government should 1, conclude a treaty of mutual assistance with Germany; 2, come to an immediate decision in the question of a war against the Soviet Union; and 3, reach an agreement with Germany over the terms of collaboration in this war. Another of Werth's memoranda followed at the end of the month, in which the Chief-of-Staff again emphasized his belief that Berlin was counting on Hungary's participation in the Russian campaign.[12] Finally, on the 14th of June, he made still another attempt to convert the government to his views. On this occasion, Werth stated that, according to latest reports from very reliable sources, the German-Russian war would break out within the next 9-10 days. He used every possible argument to convince the civilian leaders of his country of the necessity of immediate preparation for participation in this conflict. He stated that, should the government neglect to do this, the Germans will themselves take over the defence of the eastern border, which will in turn bring upon the country the wrath of Soviet Russia. He also pointed out how dangerous it would be for Hungary to abstain from a war which Rumania would join. Such a situation would not only destroy the chance of further revision in the former's favour, but might end in the loss of Hungary's recent gains. In conclusion, Werth warned that the Germans would not inform Budapest until the last day or last hour. The government therefore, should immediately get in touch with Berlin and make an offer of "our voluntary participation in the German-Russian war."[13]

Somewhat different ideas prevailed in Hungary's leading civilian circles. To be sure, there were many in Parliament, in the country's diplomatic service and a few even within the Cabinet who shared the views of Werth. One of these was Sztojay who, in his reports to the Foreign Ministry, stressed the urgency of the situation and the necessity of Hungarian participation.[14] The majority of the Ministers and the new Prime Minister, however, held different views.

The composition of the Ministerial Council in May and June of 1941 was much the same as it had been during Teleki's last days. Following his death, the Regent first asked Keresztes-Fischer to assume the leadership of the country's government. The fact that Horthy called on a man who only a few days ago had taken a stronger stand against involvement in the war on Germany's side than Teleki himself, demonstrates clearly that the old Hungarian Head-of-State was not as singlemindedly in favour of collaboration with Hitler as communist historians suggest. Kereszter-Fischer, however, declined to accept the position. He pointed out that his anti-German views were known and his appointment would arouse hostility in Berlin. He proposed that Bardossy should succeed the late Prime Minister. Similar advice was given to Horthy by Bethlen.[15] Accordingly, the Regent invited the Minister of Foreign Affairs to assume the leadership of the government.

Laszlo Bardossy was a career diplomat with little political experience. Death had cleared the way for his rise to prominence. In January he replaced Csaky as Foreign Minister, and in April he assumed Teleki's office. Although during the crisis-ridden last days of March Bardossy had supported the viewpoint of his Prime Minister, he was not known to have been committed either against or for a pro-German line in foreign politics. This, perhaps, was the main reason for his appointment.

In his personal habits, the new Prime Minister was very much different from Teleki. While the deceased statesman tended to be somewhat of a procrastinator when it came to important decisions, and could never draw a clear distinction between his own high moral standards and politics, Bardossy could resolve the greatest issues at an instant without deep personal involvement. In fact, his quickness in decisions almost bordered on rashness. Hory relates in his account of the negotiations with the Rumanians in Turnu-Severin, that on one occasion, Bardossy wanted to act upon a message from Budapest without having deciphered it completely.[16]

The history of the Bardossy administration's first days has already been told. It might just be added that, on the day of the new Prime Minister's accession to office, Bethlen reputedly made a speech in which he warned that "to enter a war was easy, but to finish it was extremely difficult" and asked the new government to do everything humanly possible and more, to keep the country out of the war.[17]

As far as the coming German-Russian war was concerned, Bardossy and his colleagues made every effort to adhere to the old statesman's words of advice until the very end of June. The Prime Minister consistently rejected Werth's suggestions. The Ministerial Council did the same. When, on 14 June, it met to consider the Chief-of-Staff's latest memorandum, the majority of its members voted against the idea of voluntary entry into the coming German-Russian war.[18] The Cabinet decided, however, to make an enquiry whether the German Government intended to inform Budapest of any expected major changes in German-Russian relations. Bardossy also asked Sztojay to find out what role the Germans planned to assign Hungary in a possible confrontation between the *Reich* and the Soviet Union.[19]

Before the Hungarian Minister to Berlin had a chance to contact the officials of the *Wilhelmstrasse,* the message arrived from Ribbentrop that Russian-German relations would be clarified "by the beginning of July at the latest." Hungary was asked "to take steps to secure her frontiers." Nothing more was said of her role in the upcoming developments.[20]

On the 16th of June then, the Hungarian Government at last got an official hint of Hitler's plans in the East. When the country's military leaders were told about Operation Barbarossa is not certain. Weizsäcker suggested in his memoirs that Hitler had Hungary's top officers informed already at the end of May.[21] This seems unlikely, however. According to Juhasz, it was not until the 19th of June that General Halder told Werth about the coming invasion of the U.S.S.R. At that time the German military chief made no demands for Hungarian participation. He only asked that Hungary disarm Soviet soldiers who fled across her border, and place certain railways at the disposal of Germany if it became necessary. Finally, Halder stated that, should the need arise for further measures on the part of Hungary, a German officer assigned to Budapest, General Himer, would contact Werth personally.

In the early hours of the 22nd of June 1941, the German invasion of Russia began. The Hungarian authorities were informed of the development within hours.[23] That morning Erdmannsdorff paid a visit to Horthy. Announcing the news, he delivered a note from the *Führer.* In it Hitler explained the reason for his decision to invade Russia. He also thanked Hungary for reinforcing her eastern frontiers. The *Führer,* however, made no request for direct Hungarian participation in the campaign.[24] Reporting on his conversation with the Regent, Erdmannsdorff stated that Horthy had expressed his delight over the news and had wished Germany good luck in the enterprise. Contrary to various contemporary rumours, however, the Regent made no offer of Hungarian help.[25]

Although Hitler had not asked for Hungary's entry into the war, the Germans were not at all opposed to the idea of accepting Hungarian help in the war effort. General Jodl that day told General Himer that Germany would be grateful for any assistance Budapest might offer.[26] This attitude on the part of the Nazis became more and more evident in subsequent days.

The next day, 23 June, several important developments took place. For a change, the first of these happened neither in Berlin, nor in Budapest, but in Moscow. In the forenoon of the day Jozsef Kristoffy, the Hungarian Minister to the U.S.S.R., was summoned to an audience with Molotov. The Soviet Foreign Minister expressed his hope that the Hungarian Government would stay out of the war. He gave assurances of his country's friendship toward Hungary. He even hinted that the Soviet Union would make no objections to a further revision in Transylvania in Hungary's favour. Finally Molotov asked the Hungarian diplomat to find out immediately what the Budapest government's attitude would be in the crisis.[27]

Long before Kristoffy's report on this interview arrived from Moscow, the Hungarian Cabinet met to consider precisely this problem of the country's attitude to the German-Russian war. Feeling the necessity of taking some form of action, the Ministers decided to break diplomatic relations with the U.S.S.R. The only one to voice his opposition to the idea was Keresztes-Fischer. The decision was communicated to the Soviet Government later in the day. The main reasons for the Cabinet's decision were, no doubt, the desire to please Hitler, and to take the wind out of the sails of rightist agitators who demanded some show of solidarity with the German "crusade" against bolshevism. The German Minister to Budapest, incidentally, was not at all impressed with the Hungarian Government's move. When asked what he thought of the measure, Erdmannsdorff replied that this was the least Hungary could do.[28]

163

Almost simultaneously with the Molotov-Kristoffy interview and the meeting of the Cabinet still another discussion took place: this one between General Himer and General Werth. "In this very plain and emphatic conversation..." reported the German officer to Berlin later on that day, "I once again personally transmitted the view of the OKW and of General Halder, that every support by Hungary was most welcome to Germany. However, no demand would be made." The Hungarian Chief-of-Staff apparently tried to convince his German colleague that Hungary could not intervene because the move had not been prepared politically, and because it was too late for effective Hungarian military action. To this Himer replied that it mattered little whether or not the move had been prepared, since "now the soldiers were talking," and "it was still a little before 12:00 o'clock, and Hungary could still participate in the crusade against Bolshevism in the otherwise solid front."[29]

The German view communicated to Werth by Himer, was a virtual demand for an immediate Hungarian entry into the war. Now the Nazis had made their attitude clear. They, however, also put it on record that Hungary's politicians were not to expect an official request for help in the campaign. Hitler, after all, would not beg for a small power's assistance, especially since all the aid he got so far had been offered voluntarily. His generals, who had always favoured as wide a participation in the campaign as possible, were now clamouring for any help they could get. The reason for this was the fact that soon after the beginning of the *Blitzkrieg*, the *Wehrmacht* had run into strong resistance in the South, and was behind schedule.[30]

On the morning of the 24th Bardossy received two messages. One was Kristoffy's report on his conversation with Molotov; the other was Werth's note on his talk with Himer. Bardossy paid no attention to the message from Moscow. He did not inform anyone of its contents, not even the Regent.[31] He was much more concerned with what Werth's memorandum had to say.

In his report to the Prime Minister, the Chief-of-Staff had outlined the German General Staff's evident eagerness for

Hungarian participation. He also suggested that in view of this, the government should declare war on Soviet Russia. Bardossy immediately conferred with Werth and Bartha, and then with the Regent. Finally, it seems, another meeting of the Cabinet was called. On this occasion Werth's recommendation was almost unanimously voted down.[32]

In the early afternoon Bardossy also had a long discussion with the German Minister to Hungary. In the course of this interview, the Prime Minister asked Erdmannsdorff if what General Himer had said to the Hungarian Chief-of-Staff was true. Then Bardossy outlined at length why Hungary at the time could not mount a major war effort. He explained that the situation in Transylvania was still unsettled, the Slovaks were still resentful about the First Vienna Award, the Hungarian railroad network was already tied up by deliveries for Germany and, finally, that "the Hungarian Government had to take into account the impending start of the harvest in view of the very serious food situation." In conclusion Bardossy stated that in spite of all this "the Hungarian Government would be willing to review the question of participation by parts of the Hungarian Army in the advance against the Soviet armies, and to submit this to the Regent, in case this were desired by Germany and he were informed of this . . . through diplomatic channels."[33]

In the course of this conversation Bardossy did not quite conceal his resentment against the Germans' technique of bringing pressure upon Hungary's Government through the country's General Staff. He did not fail to emphasize that the question of Hungary's participation was a political one which was to be decided by her civilian authorities. The Prime Minister hinted that if the German leaders wanted help, then they should make a formal request.

It is not easy to speculate on Bardossy's motives behind his statements to the German Minister. It is evident, however, that the Hungarian statesman was not at all anxious to enter the war between the two dictatorships. This is why he referred to the railways of the country already being used to capacity, and this is why he mentioned the "impending start of the harvest" and the "very serious food situation."

He knew well that the supply of food was one of the Nazi leadership's major headaches. Moreover, in the light of the experience of the past few weeks, and of Himer's statement that no official demand for Hungarian help would come from Berlin, Bardossy also suspected that if he made his country's participation conditional on a formal request, he would have a good chance of staying out of the war — for a while at least. The Hungarian Prime Minister, however, went even further. By bringing up the question of Transylvania and Hungarian-Slovak relations, he made the impression that his government wanted to exact a price for any help it would render Germany. Bardossy knew that at the moment Hitler was in no position to offer Hungary anything which could be considered as unfair by the government of Slovakia and Rumania. After all, the Germans needed the co-operation of these countries more or less as much as they needed that of Hungary.

The German request for Hungarian help, which Bardossy hoped to avoid, never came from Berlin. Hungary, however, still became involved in the war within a few short days.

The next day, the 25th of June, witnessed several developments which made the position of the Hungarian Government still more difficult. In the morning, General Himer brought together several German diplomats, a few pro-German Hungarian officers and representatives of the German minority. At this meeting, plans were concocted for the raising of a volunteer-force from the ranks of the country's German-speaking population.[34] Later on during the day, a message arrived at the Foreign Ministry in Budapest from Rome warning that Hungary's refusal to join the Russian campaign "may have harmful repercussions."[35] As if this was not enough, June 25th also saw the entry of still another country into the war on Hitler's side: Slovakia.

The involvement of this state in the Russian campaign was a very serious development from the point of view of the Hungarian Government. Slovakia's participation had not been planned originally. That state did not have the military forces it could readily afford to send off to a distant campaign. She was not even contiguous to the Soviet Union. The seemingly unsolicited entry into the war of the weak and unprepared Slovak state, which could not claim as much as a border dispute with the U.S.S.R., left the Hungarian Government with no excuse for not doing the same. In spite of this, Hungary's civilian leaders refused to yield to the increasing pressure. Not for long, however. For, on the following day, an event took place "which" in Professor Macartney's words, "changed the whole course of events."[36]

2. The Kassa Incident.

In the early afternoon of the 26th, various points in northeastern Hungary were attacked by unidentified aircraft. The incidents took place in the vicinity of the town of Raho, near the Russian border; at Munkacs, a town of central Ruthenia; and at Kassa (Kosice), a provincial centre just South of the eastern tip of Slovakia. Heaviest hit in the raid was Kassa, where some 27 bombs were dropped causing loss of life and considerable material destruction.

The story of the bombings of the 26th has been told many times in many different ways. This is not surprising, considering the fact that precise information on the event is remarkably difficult to obtain. Even the raid on Kassa remains to some extent a mystery, in spite of the fact that it took place in broad daylight and in the presence of Hungarian military personnel.

That the attack at Raho did in fact take place is almost beyond doubt. It was mentioned in the evidence produced by the Soviet Prosecutor at Nuremberg.[37] It is also admitted by communist historians.[38] About the bombing of Munkacs very little is known. Indeed, some reputable historians make no reference to it at all. Somewhat more familiar is the story of the attack on Kassa.

A few minutes after 1 p.m. three[39] planes approached the town at a low altitude, dropped their bombs and departed. The attack came as a complete surprise to the local detachment of the Hungarian air force. The personnel of the Kassa air-field, on sighting the planes, at first assumed that friendly aircraft were coming in for an unscheduled landing.[40] Apparently, a Russian attack at the time was not expected, although air force units in the region had been alerted as early as the first day of the German invasion against the U.S.S.R.[41]

The identity of the planes has never been established. Their national markings could not be seen from the airfield. In the town very few competent witnesses were found. Some of those who saw the aircraft from a shorter distance, recalled having observed yellow markings on them, a fact which would indicate that they were of Axis origin.[42] According to Professor Macartney, an inquiry conducted into the affair during the war by the Hungarian Government, came to the conclusion that from their shape, the planes might have been of Soviet, German or Czech manufacture. The bombs and shells used in the attack, however, were found to be of Russian origin.[43]

Ever since the afternoon of the 26th of June 1941 politicians, journalists and lately historians have been trying hard to find an answer to "the salient mystery," as Professor Macartney put it — "who bombed Kassa, and why?"[44]

The question has already been answered on many occasions. The fact remains, however, that a satisfactory solution to the riddle has yet to be offered.

Rumours began to circulate immediately after the incidents took place. A few of the witnesses swore (as some apparently still do) that the planes were Russian. Others, however, thought differently. Only two days after the attack the Hungarian journalist Dezso Saly made the following entry in his diary: "according to 'M', the bombing was done by the Germans to involve Hungary in the war."[45] This version gained almost universal acceptance in Hungary during the war. It is still argued by communist historians. Another theory which became current soon after the incidents was that the raid was perpetrated by Slovak pilots who stole some German planes and fled with them to Russia, using up their bombs and ammunition as they passed over Hungarian territory.[46] This story was eventually accepted by Professor Macartney as the most likely explanation of the mysterious affair.

In the course of time the rumours, supplemented by a large amount of often futile research, crystallized into two basic historical theories on the Kassa incident: 1, that the bombing was perpetrated by the Germans to force Hungary's entry into the war; 2, that it was carried out by pilots from Slovakia fleeing to the Soviet Union. The idea that the aircraft might have been really Russian has been almost completely discounted.

The first of these hypotheses was held by many in Hungary during and after the war. In his memoirs, Horthy himself subscribed to this view.[47] Communist historians, as it has been mentioned, have also steadfastly held to this explanation of the incident.[48]

The theory that the attack on Kassa, and presumably on the other points as well, was carried out by the Germans has been based on two different sources of evidence, namely, the revelations of two former Hungarian officers: Colonel Adam Krudy and Major General Istvan Ujszaszy.

Krudy was an air-force captain assigned to duty in Kassa at the time of the incident. He was one of the few competent officers to have witnessed the attack, and apparently the only one who from the very day of the bombing contended that the planes were German. In fact, Krudy had communicated his observation to the authorities in Budapest only a few hours after the incident, but was told to keep quiet. This he did, almost until the end of the war, when he might have made some unguarded remarks on the matter. In any case, he was imprisoned by the Nazis. Since 1945 Krudy has made several public statements in Hungary reaffirming his original argument.[49]

Ujszaszy had been the Chief of the Intelligence and Counter-intelligence Services of the Hungarian General Staff from 1939 to 1942. His testimony was presented to the Nüremberg Tribunal by the Soviet Prosecutor. According to this evidence, the plot to involve Hungary in the war was hatched by a few high-ranking German and Hungarian officers, and the bombings in northeastern Hungary were "carried out by German planes with Russian markings."[50]

At this point one must ask the question what are the strong points and the flaws of this theory based on the revelations of Krudy and Ujszaszy. The main strength of the theory lies, no doubt, in the fact that the story is quite plausible. The

German military did have an interest in involving Hungary in the war, and there was nothing like a neat little provocation to attain this. Nor could it have been difficult to interest one or two Hungarian generals in the matter. The planes, bombs, ammunition and pilots necessary for the venture could have been obtained right in Slovakia. The German planes were there: all that had to be done was to paint over their markings. Bombs and shells of Russian manufacture could have been obtained from the stores of the former Czecho-slovak air force. Kassa was only a few minutes' flying time from some of the Slovak air-fields. The fact that nothing of major strategic importance was attacked, (the railway station escaped the raid unscathed, and the invaders did not go any-where near the airfield) also tends to prove that the whole affair was a staged provocation.

Besides this "plausibility" of the story, however, the theory cannot be accepted without reservation. First of all, the evidence upon which it is based is by no means completely reliable. It must be remembered that Ujszaszy's testimony was obtained by Soviet authorities, probably by the usual Soviet methods. More important still, the Chief of the Intelligence and Counter-intelligence Services did not admit having ever found any material evidence of the plot. A closer examinations of portions of his testimony that were read by the Soviet Prosecutor at Nuremberg, reveals that Ujszaszy had come to the conclusion that the bombings had been carried out by the Germans not because he had received any concrete information or evidence on the matter, but only as a result of having observed the behaviour of the officers he had thought to have been involved in the plot.[51] In reality then, Ujszaszy's testimony is based on nothing but pure speculation on his part.

Krudy's evidence is just as doubtful. True, he was an eye-witness. But the plain fact is that it was not possible for any-one to identify the planes from as far as the airfield.[52] The communist military historian, Major Jozsef Kun claims, how-ever, that during the attack Krudy took to the air, gave chase to the invaders and succeeded in observing their mark-ings. If this is true, which is highly questionable, then he must have followed them over Slovak territory, unless of course the attacking planes headed for the East, toward the Russian border.[53] In connection with Krudy's post-1945 revelations it might also be remembered that this man had tasted life in a Nazi prison and that at present he is living in a communist country. Under these circumstances it is not likely that he would change his original story and thereby exonerate his one-time enemies and displease his present masters.

Another factor which detracts from this theory is the rather inconsistent way in which some communist historians have treated it. A few of them, for example, had argued that the aircraft in question were "camouflaged as Russian planes." Probably realizing that this was sheer nonsense — aircraft can be smeared with paint but cannot be camouflaged — others had stated only that Russian markings had been painted on them. Kun, in his effort to prove that the airplanes had been German, cited the fact that they had been seen (by Krudy) flying in a formation "which in 1941 was flown only by the German air force."[54] Why the Nazis would take the trouble of "disguising" their planes and then parade them around in a typically German formation is beyond the understanding of this writer.

The second theory, according to which the attack was committed by Czech or Slovak pilots fleeing to the Soviet Union, has even less evidence to support it. In spite of this fact, Professor Macartney considers it to be "the most likely version." Indeed, one great asset of this theory is that it explains why the Post Office, rather than a location of greater strategic importance was singled out as the target. By bombing a government building, the pilots made sure that most of the victims would be Hungarians rather than Slovaks. In 1942 a story was published in a Hungarian newspaper, which lent further weight to this hypothesis. According to it, a Hungarian officer was billeted in a house in one of the towns of occupied Russia. There he learned that a previous occupant of his room had been a Czech-born pilot of the Soviet air force who had acknowledged his own participation in the raid on Kassa.[55]

This is indeed an ingenious theory, which answers almost

all of the questions connected with the bombings: the attack on the Post Office, the incidents all the way from Kassa to southeastern Ruthenia, and even possibly the Russian bombs. There is, however, one problem with this explanation. According to Ujszaszy, the attack on Raho took place at 12:30 noon,[56] while the bombing of Kassa did not occur until after 1 p.m. Would this not suggest that the invading aircraft came from the East, from Russia, rather than Slovakia?

In the light of the questionable adequacy of the two traditional explanations of the events of the 26th, it becomes necessary then to consider the possibility that the culprits were the Russians after all. In a re-examination of this historical problem one might start with the question: how valid were the reasons that historians, behind the Iron Curtain as well as in the West, had for rejecting this version of the story? Communist authors have invariably argued that the Soviet Government had no reason for attacking a neutral state thereby causing its entry into the war against the U.S.S.R. They have also contended that at the time the Soviet air force was in no position to send aircraft against Hungary. "The suggestion", wrote Kun, "that the bombing of Kassa was carried out by Soviet planes, seems absurd from the military point of view also."[57] Professor Macartney has also discounted the theory that Russians were involved in the attack. He seems to have had impressive reasons for doing so. It is not clear, he stated, why the Russians "should have wanted to bomb Kassa at all." He argued, furthermore that they "might have done so by mistake for a town in German occupation . . . but the German air force was at that date in complete mastery of the air, and observers testified that no hostile aircraft had crossed the Carpathians anywhere near Kassa at the relevant time."[58] Finally even Horthy admitted in his memoirs that in view of the weakness of Soviet air power at the time, and the evident interests of Moscow that Hungary should remain neutral in the conflict, Russian guilt in the affair had to be ruled out.[59]

At this point one might ask the question whether it is possible that both the communists and Horthy as well as an eminent neutral observer could all be mistaken? This can only be established if their arguments are analized in detail. First of all let us consider the statement by Professor Macartney that no hostile planes were seen crossing the Carpathians near Kassa, that is, in northern Ruthenia. This might be perfectly true. If, however, the aircraft which bombed that city were the same as the ones which attacked Munkacs and Raho, then they would not have crossed the Carpathians north-east of Kassa, but somewhere in the vicinity of the town of Körösmező, in southeastern Ruthenia.

Next, we might consider the question why the Soviets would attack a neutral country at all. At the time, the Russians, in their agony, apparently made no careful distinction between the countries that had entered the war against them and those that had not. It might be pointed out, that Soviet aircraft had attacked a Finnish fortification and two ships as early as the 22nd of June, before Finland gave any indication of her intention to participate in Hitler's invasion of Russia.[60] It could be argued, of course, that the Soviet leaders expected Finland's entry into the war, while they might have hoped to keep Hungary neutral. This, indeed, might have been the case originally. Otherwise Molotov would not have promised, on the 23rd, to support the cause of Hungarian revision in Transylvania should Hungary maintain her neutrality. Soon, however, this situation changed. By the 26th almost every country in the Axis orbit had joined Germany in her attack against the U.S.S.R. The Soviet leaders could not have had much hope left that Hungary would fail to do the same. If they still had any, their expectations were probably shattered when the news arrived that Budapest decided to break off diplomatic relations with Moscow. The Soviets had offered their help to Hungary against the Rumanians. The Hungarians replied with a serious affront. Surely this response could have been taken in the Kremlin as proof of the Hungarian Government's belligerent attitude towards the U.S.S.R.

We have now come to the last question to be considered: was it possible for Soviet aircraft to leave Russian air-space and attack towns in Hungary? As it has been seen, this query has been answered in the negative by communist historians as well as Professor Macartney and Horthy. Indeed, the accepted view among historians in general is that Soviet air power had been almost completely shattered in the first hours of the German invasion. Evidence for this is not difficult to find. On the third day of the conflict, for example, General Halder remarked in his diary that the Russian air force was in complete retreat.[61] This observation, however, creates a misleading picture. Halder was thinking of northern and central Russia only. A more accurate account of Soviet strength in the air during those days is presented by the official record of the German High Command, the *Kriegstagebuch des Oberkommandos der Wehrmacht*. This source emphasizes that Russian air power in the South was still "very strong" at the time.[62] In the light of this evidence the traditional argument that it was impossible for Russian aircraft at the time to penetrate the Carpathian basin, must be taken with grave reservations.

All this, however, leaves one important question still unanswered. If it was the Russians who carried out the bombings, why did they single out Kassa for special attention and not another city nearer to Raho, where the planes evidently crossed the border? It is here, however, that the Czech-born officer of the Soviet air force, mentioned in the Hungarian newsreport of 1942, comes into the story. Could it be that this man did not defect to Russia on 26 June, 1941, as Professor Macartney has suggested, but had been in the Soviet Union all along? For if he had, then the riddle is solved: what happened on the 26th of June then was that Soviet aircraft, piloted by Czech and possibly also Slovak members of the Russian air force, took off from an airfield somewhere in the western Ukraine, crossed the Carpathians, hit a few strategic points in Ruthenia, (at Raho trains were attacked), and then flew straight on to Kassa, a town which had long been a bone of contention between Magyars and Slovaks. There they settled an old score against Hungary and returned to their bases.

This, of course, is just another theory. To convert it into an exact account of events will be impossible unless more evidence will come to light on the whole affair. More will have to be known on the precise timing of the attack, especially at points other than Kassa. To find more evidence might prove very difficult. Captured Nazi sources have already been combed through fairly systematically. So far they revealed nothing on the matter. It is not very likely that they would yield anything in the future. The communists will not divulge any evidence prejudicial to their version of the story. And even if more will be found, who knows what it will reveal? Perhaps it will turn out that Raho was hit by the Russians, while Kassa was bombed by the Germans who were just wait-ing for the first news of a Soviet violation of Hungarian air-space to carry out their provocation with an excellent chance that it would be blamed on the Russians. Or perhaps, we shall learn that Ujszaszy was an hour out when he put the time of the attack on Raho at 12:30, and the whole affair was really the work of pilots who took off from Slovakia with a few planes and escaped to Russia dropping their bombs on the way.[62A]

The incidents of the 26th of June served as a climax to a series of internal and external developments which had exerted great pressure on Hungary's leadership. By that date many countries had already joined Hitler's invasion of the U.S.S.R. Italy and Rumania declared war on the Soviet Union on the first day of the attack. Slovakia followed suit on the 23rd. Two days later Spain announced that she would also send a contingent against Russia. Next, Finland's entry into the war became official. The Nazi propaganda machine, more-over, used every means to build up the campaign as a "crusade against bolshevism". As the hours went by, the pressure for action continued to mount in Budapest. The military called for war. Rome warned against continued inaction. Nazis and Germans in Hungary were plotting to organize a "volunteer army". It was at this juncture that the news arrived from Kassa that "Soviet aircraft" had bombed the city. From there on, events came to a rapid conclusion.

Upon hearing the news, General Werth and Defence Min-ister Bartha hurried to consult with Horthy. When the report reached Bardossy, his first reaction was to give orders that the news of the affair should be suppressed for the time being.[63] Next, the Prime Minister also went to see the Regent.

What happened then has been described by Professor Macartney: "(Bardossy) found (Horthy) in a state of high excitement, convinced that Hungary had been the victim of a dastardly and unprovoked attack. The attack had got to be 'answered'. He had already given orders to the air force to carry out reprisals."[64]

It is difficult to know what exactly transpired at the meeting of Horthy, Werth, Bartha and Bardossy. It seems evident that pressure was put on the Prime Minister to abandon his efforts aimed at avoiding a voluntary entry into the war. Bardossy gave in. When the Cabinet met later on that afternoon, the Prime Minister himself sponsored a motion calling for a declaration to the effect that Hungary considered herself at war with the Soviet Union.

What caused this sudden *volte-face* in Bardossy's policy is not easy to explain. Undoubtedly the whole course of events during the past few days, climaxed by the bombings, had a great deal to do with it. Horthy's impulsive reaction to the attack, abetted, no doubt, by the advice of Werth and Bartha, made matters even worse. Unlike the Regent, Bardossy was not at all sure that the intruding planes were Russian. During those fateful hours Hungary's Prime Minister seems to have come to the conclusion that the attack was a staged provocation to force his country into the conflict. He explained to Antal Ullein-Reviczky, an official of the Foreign Ministry, that "when the country's military, in connivance with the Germans, refrained from nothing in order to draw Hungary into the war, and as Rumania was already belligerent," involvement could not be avoided. "I have realized that in five minutes," he added.[65] And when, later on in the afternoon, the Prime Minister received the confidential message from Krudy that the invading aircraft bore "Axis markings", he became convinced "that the bombing", to use Professor Macartney's words, "was a German trick ... and ... that the time when Hungary could exercise any freedom of choice was past."[66]

Once Horthy, Bardossy, Bartha and Werth had made up their minds, the question of peace or war was in effect already settled. At the emergency session of the Ministerial

Council during the afternoon only three of those present (Ke-resztes-Fischer and two others) voiced their opposition to the idea of entering the war in view of the day's developments;[67] and when Parliament met the next morning, it was confronted with a *fait accompli*. Here, it was simply announced that, as a result of the Soviet attack, a state of war existed between Hungary and the U.S.S.R. No debate was allowed, and no vote was taken.

By this time it would have been too late to reverse the decision in any case. The orders for the mobilization of the country's mobile corps had already gone out, Berlin had already been informed of the Hungarian Government's intention to contribute to the German war effort,[68] and a reprisal by the air force against Stanislav, a Russian city on the eastern slopes of the Carpathians, was already under way.

Ever since June of 1941, Horthy and Bardossy have been severely criticized for their handling of the whole affair. Much of this criticism is, no doubt, well deserved. Indeed, Horthy's impulsive reaction to the attack and Bardossy's very sudden change of policy revealed that in those historic days the fate of Hungary was not in the hands of statesmen of great political acumen and foresight.

Yet, in passing judgement on Horthy's and Bardossy's moves during those critical hours of the 26th, the political atmosphere of the day should not be forgotten. It must be remembered that these men evidently feared that should Germany win the war, Hungary's interests would be disregarded at the time of the peace settlement in Europe unless the country, like all the other allies of the Third *Reich*, could claim to have had a helping hand in German victory. They considered it highly probable that in case of a Nazi victory, to which Hungary had contributed nothing, all prospects for further revision would vanish, and the threat of a reversal of the Vienna awards could become a menacing reality. The developments preceding the incidents of the 26th, no doubt greatly accentuated these feelings of fear and uncertainty, while the raid on Kassa and other points served as a catalyst in precipitating Hungarian involvement in the war. The attack could not be ignored. A refusal to react promptly and vigorously to the Kassa bombing would have placed the Bardossy government in an impossible position. The Nazi propaganda machine, inside and outside the country, would have launched an immense campaign of denunciation against the Hungarian leadership for failing to defend the nation's honour in the face of unprovoked Russian aggression. To make Krudy's message public, that is, to announce that the attack might have been prepetrated by the Germans and not the Soviets, would have been disastrous for Hungary in 1941.

Faced with such prospects, Horthy and Bardossy gave in to the demands for Hungarian participation in what was expected to be a short and victorious German campaign against Soviet Russia. Hungary's leaders had been under mounting pressure even prior to the bombing of Kassa. The additional stress generated by this incident proved unbearable for them. Consequently, they decided to make a token contribution to Hitler's war effort.[69] Once this step had been taken, however, the country's increasingly deeper involvement in the gigantic and protracted struggle became unavoidable.

CONCLUSIONS

On the 26th of June, 1941, Hungary at last became involved in the Second World War. This turn of events was, to a considerable extent, the outcome of international developments in Europe during the preceding half decade. The phenomenal rise of German power, manifested by the rearmament of that country, the expansion of her economic influence in the Danube Basin and the extension of the area under direct German control through sudden military moves, had a very strong effect on the conduct of Hungarian foreign and, to a lesser extent, internal policies.

The reaction of Hungary's policymakers to the revival of German strength was basically twofold. The re-emergence of Germany as a great power in Europe heightened Hungarian expectations about a revision of the peace settlements of 1919-1920. At the same time is caused many of the country's leaders to fear the prospect of unchecked German economic, political and even military expansion in East Central Europe and the Balkans. The result was that, starting with the mid-1930's, two major tendencies began to predominate in Hungarian foreign policy. One of these aimed at exploiting the changes in the European international structure for the revision of the Trianon settlement. The other had as its goal the containment of German influence in the Danube Basin so that Hungary's freedom of action would not be seriously threatened. It must be emphasized that these tendencies did not cause the rise of two different and easily distinguishable sets of foreign policies. The two were inseparably intertwined in almost every move of Hungary's policymakers.

Of the two aspirations in Hungarian foreign policy, the first one, the desire for revision, is obvious. The Magyar nation, with a deep sense of its thousand year old past, and of its historic mission in the Carpathian Basin had not acquiesced in the judgment of Trianon. In response to the lasting sense

179

of injustice which the peace settlement had left in the people of Hungary, the leadership of the country considered it to be one of its primary tasks to aim for the recovery of some of the territories which had been lost in the wake of the First World War, territories that, with a few interruptions, had belonged to the Hungarian state ever since the Eleventh Century.

It has been argued many times that the desire for revision drove Hungary into the German orbit. This argument, however, is valid only to a certain extent. True, in the minds of many Magyar nationalists the cultivation of Berlin's friendship was closely connected with the expectation of territorial re-adjustments in the Carpathian Basin. It must also be admitted that co-operation with Germany eventually netted certain territorial gains to Hungary. It has been pointed out, however, that in some cases these gains were not much more than periodic alms handed out to the country's government to make it feel obligated toward the Third *Reich*. Hitler furthered the cause of Hungarian revision only when it served his own ambitions. It should also be remembered that several of the leading Hungarian politicians of the time had no desire to attain revision at the price of direct collaboration with Germany. Men such as Bethlen, Kanya, Keresztes-Fischer and Teleki realized that nothing would harm the cause of Hungarian revision more than participation in Hitler's grand schemes for the aggrandizement of the Third *Reich*, schemes which were doomed to eventual failure because of the material and moral superiority of the forces opposed to them.

The other aspiration of Hungary's leadership, the desire to contain the spreading influence of Germany, is also understandable. The undue expansion of German economic and political influence threatened Hungary with the reduction of her freedom of action. The loss of the "free hand" in foreign policy would have doomed all her ambitions in external affairs, and would have reduced the country's chances of staying out of a European conflagration. In fact, it would have been the first step toward a complete and inevitable enslavement of Hungary.

Hungarian efforts for the containment of German power

were not pursued with equal force and determination through the years which preceded 1941. In the days of Gombos, when the danger was less acute and less apparent, the leaders of Hungary satisfied themselves with counselling an Austro-German reconciliation both in Vienna and Berlin. They probably believed that amity between the two German-speaking states would make annexation less necessary in the eyes of Germany's leaders. The Hungarian Government also continued its participation in the Rome bloc with the intention of bolstering Austria's position *vis-à-vis* the Third *Reich*. Through such measures it hoped to lessen the threat of *Anschluss,* and to prolong the division of the German world, a division which some of the more astute politicians in Budapest considered to be an asset to Hungarian diplomacy.[1]

As a result of the continued growth of the Third *Reich's* power and prestige, the increasing economic penetration of the Danube Basin by Germany, and the proliferation of local neo-Nazi movements in this region, the threat to Hungary's freedom of action increased. To combat this danger, Hungarian diplomacy tried to work for the creation of a power-balance in Danubian Europe between the Third *Reich* and a number of states interested in the containment of Germany. This was the main purpose of Hungary's policy of friendship with Italy.[2] As time went on, and as Italy's disinterest in the Danube region increased, Hungary's leaders realized that other states had to be brought into the picture if German influence was to be effectively counterbalanced.

It was in this context that the idea of an alignment of East Central European states along the Vistula and the Danube rivers emerged early in 1938. Based on close Polish-Hungarian co-operation and a common boundary between the two states, along with Hungarian *rapprochement* with Belgrade and even Bucharest, the support of Italy and possibly of Britain, this bloc of nominally pro-German, but hopefully independent states was to form a political front against further penetration of German influence into the region. It was largely for the attainment of this aim that the Budapest regime sought close ties with Warsaw, unfailingly cultivated the friendship of Rome, sought the support of London, and worked for a

181

modus vivendi with Belgrade and Bucharest. To increase the effectiveness of this policy it even made modest and vain attempts to improve Anglo-Italian relations.[3]

Under the strain of German hostility to Poland the plans for the Danube-Vistula alignment disintegrated. Hungary could do no more for Poland at the outbreak of the war in 1939 than to deny co-operation to the Germans and to offer help to Polish refugees. The ties of Hungarian diplomacy with Rome and the British Foreign Office were, of course, maintained even after the disappearance of independent Poland from the map. Good relations were cultivated with Yugoslavia, and it seems that the makers of the country's foreign policy even entertained, quite unrealistically, ideas of attaining better relations with Rumania once the Transylvanian issue was settled.

After the demise of Yugoslavia, Hungary's last "window to the West", the possibility of finding some means to counterbalance, at least to some extent, the predominant influence of the German *Reich* in the Danube region became very slim indeed. The country was now almost completely isolated from the forces that worked towards the containment of Nazi Germany.

Ever since the mid-1930's one of the most important means of Hungarian diplomacy for the containment of Germany was, unusual as it may seem, the policy of friendship with that country itself. Good relations with the *Reich* were not initiated for this purpose. They actually pre-dated the years of the German danger. As time passed, however, friendship with Berlin came to be the best assurance against the chance of German military expansion into the heart of the Danube Valley. A weak Hungary, hostile to the *Reich,* would have been not only a provocation but also an enticement for adventurers like Hitler and Göring to test their country's new-born military might. After all, they almost did just that to Czechoslovakia, a state which had a more powerful army and a greater number of potential allies than Hungary. The issue of German minorities in Hungary could easily have served as a pretext. Probably realizing, but for good reasons never admitting this, Hungary's policymakers were most reluctant all through these years to take any measures that might have brought down the wrath of Hitler upon the country. After 1940 this became almost a permanent feature of Hungarian-German relations. "(Hungary) went to the limit to preserve her independence, her freedom, her wealth, and her humanity," wrote Kallay in his memoirs, "without, however, so straining the bow as to provoke brutal intervention from the Germans and the destruction of all of these."[4]

In the end, however, neither the policy of containing the spread of German influence, nor that of appeasing the Third *Reich* prevented the serious impairment of Hungary's freedom of action. The question which might be asked here is whether there were any feasible alternatives open for Hungary's leaders to follow in order to avoid this turn of events? The answer to this query will have to be a negative one. First of all, no single Danubian state, and probably not even a combination of them could have successfully resisted the German onslaught, diplomatic or economic, not to mention the military. Secondly, Hungarian association with an openly anti-Nazi bloc, such as an alignment between Hungary and the Little Entente, or the Prague-Vienna-Budapest "triangle", could have proved tantamount to an invitation for drastic intervention by Germany. From this it might be concluded that, in view of the preponderant power of the Third *Reich* and the ever increasing threat of a German military occupation, a considerable limitation of Hungary's freedom of action sooner or later became inevitable.

Another question which needs to be answered is whether this weakening of Hungary's free hand in external and, to some extent, even in internal affairs could have been stopped short of the country's involvement in war on Germany's side. Before answering this question it might be pointed out that most of Hungary's leading politicians had no desire to get involved in an all-European conflict either on Hitler's side, or on that of the Allied Powers. As has been mentioned, many of them believed that revision, attained at the cost of collaboration with the Nazis, would prove useless in the long run. They also knew that to expend the nation's energies in a European struggle and thereby to leave the country weak and defenceless for the aftermath of the war could lead to precisely the same kind of catastrophe that had overtaken Hungary in the wake of the First World War. Exactly a month before his suicide, Teleki stated in a foreign policy memorandum that at the end of the war chaotic conditions could arise in Eastern Europe, especially in case of a partial or complete German defeat. The Prime Minister envisaged the rise of a situation which could seriously threaten an enfeebled Hungary. He pointed to the danger of expansionist attempts by the country's neighbours, especially Russia, and to the possibility of a general spread of communism. Teleki concluded from this that the first and foremost task of the country's leadership was "to keep Hungary strong and intact to the end of the war."[5] Moreover, Hungary's leaders were convinced, especially before the spring of 1940, that Germany would lose the war in the end. In fact, before the outbreak of the conflict, this belief was almost universal in the top political circles of Hungary. Horthy was bold enough to reveal his feelings to the Nazi leaders about the chances of German victory in an all-out confrontation. In December 1937 he warned them that it would be a grave mistake to underestimate England's power, which was still "enormous" in spite of "signs of decadence" among the British youth.[6] In a message to the Polish Government in September 1938, Kanya also expressed the view that if war came over Czechoslovakia, Britain and France would intervene and Germany would lose the ensuing long struggle.[7] It might be recalled that in April of 1939 Hory prophesied the defeat of Nazism after initial victories,[8] and a year later Bethlen, in a memorandum on the Hungarian position regarding a post-war peace settlement, refused to consider the possibility of a German victory.[9] As late as March of 1941, Teleki could still write that the "outcome of the war" was "uncertain".[10]

After Germany's stunning victories in the spring of 1940, however, faith in Western superiority declined. Some influential persons in Hungary gradually abandoned their former resolve to oppose involvement in German military ventures. Others, among them Sztojay, Defence Minister Bartha and General Werth, openly voiced the view that the Third *Reich* would win the war and that Hungary's interest would be best served if she voluntarily entered the conflict on Germany's side. Consequently, two schools of thought emerged within the country's leadership. One of them called for Hungary's entry into the war, while the other maintained that the national interest demanded the country's neutrality in the conflict. For a long time the second had by far the greater influence. However, as Nazi power in Europe grew and as pressure on the Hungarian Government increased, the balance of power between the forces of peace and war became more and more delicate. On the 26th of June 1941 an incident, the attack on Kassa and other points, tipped the scales. At that moment the country's leaders yielded to overwhelming pressure and Hungary became involved in the war. That eventually it had to come to this was probably inevitable. For even if the country, through a combination of good luck and astute leadership, had succeeded in avoiding entry into the conflict during the summer of that year, it could not possibly have prolonged its neutrality for too long. One merely has to remember the enormous pressure the Germans put on Budapest for a greater contribution to the war effort as soon as the *Wehrmacht* ran into serious trouble in Russia during the winter of 1941-42.[11]

Once the country became involved in the conflict there was no way out. In vain were Werth and Bartha replaced by more sober men, and in vain was the anglophile Kallay appointed in place of Bardossy early in 1942, and in vain did Horthy try to pull the country out of the war two and a half years later, Hungary remained in the conflict till the conclusion of the hostilities. Early in 1944, moreover, she was occupied by the Germans. The country became ruled by Quislings. At the end came the Russian occupation, followed, in due course, by the establishment of a communist dictatorship.

It might be asked here whether or not Hungary would have escaped this fate if she had not participated in the war on Hitler's side. The answer to this question must be in the negative. One does not need to look further than the example of Bulgaria. The leaders of that country seem to have convinced Hitler that the Slav and Orthodox Bulgarians would not make reliable soldiers in a struggle against their Slav and Orthodox Russian brothers. In this way Bulgaria had avoided involvement in the war. Yet she did not escape the fate of the other East European nations. When the Red Army approached her borders in September 1944, the Soviet Union declared war on her, occupied the country and turned it into a Soviet satellite. Or let us take the example of Poland. That country refused to yield to German pressure. Did it escape Soviet occupation and the loss of its independence?

During the decade which preceded the catastrophe of World War II, Hungary's leaders sought to serve their country's national interest amidst a rapidly changing situation. They were eager to exploit the opportunities offered to them by the dislocations in the European power structure for the revision of the Trianon settlement. They were also anxious to preserve their country's basic freedom of action. These two aspirations often led to contradictions in Hungary's foreign policy. The efforts at revision often tended to prejudice the effectiveness of the policy of protecting the country's "free hand" through the containment of German influence. Hungarian revisionist moves on some occasions helped to reduce the power of resistance of Hungary's neighbours to Nazi pressure. Occasionally they also tended to reinforce the determination of the leaders of some of these states to turn to Hitler for protection and align their policy with that of the Third *Reich*. The result in both cases was an even faster expansion of Nazi power in the Danube Basin. At the same time, the Hungarian Government's desire to retain the "free hand" and not to align the country's foreign policy irrevocably with that of the Third *Reich* reduced the success of the policy of revision. The reluctance to cooperate more fully with Hitler probably deprived Hungary of some opportunities to make even more extensive changes in the onerous territorial provisions of the Treaty of Trianon.

Hungary's leaders have often been criticized, by those who stand on the vantage ground of hindsight, for not relinquishing their revisionist aspirations and for failing to offer a helping hand to their neighbours when these were threatened by Germany. Those who make such criticism, however, reveal a certain lack of understanding for the workings of diplomacy in a passionately nationalistic environment. Deep-seated antagonism, heightened by the existence of serious territorial disputes, cannot simply and suddenly be erased. It is also unrealistic to expect countries, which had been mortal enemies for decades, to risk defeat and destruction to protect each other. Not long before Hungary's involvement in the Yugoslav affair, Teleki himself stated this clearly. "We may risk", he wrote, "the country, our youth, our military power for ourselves only and for *no one* else..."[12]

The existence of national antagonism and territorial quarrels in the Danube Basin was, of course, very unfortunate. It made the whole area more vulnerable to German pressure, for Hitler exploited the rivalries of these states with great cunning. By inciting them against each other and by holding out the prospect of favourable change to one and then to the other, the *Führer* perfected the game of "divide and rule" to a fine art probably never equalled in the history of this part of Europe. It would be a mistake, however, to attribute all of Hitler's success to the existence of territorial disputes in this area. The German penetration of East Central Europe was basically the result of the overwhelming power position the Third *Reich* attained in Europe by the end of the 1930's.

Once all hope was lost for the containment of German influence in this general region, Hungarian diplomacy had to rely more and more on a policy of appeasing the Nazi leaders in Berlin. This remained Hungary's only means of averting the loss of all her freedom of action as a result of a direct intervention by the Germans in the country's affairs. Of course, such a policy could not be conducted without considerable moral and material cost to the country. It involved an ever increasing economic and military contribution to Germany's war effort, as well as concessions to the Nazis in the field of external and, to a lesser extent, internal politics. Through this policy, however, Hungary retained a considerable measure of control over her internal affairs for the major part of the war. As a result, until the last year of the war, she could offer refuge to persons fleeing violent persecution in German-controlled areas. For years she also avoided the miserable experience of being ruled by National Socialist revolutionaries and similar extremists. All this, of course, came to an end after the Germans occupied Hungary in 1944.

When the end of the Second World War came with the collapse of the Third *Reich* in the spring of 1945, the plight of Hungary, like that of the other states of East Central Europe, did not come to an end. Within a brief period of time, most countries in this area were transformed into Soviet satellites. Although at the present time there seems to be little hope for a termination of this state of affairs, history is full of surprises. One day, perhaps, Russian domination over this part of Europe will also cease. When that time comes, the nations of East Central Europe will have to find themselves an overall organizational framework which would enable them to resist any new expansionist thrust on the part of their great power neighbours into this region. It would probably be a mistake, however, to seek this new political setup in the restoration of the interwar system based on the division of this area into numerous inadequately small sovereign states. Rather, the peoples of this unfortunate region should seek the creation of a federal state of their own, or participation in an all-European federation. Within such an organizational structure there would be a better chance of achieving a high degree of economic prosperity, a large measure of individual freedom and the unhindered social and cultural development of all regardless of national origin. When this will become a reality, the peoples of East Central Europe can look forward to being masters of their own destiny at last.

NOTES

List of Abbreviations.

Ciano's Papers — Ciano's Diplomatic Papers.
DIA — Documents on International Affairs.
DBFP — Documents on British Foreign Policy.
DGFP — Documents on German Foreign Policy.
DIMK — Diplomáciai Iratok Magyarország Külpolitikájához.
Horthy's Papers — Horthy Miklós Titkos Iratai.
IMT — The Trial of the Major War Criminals before the International Military Tribunal, Nuremberg.
MMV — Magyarország és a Második Világháború.

NOTES TO THE INTRODUCTION

1. *The Central European Observer,* vol. XVIII, no. 6, (15 March 1941.) p. 62. The Holy Crown of St. Stephen was the symbol of the Hungarian Monarchy.
2. In J. Opocensky (ed.) *Eduard Benes: Essays and Reflections,* London: Allen and Unwin, 1944. p. 164.
3. H.L. Roberts in G.A. Craig and F. Gilbert, (eds.) *The Diplomats,* New York: Athenaum, 1965. Vol. II. p. 593.
4. Borsody, S., *The Triumph of Tyranny,* London: Cape, 1960. p. 106.
5. Macartney, C.A., *Hungary, a Short History,* Chicago: Aldine, 1962. p. 226.
6. Pushkash, A.T., *Vengriia vo Vtoroi Mirovoi Voine,* Moscow: Institute for International Affairs, 1963. p. 9f.
7. Adam, M., "From the History of Hungarian-Czechoslovak Relations on the Eve of the Second World War." (in Russian) *Voprosy Istorii,* 1960. p. 91.
8. Juhasz, Gy., *A Teleki-Kormány Külpolitikája,* 1939-1941, Budapest: Akadémiai Kiadó, 1964. p. 11.
9. The material published to date includes a small collection of documents on foreign policy which appeared in 1959, a volume of the confidential papers of Miklós Horthy which left the press in 1963, and three bulky volumes of the records of the interwar Hungarian Government's Ministry of External Affairs, published from time to time since 1962. The latter series is still not complete.

NOTES TO PART I. *A Burdensome Heritage*

1. As an equal partner of Austria, Hungary shouldered a share of the responsibility that can be placed upon the imperial government of the Habsburg state for the origin of the First World War. Her share is perhaps lessened by the fact that in the summer of 1914 her Prime Minister, Count Istvan Tisza, at first opposed the declaration of war on Serbia. Tisza's reasons for opposing the invasion of that country and for abandoning his original stand on this question have never been explained satisfactorily. The Prime Minister did not live to write his memoirs: he became the victim of the wave of revolutionary violence that overtook the country at the end of the war. Possibly he opposed the invasion of Serbia because he feared that it might lead to the inclusion of new and unmanageable national groups into the Dual-Monarchy which already contained large minorities that were neither of Magyar nor of German nationality; and he changed his stand on realizing that within the leading circles of the realm he alone opposed action against Belgrade.
2. Low, A.O., *The Soviet Hungarian Republic and the Paris Peace Conference,* Philadelphia: The American Philosophical Society, 1963. pp. 13, 27.
3. Bethlen, S. Count, "Hungary in the New Europe." *Foreign Affairs,* vol. III. p. 452.
4. Also called the "revolution of Michaelmas roses" (őszirózsás forradalom).
5. Karolyi, M., *Faith Without Illusion,* London: Cape, 1956. p. 126.
6. Low, p. 27.
7. *Ibid.,* p. 27.
8. According to Professor A.J.P. Taylor, Karolyi "had too great faith in human goodness and too little awareness

192

of human evil." (Taylor in his introduction to Karolyi's book, *cit.*, p. 9.)

9. This treaty, which has often been labelled the "Shameful Peace", inflicted heavy losses on the young Soviet-Russian state.

10. Jaszi's views on the problem of national minorities are expressed in his book: *A nemzeti államok kialakulása és a nemzetiségi kérdés*, Budapest: Grill, 1912.

11. Macartney, C.A. *Hungary and Her Successors*, New York: Oxford University Press, 1937. p. 106. Jaszi later claimed that the chief negotiator for the Slovaks, Milan Hodza, was prevented from accepting some form of an agreement by Prague. (Jaszi quoted *ibid.*, p. 103.)

12. Jaszi, O., *Revolution and Counter-Revolution in Hungary*, London: King, 1924. p. 59. It is interesting that in 1933, in a lecture delivered in London, Bethlen proposed a similar solution to the Transylvanian problem. See Count S. Bethlen, *The Treaty of Trianon and European Peace*, London: Longmans and Green, 1934.

13. On this see Macartney, *Hungary and Her Successors*, p. 276.

14. Jaszi, *Revolution*, p. 38.

15. Low, p. 26.

16. *Ibid.*, p. 28f.

17. Actually trickery as well as pressure were applied. The government of Kun was informed that if it withdrew from this region the Rumanians would abandon a part of the area they had occupied. Kun's armies retreated, but the Rumanians stayed where they were before.

18. Professor Low suggests that this was done to reward Austria for resisting the temptation of joining the communist revolution. (Low, p. 38f.)

19. The economic effects of the Rumanian occupation are discussed in D. Laky, *Csonka-Magyarország Megszállásának Közgazdasági Kárai*, Budapest: Magyar Tudományos Akadémia, 1923.

20. Jaszi, *Revolution*, p. 122.

21. Borkenau, F., *World Communism*, AnnArbor: University of Michigan Press, revised ed. 1962. p. 113.

22. The promise of a radical land reform was first made by Karolyi. Nothing came of it aside from the Count's own estates being parcelled out among his peasants.

23. On this see A. Cattel, "Soviet Russia and the Hungarian Revolution of 1919." M.A. thesis, Columbia University, 1948. pp. 85-100. The communists learned from the lesson. After 1945, when they returned with the Russian armies, they began by pushing for the distribution of all the land among the peasants.

24. Ninety-five *per cent,* according to Jaszi. *(Revolution,* p. 122.)

25. Prior to this time Jewish-Gentile relations in Hungary were generally good.

26. Macartney, *Hungary and Her Successors,* p. 461.

27. Buday, L., *Dismembered Hungary,* London: Richards, 1923. p. 116.

28. *Ibid.,* p. 196.

29. A scholarly work of this type is F. Deak's *Hungary at the Paris Peace Conference,* New York: Columbia University Press, 1942.

30. The fact that the leaders of the Czechs, Rumanians and Serbs rejected the idea of plebiscites for the disputed areas for many Hungarians constitutes the best proof that these regions did not desire to separate from Hungary at all.

31. Buday, p. 24.

32. For an eloquent argument along these lines see Bethlen's *The Treaty,* especially part I.

33. Jaszi, O., "Neglected Aspects of the Danubian Drama." *Slavonic Review,* vol. XIV. July, 1934. p. 65.

34. Hungarian writers have always been quick to point out that, in contradiction to this principle of national self-determination, the successor states were multinational entities.

35. In connection with this, Hungarian communist historians have come up with the most unusual version of the famous "stab-in-the-back" theory. They claim that the "reactionary regime" of 1920 accepted the Treaty of Trianon in return for imperialist support against the

socialist revolution in the country. By doing this, the communists argue, the rulers of Hungary betrayed their people, "stabbed them in the back."

36. On its way to the North, Horthy's force was joined by many White detachments which had sprung into existence during the past few months in the western regions of the country.
37. By 1920 the Social-Democrats were either squeezed out of political life or left it in protest. The Left continued to be represented in Parliament by the members of the Smallholders' Party.
38. Macartney, C.A., *October Fifteenth,* Edinburgh: University Press, 1961. Vol. I, p. 36.
39. Bethlen, "Hungary", p. 456.
40. Macartney, C.A., *Hungary, A Short History,* p. 226.
41. Dernoi Kocsis, L., *Bajcsy-Zsilinszky,* Budapest: Kossuth, 1966. p. 36.
42. For some time the bad publicity contributed to Hungary's difficulty in getting the international loans she needed for reconstruction.
43. The title of the Hungarian version of the work was: *A Magyar Kálvária.*
44. Jaszi, "Neglected Aspects," pp. 54-55f.
45. See O. Jaszi, "The Choices in Hungary." *Foreign Affairs,* vol. XXIV. 1946, no. 3. p. 463.
46. Referring to this Horthy remarked in his memoirs that Hungary of the time was a prison and Benes and his company were its gaolers. M. Horthy, *Memoirs,* New York: Speller, 1954. p. 128.
46. The claims for a change in the *status quo* established at Trianon were based on Article XIX of the League of Nations Covenant.
48. Macartney, *Hungary and Her Successors,* p. 464.
49. *Ibid.,* p. 469.
50. Horthy, p. 136.
51. Kallay, N., *Hungarian Premier,* New York: Columbia University Press, 1954. p. 30f. See also M. Szinai and L. Szucs (eds.) *Horthy Miklos Titkos Iratai,* Budapest: Kossuth,

1963. (Cited hereafter as Horthy's Papers) document no. 16 part 2.

52. Horthy, p. 139.

53. (Gombos egy évet kapott az országlásra.) Dernoi Kocsis, p. 20f.

54. In 1920 Horthy told Borviceny the following about Gombos: "He is a climber, but with good intentions ... I am sure Gombos has only military ambitions, ... Anyway, Gombos is in my hands like this!" (and showed his clenched fist). Horthy's Papers, editors note to document no. 4.

55. Dernoi Kocsis, p. 36.

56. Kallay, p. 33.

57. *Ibid.*, p. 31.

58. Bajcsy-Zsilinszky, for example, repeatedly warned against the alignment of Hungary's foreign policy with the expansionist ambitions of Hitler. In 1933 he told Gombos on the floor of Parliament that he, Bajcsy-Zsilinszky, would go as far as the "bullet and the gallows" to prevent the establishment of a "German world" in Hungary. (Dernoi Kocsis, pp. 23f and 27.) In 1945 Bajcsy-Zsilinszky was executed by the Nazis for his leadership of the resistance movement in Hungary.

59. For Horthy's disposition toward the Soviet Union see Horthy's Papers, no. 22. The Regent and his associates were equally hostile to communism at home. After 1919 they drove the communist movement in Hungary out of existence. The local leaders of the party spent long years in maximum security prisons. Actually, they were more fortunate than some of their exiled comrades in Russia, for in the prisons of Hungary they were securely beyond the reach of Stalin's merciless hand.

60. Revealing of Horthy's antagonism toward the Czech leaders was the fact that once during the 1930's he thought of challenging Masaryk or, in the old man's place Benes, to a duel. The letter which was to announce his intentions, however, was never finished. Apparently Horthy thought the matter over. (Horthy's Papers, no. 30.)

61. According to Professor Macartney, Horthy believed that

wars were won not by land powers but by those which commanded the seas. (*Hungary, A Short History,* p. 226) For a similar view see T. Eckhardt, *Regicide at Marseille, The Recollections of Tibor Eckhardt,* New York: American Hungarian Library, 1964. p. 244f.

62. Hory, A., *A Kulisszák Mögött,* Vienna: 1965. p. 23. Hory was the Permanent Undersecretary in the Hungarian Foreign Office at the time.
63. Ottlik, G., "Coloman Kanya de Kanya." *The Hungarian Quarterly,* 1938, p. 211f. (A quite laudatory treatment.)
64. Hory, p. 217.
65. Ottlik, p. 217. On Kanya's ideas on diplomacy, international relations, collective security etc. see also DIMK vol. I. no. 167.
66. Montgomery, J.F., *Hungary, the Unwilling Satellite,* New York: Devin-Adair, 1947. p. 78.
67. Horthy, p. 140. Hory states, on the other hand, that Hungary's foreign affairs were directed by Kanya right from the time of his appointment to the Cabinet. (Hory, p. 23.)
68. Ottlik, p. 217.

NOTES TO PART II. *Foreign Policies in the Gombos Era.*

1. Hory, p. 14.
2. Until the Abyssinian campaign Mussolini actively encouraged Croat separatism. (E. Wiskemann, *The Rome-Berlin Axis,* Oxford University Press, 1949. p. 41.)
3. *Ibid.,* p. 31.
4. Eckhardt, p. 109.
5. *Ibid.,* p. 113.
6. Horthy, p. 140. (British edition.)
7. Macartney, *October Fifteenth,* p. 136.
8. The text of the first two protocols is given in DIMK vol. I. p. 75. See also D. Halmosy (ed.) *Nemzetközi Szerződések,* Budapest: Közgazdasági és Jogi Könyvkiadó, 1966. pp. 339-346.
9. Basch, A., *The Danube Basin in the German Economic Sphere,* New York: Columbia, 1943. p. 160. Some details of the marketing and monetary exchange agreements were not made public.
10. *Ibid.,* pp. 162-164.
11. DGFP Series C. Volume II. no. 16. (At least according to the information of the Germans.)
12. DIMK I. no. 41.
13. *Ibid.* He suggested to the Italians that Mussolini should scold the Austrians for this.
14. *Ibid.,* no. 70. Also, DGFP C. II. no. 16.
15. "The Rome Protocols", wrote Schuschnigg in his memoirs, "... safeguarded economic freedom and the vital needs of (Austria) at a critical moment." (K. von Schuschnigg, *Farewell Austria,* London: Cassel, 1938. p. 190.)
16. Horthy's Papers, no. 21.
17. Eckhardt, p. 244f.
18. Macartney, *October Fifteenth,* p. 137.
19. Horthy, p. 137.
20. DGFP C.I. no. 400.

21. DGFP C. IV. no. 424.
22. Basch, p. 37.
23. *Ibid.*, p. 160f. Also H.G. Meyer, *Mitteleuropa in German Thought and Action*, 1815-1945, The Hague: Nijnoff, 1955. p. 313.
24. Basch, p. 38. table 2.
25. Meyer, p. 313f.
26. Horthy's Papers, no. 21.
27. DGFP C. II. nos. 175, 189.
28. *Ibid.*, no. 322.
29. Boldizsar, I., *The Other Hungary*, Budapest: New Hungary, 1946. p. 39.
30. Basch, p. 189f. Exports to Germany rose from 11.4 *per cent* of the total exports in 1933, to 23.9 *per cent* in 1935. In contrast, Hungarian exports to Britain, the country's best free market customer, was only 8 *per cent* that year.
31. DGFP C. I. no. 329.
32. When, however, the Germans hinted at the annexation of Austria, Gombos disagreed. Macartney, *October Fifteenth*, p. 139.
33. DGFP C. II. nos. 444 and 455.
34. *Ibid.*, III. no. 150.
35. Horthy's Papers, no. 31. Szinai, a historian in present-day Hungary, maintains that Goring was seeking support for *Anschluss*, and wanted a promise of Hungarian neutrality toward Yugoslavia in case it came to an armed conflict between Italy and Austria on the one hand, and Yugoslavia and Germany on the other. (M. Szinai and L. Szucs, "Horthy's Secret Correspondence with Hitler." *New Hungarian Quarterly*, 1963. vol. IV p. 182.)
36. DGFP C. IV. no. 311.
37. *Ibid.*, no. 337.
38. DIMK I. no. 102. Communist historians often refer to these talks as the origins of the German-Hungarian military plans against Czechoslovakia. In reality, however, the discussions were neither binding, nor was there anything definite committed to paper.
39. For a German view of the Gombos government's attitude to Hungarian-German relations see DGFP C. IV. no. 307.

40. *Loc. cit.*
41. Horthy, p. 142.
42. Montgomery, p. 72.
43. The phrase is H. Seton-Watson's. See his book: *Eastern Europe Between the Wars*, 1918-1941. Third ed. Hamden: Archon, 1962. p. 194.
44. Until 1939 these groups had only a weak representation in Parliament. With the introduction of the secret ballot into the voting procedures of all the electoral districts in 1939, 43 Nazis were elected to the Lower House. (Seton-Watson, p. 196.)
45. Basch, p. 164.
46. DIMK I. nos. 283, 286.
47. Boldizsar, p. 39.
48. Basch, p. 190.
49. Wiskemann, p. 40.
50. *Ibid.*, 33.
51. DIMK I. no. 158. Göring, incidentally, seems to have been worried about a possible change in the direction of Hungary's foreign policy as a result of Gombos' death. The fact that the General received a civilian funeral was probably considered by the Prussian leader to be a sign of the slackening militancy of the new Hungarian administration. Kanya, of course, assured Göring of Hungary's continued good will toward Germany.
52. *Ibid.*, no. 229
53. *Ibid.*, no. 254
54. As a result of *Anschluss*, Germany would have acquired the banks, industries, railway companies etc. Austrian firms possessed in Hungary.

NOTE TO PART III. *The Search for a Danubian Solution.*

1. Macartney, *October Fifteenth*, p. 146.
2. Eckhardt, p. 228; also p. 207.
3. DIA 1934, p. 111.
4. Horthy, p. 41.
5. The Yugoslav delegation at Geneva produced photographs, allegedly taken at Jankapuszta, of men training with weapons. On closer examination, however, it became evident, that the topography visible on the photographs did not match that of the region where Jankapuszta is situated.
6. DGFP C. II. no. 336.
7. Horthy's Papers, no. 29. The unsigned memorandum was probably prepared by an editor of the government inspired paper, the *Pester Lloyd.*
8. *Ibid.* The policy of seeking friendship with Yugoslavia was part and parcel of Germany's annexationist designs on Austria. During the summer of 1934, when Mussolini moved his troops to the Brenner, there was a counter-mobilization in northwestern Yugoslavia.
9. Eckhardt, p. 209.
10. *Ibid.,* p. 209. A weakened Italy might have to rely more on France than a strong one, or at least this is how Laval reasoned according to Eckhardt.
11. *Ibid.,* p. 210.
12. DIA 1934, pp. 111-113.
13. Horthy's Papers, no. 29.
14. For such a view see for example Sir C. Petrie's *The Twenty Years Armistice — and After,* London: Eyre & Spottiswoode, 1940. p. 206.
15. DIMK I. no. 230.
16. *Ibid.,* no. 333.
17. *Ibid.,* no. 112.
18. *Ibid.,* no. 201.

19. *Ibid.*, no. 112.
20. *Ibid.*, nos. 110 and 201.
21. DGFP D. I. no. 157.
22. DIMK I. no. 204.
23. DGFP D. I. no. 204.
24. DGFP C. IV. no. 269.
25. *Ibid.*, no. 292.
26. DGFP D. I. no. 209. In 1936 a Hungarian confidential report on Croatia asserted that loyalty to the Habsburgs was still strong among the Croats, and Croatian peasants still displayed pictures of Francis-Joseph in their homes. The report concluded that Belgrade had good reasons to prefer *Anschluss* to restoration. (DIMK I. no. 43.)
27. Hodza, M., *Federation in Central Europe*, London: Jarrolds, 1942. p. 127.
28. DIMK I. no. 230.
29. DIMK I. no. 234.
30. Horthy's Papers, no. 25.
31. Macartney, *October Fifteenth*, Vol. I. p. 183f. The whole affair, according to Professor Macartney, was an anti-Nazi demonstration.
32. *Ibid.*, p. 183.
33. DIMK I. no. 189.
34. *Ibid.*, no. 196.
35. Basch, p. 63.
36. DGFP C. IV. nos. 253, 249 and 307.
37. DIMK I. no. 35.
38. Hodza's ideas were in many ways similar to those of the well-known Czech historian Palacky.
39. Hodza, p. 125f.
40. *Ibid.*, p. 131
41. DIMK I. no. 164.
42. *Ibid.*, no. 57. Cf. DGFP C. IV. no. 542.
43. DIMK I. no. 274.
44. Hodza, pp. 128, 130.
45. DIMK Vol. II. no. 78.
46. DGFP D. I. no. 259.
47. Chancellor Schuschnigg, his Foreign Minister Berger-

Waldenberg, Gombos and Kanya took part in the meeting. It seems Kanya did most of the talking.

48. DIMK I. no. 62.
49. *Ibid.,* no. 167.
50. *Ibid.,* no. 62.
51. *Ibid.,* no. 167.
52. DIA 1937 p. 318.
53. *Ibid.,* p. 310. The Hungarian Government had probably toyed with the idea of declaring its military equality unilaterally. The Hungarian Chief-of-Staff, General Somkuthy, fearing military countermeasures by the Little Entente, advised against the idea. (DIMK II. no. 15.)
54. DIMK II. nos. 83-87. (especially 85 a.)
55. *Ibid.,* no. 90.
56. The Czechs seem to have been dissatisfied with the conduct of the Rumanians. Krofta, for example, blamed Antonescu for the delays in the negotiations. (DIMK II. nos. 95, 98.)
57. Hodza, p. 130.
58. *Ibid.,* p. 138.
59. *Ibid.,* p. 139. Hodza blames the new Rumanian Prime Minister, Goga, "an impossible politician", for this turn of events.
60. "I am able to state", wrote Hodza in his memoirs, "that in spite of the delicate Hungaro-Czecho-Slovak situation I found some Hungarian politicians who in principle agreed with the scheme of Danubian co-operation." (Hodza, p. 130f.)
61. For French suggestions urging Hungarian-Czech raprochement see DIMK Vol. I. no. 81 and Vol. II. no. 109.
62. DIMK Vol. II. no. 32. Benes stated during the conversation that he was expecting a democratic revolution to take place in Hungary. Benes' memoirs are revealing on his attitudes on co-operation with "unreformed" Hungary. "Any attempt", he wrote, "to establish some other combination (of East European small powers), with Hungarian participation, ... would, on our part have been futile if not indeed ridiculous so long as Hungary did not

change socially." (Benes, E., *Memoirs of Dr. Eduard Benes,* London: Allen & Unwin, 1954, p. 8.)

63. DIMK II. no. 54.
64. *Ibid.,* no. 62.
65. *Ibid.,* no. 111.
66. In 1930 a tariff war broke out between Hungary and Czechoslovakia which badly hurt Hungarian agriculture. Benes said that he regretted this development, but at the time he had not been able to prevent it because of the internal political situation in his country.
67. DIMK I. no. 226. Cf. DIA 1938 Vol. I. p. 270.
68. Eckhardt, p. 112.
69. DGFP C. III. no. 336.
70. DIMK I. nos. 23, 163.
71. DIA 1938 Vol. I. p. 270.

NOTES TO PART IV. *The Danube-Vistula Axis.*

1. DIMK I. no. 389.
2. On Horthy's views see his *Memoirs,* p. 152.
3. Ciano, in his diary, was more outspoken on this problem of the impossibility of preventing Austria's annexation. "What in fact", wrote the Italian Foreign Minister on February 23, 1938, "could we do? Start a war with Germany? At the first shot we fired every Austrian, without a single exception, would fall behind the Germans against us." (Ciano, p. 79.) Although Ciano was exaggerating, he had a point. The Italian decision not to oppose *Anschluss* was brought to the attention of the Hungarians by an Italian staff officer early in February. (DIMK II. no. 110.)
4. On this see DIMK I. nos. 314, 337 and 339.
5. Unity in the Rome bloc was, by this time, not much more than appearance. In 1936 the leaders of the three states decided to conduct non-binding staff talks. "On Schuschnigg's request", wrote Kanya, "we obliged ourselves to handle this decision as strictly confidential even with respect to the Germans."(DIMK Vol. I. no. 174.) The ensuing talks, however, concerned themselves little, if any, with the problems of Austria's military security. (Ibid., nos. 200 and 212.) By early 1938 this idea had been dropped completely.
6. Ottlik, G., "Hungary's Foreign Relations." *Hungarian Quarterly,* Vol. IV. 1938. p. 28.
7. On the margin of a secret military report on the Austrian situation of December, 1937, which asserted that "the Austrians will resist with arms" the marks "?!" appear. They were probably made by Kanya. (DIMK Vol. I. no. 332, editor's note.)
8. DIMK I. no. 382.
9. *Ibid.,* I. no. 389. The instructions were sent from Vienna

where Kanya was "visiting relatives" i.e. he was conducting secret discussions with Schuschnigg. *(Ibid.,* no. 366.)

10. Macartney, *October Fifteenth,* Vol. I. p. 217.
11. DIMK I. no. 447.
12. Horthy's Papers, no. 34. DIA 1938 Vol. I. pp. 264-267.
13. DIA 1938 Vol. I. p. 266. Cf. DIMK I. no. 448.
14. DIMK I. no. 440. To Rome and Berlin, however, the circular was dispatched without the policy of the free hand and the relations with the Little Entente being mentioned.
15. Indicative of the animosity between Czechoslovakia and her neighbours to the north and south was the fact that plans for a Warsaw-Budapest air route broke on the rock of Czech opposition. In turn, the Poles frustrated the establishment of a Prague-Moscow route. (DIMK I. no. 235.)
16. Hory, p. 14f. Bathory was Prince of Transylvania before his election to the Polish throne. Bem was the "Polish hero" of the Hungarian revolution of 1848-49. Throughout the ages Poles and Magyar struggled with and suffered from common enemies: the Turks, the Russians and the Germans.
17. Hory, p. 15f.
18. Hory writes that Kanya dismissed him from his position and appointed him to Warsaw because the differences of views over the strategy and tactics of foreign policy made harmonious relations between the two men impossible. (Hory, pp. 16-21.)
19. DIMK II. no. 17.
20. Hory, p. 21.
21. Hory, pp. 17-23.
22. DIMK II. no. 104.
23. *Ibid.,* Vol. I. no. 342.
24. Hory, p. 28.
25. DIMK II. no. 123 and note 115. The conversations between Beck and Kanya are very poorly documented. Horthy and Hory were not present, much to the displeasure of the latter. The editors of DIMK claim that

some of the documents on the talks were lost, or are not worth publishing. It seems that these documents probably contain some information on the discussion between Beck and Kanya regarding the ways and means of combatting the German and, in the case of Poland, also the Russian dangers.

26. Horthy, p. 155f. Cf. DIMK II. no. 123.
27. DIMK II. no. 135 and also no. 137.
28. *Ibid.,* nos. 191, 200.
29. *Ibid.,* no. 219. The Polish Government feared that an autonomous Ruthenia would become the center for Ukrainian nationalist agitation.
30. *Ibid.,* no. 252.
31. *Ibid.,* Vol. I. no. 422.
32. Ciano, p. 93. Cf. DIMK II. no. 136.
33. There were signs of improving Polish-Italian relations in this period. On his visit to Rome in February Beck discussed the "horizontal axis" with Ciano. The Italian Foreign Minister seems to have been very anxious for Polish participation. (DIMK II. no. 125.)
34. *Ibid.,* no. 268.
35. *Ibid.,* no. 269.
36. On these requests see Ciano, pp. 117, 138.
37. See for example the article of G. Ottlik on Hungary's foreign relations, *cit.,* p. 29.
38. Macartney, *October Fifteenth,* Vol. I. p. 220.
39. Imredy, formerly the President of the National Bank, was considered to be a financial wizzard with good reputation abroad, especially in England.
40. DIA 1938. Vol. I. p. 267.
41. Horthy's Papers, no. 29.
42. Ciano's Papers, p. 119.
43. DIMK I. no. 88.
44. It is difficult to establish just what type of military operations the Hungarian leaders had in mind, full scale war or the use of armed bands of irredentists, to disrupt Czechoslovak unity, and then to prod the Slovaks and Ruthenes toward a "Hungarian solution".
45. Nazi attitudes toward the Czechs were outlined in intel-

ligence reports coming from Berlin and Prague. (DIMK II. nos. 8, 20 and 148.)

46. The Hungarian documents throw light only on the preparations made for this unofficial call on Hitler by the Regent who at the time was on a tour of Austria. According to these, Sztojay, the Hungarian Minister to Berlin, was asked to keep his ear to the ground and find what Hitler talked about lately. The Minister communicated his observations and suggestions to Budapest. (MMV no. 8, DIMK I. no. 148.) Taking these in view, Horthy wrote his discussion plan for the meeting. In this he touched on, *inter alia*, the problem of military action against the Czechs. Anxious to make a good impression on Hitler, Horthy stated that, in view of the Little Entente threat to Hungary, any action against Czechoslovakia must be swift and decisive. The discussion plan ended in some wild statements, such as "no peace on earth till the Soviets are crushed", which, Horthy probably thought, would sound dear to the Führer's ears. (See Horthy's Papers, no. 32.) The published sources do not tell what really was discussed at the meeting.

47. DGFP D. V. no. 149. DIMK I. no. 313. Also MMV no. 16.

48. DGFP D. II. nos. 65, 66 and 114.

49. *Ibid.*, Vol. V. no. 190. Cf. DIMK II. no. 146.

50. DIMK II. no. 226. See also no. 146. The German officer is not identified.

51. The view that Hungary was an undesirable ally was expressed in a contemporary German foreign policy memorandum which concluded that "Hungarian help, which would bring new opponents to our group, would be no gain for us." (DGFP D. II. no. 367.)

52. DGFP D. II. no. 284.

53. When it is considered, however, that the lot of the Hungarians living in Czechoslovakia was better than that of those living in Rumania and even Yugoslavia, the protestations over the fate of the Magyar minority in Czechoslovakia appears less justified.

54. DIMK II. no. 53.

55. *Ibid.*, nos. 2, 7, 24 and 53.
56. *Ibid.*, no. 73; Vol. I. no. 254.
57. Ciano, pp. 42 and 43.
58. DIMK II. no. 18, 53.
59. DIMK I. no. 318.
60. DIA 1938, Vol. I. pp. 271-273.
61. DIMK II. nos. 223, 234.
62. *Ibid.*, no. 236.
63. *Ibid.*, no. 242.
64. *Ibid.*, no. 248.
65. *Ibid.*, no. 255.
66. *Ibid.*, no. 294.
67. *Ibid.*, no. 295.
68. According to Professor Macartney it did not, but in the published documents there is a mention of a telephone conversation. It is not revealed what was discussed.
69. DIMK II. no. 296.
70. *Ibid.*, no. 301.
71. *Ibid.*, no. 301, a and b. Cf. Halmosy, pp. 429-432.
72. DIMK II. no. 305. For a more detailed, though mistaken explanation of the Hungarian position see Macartney, *October Fifteenth*, Vol. I. p. 239, especially note 4.
73. Macartney, *October Fifteenth*, Vol. I. p. 239.
74. DIMK II. no. 292. The editor of this volume of DIMK claims that no other documents were found in connection with the Kiel visit.
75. DIMK I. nos. 324. 335.
76. DGFP D. II. no. 383.
77. Macartney, *October Fifteenth*, Vol. I. p. 241. Kanya managed to call Ribbentrop a *"yunger mann"*. The German Foreign Minister never forgave Kanya, nor did he ever forget the incident, except at the time of his trial, at which he claimed not to remember the details of the discussion. (IMT Vol. X. p. 339f.)
78. DGFP D. II. no. 383. Cf. IMT Vol. III. p. 51.
79. Horthy, p. 162. Weizsacker, in his very brief report on this conversation, (which avoids mention of any unpleasant exchanges between the two leaders), states that Horthy promised that Hungary would "co-operate".

It is not explained by what means, military or diplomatic, she was to do this. (DGFP D. II. no. 383.) Apparently on this basis the prosecution at the Nuremberg trials concluded that "the Hungarians, with the exception of Horthy, ... proved reluctant to commit themselves." (IMT Vol. III. p. 51.)

80. Macartney, *October Fifteenth*, Vol. I. p. 242. DGFP D. II. no. 383. Hitler never forgave Horthy for this. See DGFP D. VI. no. 784.
81. Guderian, G.H., *Panzer Leader*, London: Joseph, 1952. p. 57. Weizsacker testifies in his memoirs that on one occasion during this visit "Horthy spontaneously addressed the following remark to my wife, who had to accompany Madame Horthy: 'We must see to it that we do not get involved in a new war'." E. Weizsacker, *The Memoirs of Ernst von Weizsacker*, Chicago: Regenry, 1951. p. 138.
82. IMT Vol. XXXI. nos. 2796 and 2797. (Translated by the editors of DGFP as: "he who wanted to sit at the table must at least help in the kitchen". DGFP D. II. no. 383.)
83. Horthy, p. 162.
84. DGFP D. II. no. 390.
85. Horthy, p. 165.
86. DGFP D. II. no. 402.
87. *Ibid.*, no. 395. Imredy repeated this view to Erdmannsdorff, the German Minister to Hungary, in Budapest on the 29th. (*Ibid.*, no. 402.)
88. In German and Hungarian diplomatic circles the crisis was no secret at all. A circular of the Wilhelmstrasse openly admitted that the German leaders' surprise at the Bled events "was not concealed from the visitors." (DGFP D. V. no. 221.) Nor did the Hungarian leaders make secret of the developments. Kanya told Hory, who returned to Budapest to gain first hand information about the events, that "That idiot (Hitler) wants to start a war at all cost." (Hory, p. 33.)
89. DIA 1938, Vol. I. p. 274.
90. Macartney, *October Fifteenth*, Vol. I. p. 248.
91. *Survey of International Affairs*, 1938. Vol. II. p. 298.

92. *Ibid.*, p. 298.
93. DGFP D. II. no. 402.
94. *Ibid.*, no. 503. Cf. IMT Vol. III. p. 54.
95. Macartney, *October Fifteenth*, Vol. I. p. 246.
96. DIMK II. no. 361. Cf. DGFP D. II. no. 506.
97. DGFP D. II. nos. 554, 555.
98. DIMK II. no. 401.
99. *Ibid.*, no. 411 and no. 413.
100. *Ibid.*, nos. 180, 181.
101. *Ibid.*, no. 272. On the 31st, however, Sir Orme Sargent refused to reaffirm Vansittart's statement. (*Ibid.*, no. 308.)
102. *Ibid.*, no. 364; also no. 381.
103. *Ibid.*, no. 334.
104. *Ibid.*, no. 368.
105. DGFP D. II. nos. 603 and 658.
106. DIMK II. nos. 346, 359, 362, 363, 367 and 373; Cf. DGFP D. II. nos. 541, 551, 560 and 569.
107. DIMK II. no. 432. Cf. Hory, p. 35f.
108. DIMK II. nos. 425, 479.
109. *Ibid.*, nos. 516, 523, 539 and 559.
110. After the Munich Conference Czechoslovakia became a federal state. Slovakia and Ruthenia received autonomy. The country's name became hyphenated.
111. Macartney, C.A. and A.W. Palmer, *Independent Eastern Europe*, London: Macmillan, 1962. p. 388.
112. Early in October the German Supreme Command reminded the Foreign Ministry in Berlin that "it is in our *military interest* that Slovakia should not be separated from the Czechoslovak union" but should remain with Czechoslovakia "under strong German influence." The note also warned against the establishment of a "common Hungarian-Polish frontier." (DGFP D. IV. no. 39.) Another memorandum, prepared by the German Foreign Ministry for Hitler, called for the "rejection of the Hungarian or Polish solutions for Slovakia as well as for Carpatho-Ukraine" and noted that preparations were "already on foot" for converting these areas "in favour of our solution", i.e. a loose Czecho-Slovak federation

dominated by Germany. *(Ibid.,* no. 45, also no. 46.)

113 More precisely: autonomy for the Magyar minority and border adjustments. (MMV editor's note p. 78.)

114. Typical of the tension and animosity during the talks was Kanya's insistence that the discussions be conducted in French, which few of the Slovak representatives present knew, and not in Magyar, which would have been an acceptable alternative to all the delegates.

115. MMV no. 42.

116. *Ibid.,* p. 79.

117. (ha kell fal mellé is állni.) *Ibid.,* no. 45. (Kozma's diary entry for October 9, 1938.)

118. *Ibid.,* nos. 47 and 48.

119. *Ibid.,* nos. 49 and 50.

120. *Ibid.,* no. 53.

121. *Ibid.,* no. 51. Also, Kozma's diary entry for October 15. *(Ibid.,* no. 45.)

122. DGFP D. IV. nos. 60 and 62.

123. MMV no. 55. The British attitude seems to have been similar. The British Ambassador to Rome apparently informed Ciano that while the British Government was not opposed to a four-power meeting, it preferred an Italian-German arbitration in the case. (MMV no. 58.) For a similar view expressed by Lord Halifax to the Earl of Perth see DBFP third series, Vol. III. no. 227.

124. DGFP D. Iv. no. 64.

125. DBFP third series, Vol. III. nos. 222, 227 and also 226. The Czechs, however, rejected the idea of including Poland in the discussions when it came to the issue of Ruthenia.

126. On the 14th of October Hitler told the Czech Head -of-State that Hungary should only get "the areas in which there was a definite Hungarian majority." (DGFP D. IV. no. 61.)

127. MMV no. 59.

128. The Polish Government, while giving its wholehearted approval to the venture, out of consideration for its international reputation, refused to promise the deployment of its regular military forces against Ruthenia. Instead,

it assured Budapest of holding the Rumanians at bay. (MMV no. 68.)

129. Macartney, *October Fifteenth,* p. 312.
130. Kozma's diary entry for November 20, 1938. MMV no. 70. Needless to say, Kozma was outraged. He told the generals that by the next day new difficulties would arise. He proved to be a good prognosticator.
131. DGFP D. IV. no. 128.
132. DGFP D. IV. no. 132. MMV nos. 72 and 73.
133. Kozma's diary entry for November 21. MMV no. 70. This source seems to suggest that the decision to halt the attack came after the German-Italian note was presented. The editors of the MMV, however, suggests that the Hungarians called the plan off before this, as soon as they were warned by Mussolini of the impending German protest. The call-off, incidentally, came so late that some Polish irregulars could not be stopped from crossing the border of Ruthenia. (MMV no. 76.)
134. For Halifax's attitudes to the Czech-Hungarian dispute and its implications see: DBFP third series, Vol. III. nos. 226, 227.

NOTES TO PART V. *The Teleki Era.*

1. Macartney's foreword to Kallay's book, *cit.*, p. XXIV. For a similar view see also H. Ripka, *Munich: Before and After*, (London: 1939), p. 116.
2. DGFP D. IV. no. 62. Cf. MMV no. 75.
3. A treaty signed originally by Germany, Italy and Japan, aimed at the curtailment of the influence and activities of the Communist International.
4. MMV no. 74. Also DGFP D. V. p. 336f.
5. Hory, p. 46.
6. *Ibid.*, p. 24f.
7. Ciano's diary, p. 207.
8. Relations were not resumed till after the dissolution of the anti-Comintern pact in August 1939.
9. Ciano's diary, p. 207.
10. DGFP D. V. nos. 272 and 273. Also MMV no. 83. Hungary withdrew in April.
11. Ciano's diary, p. 207.
12. Macartney, *October Fifteenth*, Vol. I. p. 309.
13. Payr mentioned four persons who, in his opinion, would be capable of accomplishing this task: these were Bethlen, Sandor Sztranyavszky (Minister of Agriculture), Ferenc Keresztes-Fischer (Minister of the Interior) and Pál Teleki (Minister of Education). Payr also suggested that the army should be purged of rightist hot-heads by making an example out of a "few of these misled gentlemen".
14. The opposition to Imredy's policies, it seems, wanted to use the minor crisis created by the failure of the Ruthenian venture to topple the Imredy government. On the 22nd of November, many prominent M.P.'s resigned from Imredy's party. On the following day the combined vote of the Prime Minister's conservative opponents and the parties of the moderate left defeated a government

motion in the Lower House of Parliament. Following this Imredy duly resigned. His resignation, however, was not accepted by Horthy. Professor Macartney suggests that the resignation was not accepted by the Regent mainly because Horthy and some of his close advisors (including Teleki) believed that Imredy's sudden fall at such critical time would provoke large-scale rightist disturbances. (Macartney, *October Fifteenth*, Vol. I. p. 315.) See also Dernoi Kocsis, pp. 81-82. Incidentally, this was the occasion Imredy used to reorganize his cabinet and to leave Kanya and some others out of it.

15. Horthy's Papers no. 43.
16. Macartney, *October Fifteenth*, Vol. I. 327f.
17. *Ibid.*, p. 327f.
18. Indicative of this hatred is the fact that in a letter written just before his suicide in April 1941, Teleki referred to Hitler and his associates as *"gazemberek"* which translates as "villains" or "gangsters". (Horthy's Papers no. 55a.)
19. Macartney, *October Fifteenth*, Vol. I. p. 330.
20. DGFP D. V. no. 305.
21. Ciano, G., *The Ciano Diaries*, 1939-1943, New York: Doubleday, 1946. p. 42. Cf. DGFP D. IV no. 198.
22. Montgomery, the American Minister to Budapest, was convinced that Ruthenia was occupied in spite of Germany's opposition to such move. (Montgomery, p. 123.) Hory, writing 25 years after the event, still does not seem to know about an explicit German permission for the Hungarians to march. (Hory, p. 53f.)
23. DGFP D. VIII. no. 62 note 1.
24. *Ibid.*, nos. 62 and 185. Cf. DIMK Vol. IV. nos. 97 and 123.
25. DIMK IV. no. 90.
26. Ciano's diary for 1939-43 p. 47.
27. IMT Vol. X. pp. 359, 361. See also DGFP D. VI. nos. 295-296, 300 and DIMK IV. 116.
28. See for example the *Hungarian Quarterly*, Vol. V. no. 3. p. 565 and DIMK IV. nos. 139, 148 and 149.
29. DIMK IV. no. 103 a. (This is Csaky's letter to Ciano.)

30. DIMK IV. no. 98. Cf. Hory, pp. 63-65.
31. DIMK IV. no. 126. See also nos. 119, 133, 141, 156 and 158. For Polish attempt to retain Hungary's good will
32. DGFP D. VI no. 712 enclosures 1 and 2. DIMK IV. no. see nos. 157, 162.
240, note 88.
33. Ciano first reacted to the letters favourably, but on learning the German attitude, retracted his words, and expressed disapproval. (Ciano's diary for 1939-43, pp. 112-113; DIMK IV. nos. 140, 144.)
34. DGFP D. VI. no. 784.
35. Ciano's diary, 18 August 1939, p. 123.
36. The earliest came from Sztojay on June 24. Others came from military intelligence sources in Spain. Finally, on the 21st of August, Weizsacker sent a definite warning about the impending crisis. (DIMK IV. nos. 198, 233, 280 and 281.)
37. Rauschning, H., *Hitler Speaks,* London: Buttersworth, 1939. p. 128.
38. Halder's notes in DGFP D. VII. Appendix 1. p. 566.
39. Montgomery, p. 123.
40. Macartney, *October Fifteenth,* p. 367, note 10.
41. DIMK IV. nos. 432, 433, 437 and 440.
42. DGFP D. VII. no. 489.
43. DIMK IV. nos. 314-317 and especially 327, 328, 334. Sztojay panicked and demanded an immediate Hungarian gesture to sooth the Germans' anger. (no. 317.)
44. DGFP D. VII. no. 519.
45. DIMK IV. nos. 353, 355 and 367.
46. DGFP D. VIII. no. 30. Csaky, it seems, was sincere. While the Hungarians were eager to exploit the crisis and to put pressure on the Rumanian Government, they had not planned to invade Transylvania. They were probably hoping for another "Munich Conference" followed by another Vienna award.
47. DIMK IV. no. 379; DGFP D. VIII. no. 45. Cf. Beck, pp. 179f and 209.
48. DIMK IV. nos. 377, 378.

49. DGFP D. VIII. nos. 48, 49; DIMK IV. no. 381. This, of course, was of no use to the Germans.
50. DGFP D. VIII. no. 51.
51. Ciano's diary, 11 September 1939, p. 142.
52. DGFP D. VIII. no. 185; DIMK IV no. 409.
53. DIMK IV. no. 545.
54. *Ibid.,* nos. 434a and 434b.
55. Dernoi Kocsis, p. 98-99. Dernoi Kocsis was one of the journalists asked to participate in this enterprise. He attributes his own invitation to an article of his which attacked some pro-German statements of the Prime Minister. According to Dernoi Kocsis, soon after this article appeared, Teleki told him that he agreed with the criticism but, being the country's Prime Minister, he was not in a position to speak differently. (*Ibid.,* p. 88.)
56. *Ibid.,* pp. 96-99 *in passim.*
57. DIMK IV. no. 514.
58. *Ibid.,* no. 516.
59. For the text of this interesting memorandum see document no. 1. in J. Pelenyi, "The Secret Plan for a Hungarian Government in the West at the Outbreak of World War II." *Journal of Modern History,* vol. XXXVI. pp. 173-175.
60. Quoted *ibid.,* p. 171.
61. *Ibid.,* p. 171.
62. *Ibid.,* document no. 2.
63. Dernoi Kocsis, p. 105. In the course of time other individuals also left the country to take up residence in the West as a result of Teleki's initiative.
64. Juhasz, Gy., *A Teleki-kormány külpolitikája,* Budapest: Akadémiai kiadó, 1964.
65. DIMK IV. no. 581.
66. Ciano's diary, March 24-26, 1940. pp. 226-227. Ciano's diary entry on his talks with Teleki are worth quoting: "March 24, 1940

    I play golf with Teleki. He repeats that 95 per cent of the Hungarians detest Germany. He desires only to keep his country out of the conflict and hopes Italy may do likewise ...

March 25, 1940

A long conference with Count Teleki. I find him objective and reasonable as regards Magyar claims. He realizes what a danger it would be to Hungary to incorporate within itself a disproportionate number of foreign minorities ... Teleki ... has not hidden his sympathy for the Western Powers and fears an integral German victory like the plague ...

March 27, 1940

... At luncheon Teleki asks me abruptly, 'Do you know how to play bridge?' 'Why?' 'For the day when we are together in the Dachau Concentration Camp.' This is the real state of mind of this man."

67. Juhasz, p. 97. Cf. Macartney, *October Fifteenth*, p. 395.
68. Juhasz, p. 97f.
69. DIMK IV. no. 583b.

Hungary's leaders also decided that if Hitler's plan for the securing of the Ploesti oil-fields envisaged the active participation of Hungary, then the Hungarian army would assist by occupying Transylvania. If, on the other hand, the German plans only called for the passage of the *Wehrmacht*'s units through Hungary, then Budapest would insist that they be placed under Hungarian command while on Magyar territory. Finally it was agreed that in order to find out the exact intentions of the Germans the Hungarian Government should call on Berlin and Rome to hold tripartite discussions on the future of the Balkans.

70. Ciano's diary (second part) 8 April, 1940, p. 233.

Teleki told the Italians that the Hungarian Government was aware that the gradual penetration of the country by the Germans would lead to a more serious collapse than that which would follow a short-lived resistance "because what is willingly given by one government is judged by history much more severly than that what is yielded to brutal force." (Juhasz, p. 101.) Juhasz's source is *Documenti Diplomatici Italiani*, None Serie, III. no. 727.

71. Juhasz., p. 102. The original Italian text is given by Juhasz in footnote 142.

72. Ciano's diary, 8 and 9 April, 1940. p. 233f.
73. DIMK IV. no. 587. Cf. MMV no. 112.
74. Juhasz, p. 108. (This was the substence of Teleki's answer. The Prime Minister did not put it so bluntly.)
75. *Ibid.*, pp. 112, 113.
76. An indication of the change in the Hungarian leaders' estimate of the German attitude toward the Balkans was the fact that the preparations for the government in exile were discontinued. Pelenyi was instructed to return the funds entrusted to him. (Pelenyi, *op. cit.*, p. 171.) Eckhardt also returned to Hungary, just to leave again several months later.
77. Macartney and Palmer, p. 422.
78. For Sztojay's view see DIMK IV no. 576. and MMV no. 124.
79. For some reason Bethlen did not consider the possibility of the Soviet Union and the United States playing a role in the post-war reorganization and pacification of Europe.
80. DIMK IV. no. 577.
81. DIMK IV. no. 98. Cf. Hory, p. 65.
82. DIMK IV. no. 345 a, b, c, d. Teleki also informed Mussolini on the extent of the Hungarian claims.
83. Juhasz, p. 83.
84. DIMK IV. no. 512. Cf. Ciano's diary, 7 Jan. 1940. p. 331.
85. *The Times,* 23 Feb. 1940. Quoted by Juhasz, *op. cit.*, p. 89f. note 105.
86. "Nicht ausgeschlossen", said Hitler, "das England den Ungarn scharft macht... England hat Interesse daran, dass die Olquellen (in Rumanien) brennen." F. Halder, *Kriegstagebuch,* Stuttgart: Kohlhammer, 1964. Vol. I. 24 April 1940. p. 269.
87. The Russians also demanded parts of Bukovina, a province which prior to 1918 belonged to Austria-Hungary.
88. Montgomery, p. 138. Montgomery believes that the Russians expected a Hungarian invasion of Transylvania. Macartney points out that it is not clear whether Stalin meant a diplomatic move or a military attack. (Macartney, *October Fifteenth,* p. 404.)

89. Juhasz, pp. 122, 123.
90. Juhasz places the historical responsibility for Rumania's *volte-face* entirely on Hungary and Bulgaria. *(Op. cit.,* p. 125f.)
91. MMV no. 114.
92. *Ibid.,* no. 115, 116. Cf. DGFP D. X. no. 105. The Hungarian Government also reconnoitred the attitude of several other powers on the problem. Neither Yugoslavia, nor Britain, nor as a matter of fact the United States voiced any objection to a peaceful change in the *status quo* in Transylvania. (Juhasz, pp. 139-140.)
93. DGFP D. X. no. 104.
94. Horthy's Papers, no. 47.
95. DGFP D. X. no. 146. The Hungarian record of the conversation, written by Csaky, does not contain this admission. See MMV no. 118.
96. DGFP D. X. no. 146. Cf. MMV no. 118. Of the two reports Csaky's is the more detailed.
97. (Mindent vissza!) Hory, A., *Még egy barázdát sem,* Vienna: 1967. p. 34.
98. Juhasz, pp. 153, 156.
99. DBFP Series 3, VI. no. 603.
100. Juhasz, p. 159f.
101. Hory tells in his recollection of this period, that his exclusion from the active diplomatic service from the fall of 1939 to the summer of 1940 was done in conformity with the wishes of the Germans. (Hory, *Még egy barázdát sem,* p. 6.)
102. *Ibid.,* pp. 40-41. The Transylvanian problem was complicated by the fact that the largest concentration of Hungarians were in the Szekler counties of the East. Also in the East were the traditional centers of Magyar culture such as Kolozsvar.
103. Juhasz, p. 180f.
104. Hory, *Még egy barázdát sem,* p. 59.
105. For the text of the memorandum see *ibid.,* pp. 60-64.
106. The details of the Rumanian scheme for the solution of the issue were never revealed. Apparently what the leaders in Bucharest envisaged to do was to conduct a

survey for the purpose of ascertaining the number of those who wanted to live under Magyar suzerainity, and then cede a proportionate amount of land (perhaps the 11.4% of the disputed area they had earlier mentioned to Hitler) to Hungary, where the population desirous of leaving Rumania could be settled. (Juhasz, pp. 180, 186, 187.)

107. Burks, R.V., "Two Teleki Letters." *Journal of Central European Affairs*, VII. no. 1. 1947. pp. 69-70. The memorandum, remorseful in tone, sounds like a draft letter of resignation.

108. See for example DGFP D. X. no. 393.

109. *Ibid.*, no. 384.

110. Juhasz, p. 190. According to Juhasz, Hitler's decision to intervene now was not a sudden act, but the integral part of an eleborate plan designed to prepare for the annihilation of the Soviet Union. *(Ibid.*, pp. 161-166, 189, 195.)

111. *Ibid.*, p. 191.

112. Ciano's diary, 28. August. 1940. p. 288. On this conversation see also P. Schmidt, *Hitler's Interpreter*, London: Heinemann 1957. p. 188.

113. Juhasz, pp. 191, 192.

114. *Ibid.*, p. 193.

115. MMV no. 119.

116. Ciano's diary 29 Aug. 1940. p. 288. Juhasz, p. 198f.

117. MMV. no. 120. Juhasz, pp. 198-201.

118. MMV no. 120.

119. *Ibid.*, no. 123.

120. The text of the award is given in MMV no. 121. For further information see Macartney, *October Fifteenth*, pp. 418-419., Ciano's Papers, p. 386. The returned territories comprised 2/3 of the maximum Hungarian claims.

121. Schmidt, p. 189.

122. Horthy's Papers, no. 49.

123. *Ibid.*, no. 49. As after every political crisis, Teleki severely reproached himself (as well as some others), for some unfortunate turn of events. Once again he declared that he was unworthy to rule: "I have (he wrote) allowed

the soldiers to grow above my shoulders" and called for a strong man to govern the country, a man who is acceptable to the Germans, but who is not likely to be subservient to them, one who is not a professional soldier and yet can handle the military. Nor was this man to be Horthy himself.

124. MMV no. 123; also editor's note p. 234.
125. (... akárhogy is történjék a megosztás, az egyik fél mindig jajgatni fog, Erdély esetében valószinüleg mind a kettő.) MMV no. 118.
126. In November, for example, Hitler assured Marshal Antonescu in connection with the Award that "history would not come to a standstill in the year 1940." DGFP D. XI. no. 381.
127. Sztojay's report of 10 Sept. 1940. MMV no. 124.
128. Saly, D., *Szigoruan Bizalmas,* Budapest: Anonimus, 1945. p. 253.
129. Juhasz, pp. 217-219. Teleki's enemies hoped to defeat him at a party convention. Apparently, the man they had in mind to succeed him was Csaky. Cf. Saly, pp. 254-255.
130. *Ibid.,* p. 217.
131. *Ibid.,* p. 220.
132. For the Hungarian text of the agreement see MMV no. 122. For an English translation see DIA *Hitler's Europe* Vol. II. p. 322f.
133. Borsody, p. 124.
134. Juhasz, p. 205.
135. Macartney, *October Fifteenth,* p. 438.
136. Juhasz, p. 228f.
137. DGFP D. XI. nos. 80 and 131.
138. Montgomery, p. 142f. The probable chief aim of the operation, the preparation of an attack on the U.S.S.R., was not revealed by the Germans to anyone, not even to the Italians.
139. For the Hungarian text of the Pact see MMV no. 125, for the English, DIA, *Hitler's Europe,* vol. II. pp. 81-82.
140. Juhasz, pp. 221-222. Sztojay also committed the rash mistake of enquiring at the Wilhelmstrasse about the

conditions for Hungary's possible accession before he was authorized to do so. See also DGFP D. XI. no. 130.

141. According to Professor Macartney, Hitler was waiting to see whether Franco, the Spanish dictator, wanted to adhere or not. (Macartney, *October Fifteenth*, pp. 439-441.)

142. Ullein-Revitzky, A., *Guerre Allemande: Paix Russe*, Paris: 1948. p. 68.

143. Horthy, (British edition) p. 172. In his memoirs Horthy still defended Hungary's decision to adhere to the Tripartite Alliance on this ground.

144. Juhasz, p. 224.

145. Horthy, (British edition) pp. 180-181.

146. *Hungarian Quarterly*, Vol. VI. no. 2. p. 376.

147. *Ibid.*

148. In case of a conflict between Hungary and the *Reich*, Hitler, who had the habit of sharing the spoils when he wanted the recipients to become indebted to Germany, would have given a piece of the country to Rumania, just to oblige that state for assistance in the next great Nazi venture: the attack on the U.S.S.R.

149. The German occupation of Hungary did not take place until 1944.

150. One Yugoslav proposition to this effect was made on June 1, 1939. (DIMK IV. no. 176.)

151. DIMK IV. no. 188. DBFP Ser. 3. VI. 603.

152. *Hungarian Quarterly*, VI. p. 173. The U.S.S.R. was working at the time to isolate Rumania. Berlin, believing in the principle of *divide et impera*, wanted no alignment in Danubian Europe which it could not dominate.

153. DIMK. IV. page 627, editor's note 68.

154. *Ibid.*, no. 474.

155. On the 31st of the month Rumania renounced her local treaties. This cleared the way for a Yugoslav agreement with Hungary. (Macartney and Palmer, p. 438.)

156. There were many in Hungary who did not share Teleki's views. They maintained that instead of seeking friendship with Yugoslavia, the Hungarian Government should

work for the revision of the Trianon settlement in the South. (Macartney, *October Fifteenth*, p. 447.)

157. Montgomery, p. 124.
158. The recently published documentary collections are silent on this period of Hungarian diplomacy. For the details of the negotiations leading to the conclusion of the treaty see Macartney, *October Fifteenth*, pp. 447-454, and Juhasz, pp. 261-265.
159. Juhasz, pp. 255, 264f.
160. *Ibid.*, p. 269. On earlier German attitudes see DGFP D. XI. no. 478.
161. Actually, the new Yugoslav Government promised to adhere to all the existing international obligations of the country, including those imposed on it by the Tripartite Pact. The anti-German overtones of the *coup*, however, did not give weight to such promises in Hitler's eyes. (Macartney and Palmer, p. 441.)
162. Keitel, W., *The Memoirs of Field-Marshal Keitel*, New York: Stein and Day, 1966. Pp. 128, 138f. Hitler actually promised everything Horthy would desire except Croatia. The verbal message was carried to Budapest by Sztojay. (Juhasz, p. 291-293.)
163. Teleki to Apor, in Burks, p. 71f.
164. DGFP D. XII. no. 227; Horthy's Papers, no. 54; Nagy, p. 61f.
165. MMV no. 129.
166. *Ibid.*, no. 128.
167. *Ibid.*, no. 128. The matter is briefly mentioned by Juhasz, (*op. cit.*, p. 299.)
168. Ranki, Gy., "Magyarország Belépése a Második Világháboruba." *Hadtörténelmi Közlemények*, 1959, no. 2. p. 33.
169. Burks, p. 72; MMV no. 130.
170. Juhasz, p. 304.
171. *Ibid.*, p. 305. Cf. Burks, p. 72.
172. Burks, p. 72. Cf. Juhasz, p. 306.
173. See for example DIMK IV. no. 14. At the end of March 1941, moreover, there came intelligence reports to Budapest that the Germans were contemplating the setting

up of a German province in the Banat and adjacent areas. (Macartney, *October Fifteenth*, p. 479.)

174. Paulus' evidence, IMT Vol. X. p. 487f.
175. Juhasz, p. 306f.
176. Burks, pp. 71-73.
177. Dernoi Kocsis, p. 118f.
178. Juhasz, p. 95f. Teleki confided the idea to his son.
179. Many contemporary politicians seem to have held this opinion, among them Eckhardt, his successor as the leader of the Smallholders' Party Zoltan Tildy, and Montgomery as well. (On this see Eckhardt, p. 246. Dernoi Kocsis, p. 246, Montgomery, p. 127.)
180. DGFP D. XII. no. 267. (Erdmannsdorff's report on the events of the day.)
181. In his last letter to the Regent, it is these alleged provocations that Teleki alludes to. (Horthy's Papers, no. 55a.)
182. Macartney, *October Fifteenth*, pp. 487-488.
183. MMV no. 126. (Teleki's memorandum of 3 March, 1941, to the Hungarian Ministers in London and Washington.)
184. That these forces did not consist solely of German pressure was recognized by Teleki. The Prime Minister's letters written during those critical hours display a strong resentment against those in Hungary who favoured unconditional participation in the attack on Yugoslavia. See his letters to Horthy, (Horthy's Papers, no. 55.) and his lines to Apor, (Burks, pp. 71-73.)
185. Horthy's Papers, no. 56.
186. Juhasz, pp. 320-321.
187. Only one Hungarian unit ventured south of the Bacska. (Nagy, p. 67.)

NOTES TO PART VI. *War Against Russia.*

1. Halder's diary entry for 31 July, 1940, in DGFP D. X. pp. 370f.
2. The role Hungary was to play in Hitler's plans has been the object of considerable controversy. The Soviet Prosecutor at the Nuremberg trials produced evidence to the effect that during the winter and spring of 1941 the German military leaders, in collusion with their Hungarian counterparts, had been working out detailed plans for Hungary's participation in the invasion of Russia. (IMT Vol. VII. pp. 307-337 *in passim.*) The Russian Prosecutor cited the testimony of Antonescu, according to which, at the time Rumania was asked to participate in Operation Barbarossa, Hitler told the Rumanian leader that the Hungarians had already promised to take part in the planned invasion of Russia. However, neither Hitler, nor Antonescu, nor for that matter Soviet prosecutors can be regarded as the fountains of pure truth. If Hitler ever made such a statement he did it to obtain the immediate consent of the Rumanians. If, on the other hand, Antonescu invented the story, he did it to show himself in a better light.
3. Halder, vol. II. 4 May 1941, p. 394.
4. Keitel, p. 156.
5. Paulus' evidence, IMT Vol. VII. p. 229f.
6. To date, hardly any documents have come to light concerning Russian-Hungarian relations during these months.
7. DIMK Vol. IV. no. 410.
8. Macartney, *October Fifteenth,* p. 468. Professor Macartney sarcastically remarks that the Hungarians got the better of the deal because, four years later, they had both the flags and Rakosi.
9. For Horthy's letter of 3 November, 1940, see DGFP D. Vol. XII. no. 328; for that of April 1941 see Horthy's

Papers no. 58. According to Juhasz, the latter never reached Hitler. (Juhasz, p. 333 n. 204.)

10. Paulus' evidence, IMT Vol. X. p. 256.
11. Halder, 4 May 1941, p. 394.
12. Juhasz, pp. 336-337f.
13. MMV no. 141.
14. *Ibid.*, no. 142. Cf. Juhasz, pp. 338f, 341.
15. Juhasz, p. 314.
16. Hory, *Még egy barázdát sem*, p. 52.
17. Dernoi Kocsis, p. 119. Cf. Juhasz, p. 313.
18. Ranki, p. 42. Cf. Juhasz, p. 342.
19. Macartney, C.A., "Hungary's Declaration of War on the U.S.S.R. in 1941," in A.O. Sarkinissian (ed.) *Studies in Diplomatic History and Historiography*, London: Longmans, 1961. p. 158.
20. DGFP D. XII. no. 631.
21. Weizsacker, p. 254.
22. Juhasz, p. 344. Cf. Macartney, "Declaration of War" p. 159.
23. MMV no. 143.
24. DGFP D. XII. no. 661.
25. *Ibid.*, no. 667. Cf. Macartney, "Declaration of War." p. 160. Horthy, a veteran enemy of bolshevism, might have really been delighted by the prospect of Soviet Russia's demise. Whether or not he was, he was in no position to show displeasure over the developments.
26. Kun, J., "Magyarország második világháboruba való belépésének külpolitikai vonatkozásai," *Hadtörténelmi Közlemények*, 1962, no. 1. p. 29. On this day Halder recorded the following in his diary: "Ungarn ... sperrt seine Grenze. Politisch wird kein Ansuchen an Ungarn gestellt. Wenn die Soldaten mitmachen wollen, sollen sie ihre Politiker dazu veranlassen." (Halder, Vol. III. p. 6.)
27. In Ullein-Revitzky's version of the story Molotov promised to aid Hungary in her attempts to recover more of Transylvania. (*Op. cit.*, p. 101.) For a different view see Ranki, p. 44, and Juhasz, p. 348.
28. Juhasz, pp. 346-347.
29. DGFP D. XIII. no. 54.

30. Macartney, "Declaration of War." p. 159. For Halder's attitude on this matter of Hungarian help see Halder, 22 June 1941, Vol. III. p. 8.
31. Ranki, p. 45.
32. Ullein-Revitzky, pp. 104-105.
33. DGFP D. XIII. no. 10.
34. Kun. p. 33.
35. Juhasz, p. 353.
36. Macartney, "Declaration of War." p. 161.
37. IMT VIII. p. 334.
38. Juhasz, p. 353. Cf. Kun, p. 33. The editors of MMV talk of the "bombing of Kassa, Munkacs, Raho etc." (MMV p. 316.)
39. Most accounts place the number of attacking aircraft at three. One eye-witness, J. Hedervary-Konth, maintains that only two planes were involved. (J. H.-K. to N.F.D.) Kun claims that four planes were involved. (Kun. p. 24.)
40. J. Ledenyi to N.F.D.. It has been also said that the "air defences of Kassa had been caught, literally, napping." (Macartney, "Declaration of War." p. 164.)
41. E. Nemes to N.F.D.. According to Mr. Nemes, there had been reports of sporadic violations of Hungarian airspace by Soviet planes from the 23rd of June on. None of the intruding planes, however, were known to have flown deep into Hungarian territory.
42. Saly, entry for 27 June 1941, p. 371f. J. H.-K. maintains, however, that the planes had no markings.
43. Macartney, "Declaration of War." p. 164. One unexploded bomb was found. It was of Russian manufacture.
44. Ibid., p. 161.
45. Saly, entry for 28 June 1941, p. 374.
46. Ibid., p. 375. Saly's entry for the day 30 June, 1941, goes as follows: "from a military source 'L' received the information that Kassa was bombed by Slovak pilots fleeing from the airfield of Iglo to Russia on German planes . . ."
47. Horthy, p. 191. London edition.
48. See the editorial commentary in MMV p. 316f. Cf. Juhasz, p. 353f; Kun, pp. 33-34; Ranki, pp. 46-47.

49. There has been considerable confusion in historical writings in regard to Krudy's rank and position. Both Horthy and Macartney refer to him as "Colonel Krudy", while communist historians ascribe him the rank of lieutenant-colonel. Nearly all writers describe him as the commander of the air-force detachment at Kassa. The Hungarian air-force, however, had no detachment at that city in June of 1941, but only an air-force academy along with a small airfield. It was at this academy that the Captain Krudy of the time served as an instructor. He received most of his promotions only after the end of the war. (J. H.-K. and E. N. to N.F.D.)

50. IMT VII. pp. 334-335. According to Ujszaszy's testimony, the originators of the scheme included, besides the German officers Lieutenant General Fütterer and Colonel Frimond, a Hungarian, General Dezső László.

51. After the bombing of Kassa, the officers in question did their best to publicise every piece of evidence which tended to prove that the invaders came from the Soviet Union. This prompted Ujszaszy to come up with the conclusion that the attack was not carried out by the Russians but was organized by these officers themselves. (IMT VII. p. 335.)

52. This fact is admitted even by the communist historian Ranki. (op. cit., p. 46.)

53. Presuming, of course, that the invaders did not flee toward the interior of Hungary. Incidentally, none of my informants can corroborate Kun's claim. In any case, the intruders were probably miles away by the time Krudy's plane was air-born.

54. Kun, p. 33. This formation involves four planes. This is why Kun argues that four, rather than two or three aircraft were involved.

55. Macartney, "Declaration of War." p. 165. The name of the pilot was Andrej Andele.

56. IMT VII. p. 334. Ujszaszy's evidence, of course, cannot be considered completely reliable. He could not even recall the exact date of the event. There is no reason, how-

ever, why he would have forgotten or altered the time of the attack.

57. Kun, p. 35.
58. Macartney, "Declaration of War." p. 164.
59. Horthy, p. 191. British edition.
60. DGFP D. XII. no. 669.
61. Halder, 24 June 1941. Vol. III. p. 11.
62 The pertinent part of the text of this record reads as follows: "Russische Luftwaffe im Suden ebenfalls sehr stark. Dort auch neue Jagdflugzeuge ..." *Kriegstagebuch des Oberkommandos der Wehrmacht,* editor: H. A. Jacobsen, Frankfurt am Main: Bernard, 1965. Vol. I. p. 409.
62^ While this book was in the process of being printed this writer received a brief essay from one of the eyewitnesses of the Kassa incident, Mr. John Hedervary-Konth. The manuscript contains its author's reminiscences and reflections on the event.

Mr. Hedervary-Konth was a captain with the Hungarian signal corps in 1941. He, along with a few of his collegues, saw the attack from a window of the Kassa military communications headquarters which was located a few blocks south of the local Post Office. Lack of space does not allow a detailed exposé of his observations and opinions here. Briefly, his version is as follows: About 1 p.m. on the day of the incident two planes approached Kassa from the North-West, dropped their bombs and departed in the opposite direction. The aircraft were of a sand-yellow colour and bore no markings. Judging from their shape, Mr. Hedervary-Konth concludes that they were probably planes of the former Czech air-force. By hitting the post and telegraph office with three of their bombs, the raiders succeeded in knocking out the civilian telecommunications system of the Kassa area.

Mr. Hedervary-Konth also speculates on the identity of the attackers. He emphatically rejects the theory that they could have been Slovak pilots fleeing on German planes. For the usual reasons he rules out Russian guilt in the affair. Through such a process of elimination he arrives at the conclusion that the raid was an organized conspiracy, one in which Hungarian authorities, particularly General Werth, were deeply involved. By pointing out the importance of disrupting telecommunications in the area and by questioning many of the long accepted beliefs in connection with the incident, the author builds up a fairly plausible argument. However, he offers no evidence whatever which would indicate just how deeply Hungarian authorities had been involved in the plot.

Indeed, the possibility of Werth's complicity in the affair has already been brought up by some writers. Professor Macartney, for one, rejected it as being "psychologically improbable". (Macartney, "Declaration of War." p. 164.) This writer is inclined to believe that in the light of Halder's statement (see above note 26) and Bardossy's own remark to Ullein-Reviczky (see the text below) it would be certainly a mistake to dismiss it completely. However, nothing can be proved until some tangible evidence will be found.

63. Ullein-Revicky, p. 106.
64. Macartney, "Declaration of War." p. 161.
65. Ullein-Reviczky, p. 108. That Bardossy took the Kassa bombing to be a prearranged plot is also suggested in his message to Sztojay of 27 June 1941. In this note the Prime Minister remarked rather sarcastically that "We had immediately realized, without any hesitations, the meaning *(konzekvencia)* of the Soviet attack." (MMV no. 145.)
66. Macartney, "Declaration of War." p. 162.
67. Juhasz, p. 254. Cf. Ranki, p. 47.
68. MMV no. 145. Also, DGFP D. Vol. XIII. no. 22.
69. It might be asked at this point whether Bardossy was willing to do anything to "save face" as Teleki had done a few months earlier? No definite answer can be offered to this question. The Prime Minister dismissed the idea of resigning. He told Ullein-Revitzky at the time that no one could replace him as leader of the government who did not enjoy the confidence of the Germans. (Ullein-Revitzky, p. 108.) Bardossy did something else instead. He did not take the issue of war and peace

before Parliament. Not that there was any doubt in his mind that the majority of the representatives would not approve the government's decision. What the Prime Minister seems to have desired was to assume personally the responsibility for involvement in the war. By doing this he probably hoped to prevent the blame from being fixed on his nation.

The failure to consult Parliament was a violation of the Hungarian constitution. Bardossy paid dearly for his action. After the war he was condemned as a "collaborator" and died before the firing squad.

NOTES TO THE CONCLUSIONS

1. It should be remembered that the Magyars got their national autonomy within the Habsburg Empire at a time when Austria's prominence among the German states was successfully challenged by Bismarck's Prussia in the 1860's. In those years the danger of domination from Vienna was mitigated by the existence of another centre of German power in Berlin. In the 1930's, the threat from Berlin, in the opinion of some Hungarian leaders, could be lessened by the continued existence of Austria as an independent state.

2. Commenting on this aspect of the diplomacy of Hungary's leaders and, especially, her Regent, Ribbentrop remarked in his memoirs that "The *Führer* always regarded Horthy as his personal enemy and often referred to him as a great intriguer who, for instance, was trying to make mischief between Hitler and Mussolini". J. Ribbentrop, *The Ribbentrop Memoirs,* London: Weidenfeld & Nicholson, 1954. p. 167.

3. Ciano's Papers, p. 119.

4. Kallay, p. 51.

5. MMV no. 126.

6. DGFP D. Vol. V. no. 152. When referring to the "signs of decadence" among British youth, Horthy obviously had the Oxford Union resolution in mind.

7. DIMK Vol. II. no. 338.

8. Hory, pp. 63-65. Cf. DIMK Vol. IV. no. 98.

9. DIMK Vol. IV. no. 577.

10. MMV no. 126.

11. Keitel, p. 157f.

12. MMV no. 126.

BIBLIOGRAPHY*

DOCUMENTARY SOURCES

Ádám, M., Gy. Juhász and L. Kerekes (eds.) *Magyarország és a Második Világháború, Titkos Diplomáciai Okmányok a Háború Előzményeihez és Történetéhez,* [Hungary and the Second World War, Secret Diplomatic Documents on the Origins and History of the War,] Third edition. Budapest: Kossuth, 1966.

Ciano's Diplomatic Papers, M. Muggridge, (ed.) London: Oldhams, 1948.

Diplomáciai Iratok Magyarország Külpolitikájához, 1936-1945, [Diplomatic Documents on Hungary's Foreign Policy, 1936-1945,] General editor L. Zsigmond. Budapest: Akadémiai Kiadó, 1962f.

Documents on British Foreign Policy, E. E. Woodward, R. Butler *et al.* (eds.) London: H.M.S.O., 1949f.

Documents on German Foreign Policy, 1918-1945, R. J. Sontag et al. (eds.) Washington: Department of State, 1949-1963.

Documents on International Affairs, London: R.I.I.A., 1929f.

Halmosy, D., (ed.) *Nemzetközi Szerződések,* 1918-1945, [International Treaties, 1918-1945,] Budapest: Közgazdasági és Jogi Könyvkiadó, 1966.

---

* This bibliography is a selective one. It makes no attempt to list all the sources cited in the footnotes, or to cover the literature on the history of Hungarian diplomacy and politics prior to the mid-1930's. It offers only a sampling of the great number of secondary works published in present-day Hungary and other communist countries. An effort has been made, however, to provide an extensive list of the literature available in English.

Nazi Conspiracy and Aggression, Washington: Department of
State, 1946-1948.
Szinai, M., and L. Szücs (eds.) *Horthy Miklós Titkos Iratai,*
[The Confidential Papers of Miklos Horthy,] Budapest:
Kossuth, 1963.
*Trial of the Major War Criminals before the International
Military Tribunal,* 42 vols. Nuremberg: 1946-1950.

CONTEMPORARY JOURNAL
The Hungarian Quarterly, 1935-1941.

DIARIES AND MEMOIRS

Beck, J., *Final Report,* New York: Speller, 1957.
Benes, E., *Memoirs of Dr. Eduard Benes,* London: Allen and
Unwin, 1954.
Ciano, G., *Ciano's Diary,* 1937-1938. London: Methuen, 1952.
——————, *The Ciano Diaries,* 1939-1943, ed. by H. Gibson,
New York: Doubleday, 1946.
Eckhardt, T., *Regicide at Marseille, The Recollections of Tibor
Eckhardt,* New York: American Hungarian Library, 1964.
Gafencu, G., *The Last Days of Europe,* New Haven: Yale U.P.
1948.
——————, *Prelude to the Russian Campaign,* London: Mul-
ler, 1945.
Guderian, G. H., *Panzer Leader,* London: Joseph, 1952.
Halder, F., *Kriegstagebuch,* Stuttgart: Kohlhammer, 1963. 3
volumes.
Hodza, M., *Federation in Central Europe, Reflections and
Reminiscences,* London: Jarrolds, 1942.
Horthy, Admiral N., *Memoirs,* New York: Speller, 1957.
Hory, A., *A Kulisszák Mögött,* [Behind the Scenes,] Vienna:
1965. Published by the author.
——————, *Még egy barázdát sem,* [Not One Furrow,] Vien-
na: 1967. Published by the author.

Kállay, N., *Hungarian Premier;* New York: Columbia U.P. 1954.

Keitel, W., *The Memoirs of Field-Marshal* Keitel, New York: Stein and Day, 1966.

Montgomery, J. F. *Hungary, the Unwilling Satellite,* New York: Devin-Adair, 1947.

Nagy, V., *Végzetes Esztendők,* 1938-1945. [Fateful Years, 1938-1945,] Kispest: Körmendy, ca. 1945.

Papen, F., *Memoirs,* London: Deutsch, 1952.

Rauschning, H., *Hitler Speaks,* London: Butterworth, 1939.

Ribbentrop, J., *The Ribbentrop Memoirs,* London: Weidenfed & Nicholson, 1954.

Saly, D., *Szigoruan Bizalmas,* [Strictly Confidential,] Budapest: Anonymus, 1945.

Schmidt, P., *Hitler's Interpreter,* London: Heinemann, 1951.

Schuschnigg, K., *Farewell Austria,* London: Cassel, 1938.

Ullein-Reviczky, A., *Guerre Allemande: Paix Russe,* Paris: Histoire et Société d'Aujourd'hui, [1946].

Weizsacker, E., *The Memoirs of Ernst von Weizsacker,* Chicago: Regenry, 1951.

SECONDARY WORKS

Basch, A., *The Danube Basin and the German Economic Sphere,* New York: Columbia U.P., 1943.

Borsody, S., *The Triumph of Tyranny,* London: Cape, 1960.

Bullock, A., *Hitler, a Study in Tyranny,* New York: Bantam, 1961. (rev. ed.)

Churchill, W. S. *The Second World War,* Boston: Mifflin, 1948. Vols. I, II, III.

Dernői Kocsis, L., *Bajcsy-Zsilinszky,* Budapest: Kossuth, 1966.

Eubank, K., *Munich,* Norman: U. of Oklahoma. P., 1963.

Gehl, J., *Austria, Germany and the Anschluss,* 1931-1938. London: Oxford U. P., 1963.

Hillgruber, A., *Hitler's Strategie, Politik und Kriegsführung,* 1940-1941, Frankfurt am Main: Bernard & Graefe Verlag, 1965.

Hofer, W., *War Premeditated,* 1939, London: Thames & Hudson, 1955.

Hoptner, J. S., *Yugoslavia in Crisis,* 1934-1941. New York: Columbia U. P. 1963.

Juhász, Gy., *A Teleki-kormány külpolitikája,* 1939-1941, [The Foreign Policy of the Teleki Government, 1939-1941,] Budapest: Akadémiai Kiadó, 1964.

Kertesz, S. D., *Diplomacy in a Whirlpool,* Notre Dame: U. of Notre Dame P., 1953.

Kirschbaum, J. M., *Slovakia: Nation at the Crossroads of Central Europe,* New York: Speller, 1960.

Lengyel, E., *1000 Years of Hungary,* New York: Day, 1958.

Lukacs, J. A., *The Great Powers and Eastern Europe,* New York: American Book Co., 1953.

Macartney, C. A., *Hungary a Short History,* Chicago: Aldine, 1962.

————, *Hungary and Her Successors,* New York: Oxford University Press, 1937.

————, *October Fifteenth, a History of Modern Hungary,* 1929-1945. 2 vols. Edinburgh: Edinburgh U. P., 1961.

————, *Problems of the Danube Basin,* Cambridge: the U. P., 1942.

————, and A. W. Palmer, *Independent Eastern Europe,* New York: Macmillan, 1962.

Meyer, H. O., *Mitteleuropa in German Thought and Action,* 1915-1945, The Hague: Nijnoff, 1955.

Namier, Sir L. B., *Diplomatic Prelude, 1938-1939,* New York: Macmillan, 1948.

————, *Europe in Decay,* 1936-40. London: Macmillan, 1950.

————, *In the Nazi Era,* London: Macmillan, 1952.

Opocensky, J., (ed.) *Eduard Benes: Essays and Reflection,* London: Allen and Unwin, 1944.

Pushkash, A. T., *Vengriia vo Vtoroi Mirovoi Voine,* Moscow: Institute for International Affairs, 1963.

Rutter, O., *Regent of Hungary,* London: Rich and Cowan, [ca. 1939].

Schlesinger, R., *Federalism in Central and Eastern Europe,* London: Paul, 1945.

Seton-Watson, H., *Eastern Europe Between the Wars,* 1918-1941, 3rd ed. Hamden: Archon, 1962.

————, *The East European Revolution,* 3rd ed. New York: Prager, 1956.

Shirer, W. L., *The Rise and Fall of the Third Reich*, New York: Crest, 1962.

Sinor, D., *History of Hungary*, London: Allen & Unwin, 1959.

Stercho, P. G., *Carpatho-Ukraine in International Affairs*, 1938-1939, Ph. D. thesis, Indiana U. 1959.

Survey of International Affairs, A. and V. M. Toynbee (gen. eds.) R.I.I.A. London: Oxford U. P.

Szalay, J., *Igazságok Középeurópa Körül*, [Truths About Central Europe,] Paris; Collection Danubia, 1960. Vol. II.

Taylor, A. J. P., *The Origins of the Second World War*, New York: Premier, 1961.

Wheeler-Bennett, J. W. *Munich: Prologue to Tragedy*, London: Macmillan, 1966. (Revised ed.)

Wiskemann, E., *The Rome-Berlin Axis*, London: Collins, 1966. (Revised ed.)

PAMPHLETS

Boldizsár, I., *The Other Hungary*, Budapest: New Hungary, 1946.

"New Hungary", *Hungarian Economic Resistance Against German Penetration*, Budapest: New Hungary, 1946.

ARTICLES

Adam, M., "From the History of Hungarian-Czechoslovak Relations on the Eve of the Second World War." (in Russian) *Voprosy Istorii*, Sept. 1960, pp. 90-113.

Burks, R. V., "Two Teleki Letters," *Journal of Central European Affairs*, vol. VII. 1947, pp. 68-73.

Juhasz, Gy., "Beiträge zu Ungarns Aussenpolitik in den Tagen des Ausbruchs des zweiten Weltkrieges," *Acta Hitorica*, vol. VIII, 1961, pp. 137-175.

Kerekes, L., "Akten des Ungarischen Ministeriums des Ausseren zur Vorgeschichte der Annexation Österreichs," *Acta Historica,* vol. VII, 1960. pp. 355-390.

Kun, J. "Magyarország a második Világháborúba való belépésének katonapolitikai vonatkozásai." [The military-political espects of Hungary's entry into the Second World War,] *Hadtörténelmi Közlemények,* 1962, no. 1, pp. 3-39.

Macartney, C. A. "Hungary's Declaration of War on the U.S.S.R. in 1941," in A. O. Sarkission (ed.) *Studies in Diplomatic History and Historiography,* London: Longmans, 1961, pp. 153-165.

Paikert, G. C., "Hungarian Foreign Policy in Intercultural Relations, 1919-1944." *The American Slavic and East European Review,* vol. XI, 1952, pp. 42-65.

——————, "Hungary's National Minority Policies, 1920-1945," *The American Slavic and East European Review,* vol. XII, 1953, pp. 201-218.

Pavlovitch, K. S., "Yugoslavia and Rumania, 1941," *Journal of Central European Affairs,* vol. XXIII, 1964, pp. 451-472.

Pelenyi, J., "The Secret Plan for a Hungarian Government in the West at the Outbreak of World War II," *Journal of Modern History,* vol. XXXVI, 1964, pp. 170-178.

Petho, T., "Contradictory Trends in Policies of the Horthy Era," *New Hungarian Quarterly,* vol. IV. no. 12, 1963, pp. 115-131.

——————, "Hungary in the Second World War," *New Hungarian Quarterly,* vol. I, 1960, pp. 193-201.

Presseisen, E. L., "Prelude to Barbarossa: Germany and the Balkans, 1940-1941," *Journal of Modern History,* 1960. no. 4, pp. 359-370.

Puskas, A. I., "Adatok Horthy — Magyarország Külpolitikájához a Második Világháború Éveiben," [Data to Horthyite Hungary's Foreign Policy in the Years of the Second World War,] *Századok,* Vol. XVC, no. 1, pp. 83-115.

Ranki, Gy., "Magyarország belépése a második Világháborúba," [Hungary's entry into the Second World War,] *Hadtörténelmi közlemények*, 1959, no. 2, pp. 28-48.

Ranki, Gy., and I. Berend, "German-Hungarian Relations Following Hitler's Rise to Power, 1933-34," *Acta Historica*,
vol. VIII, 1961, pp. 313-347.

Szinai, M., and L. Szucs, "Horthy's Secret Correspondence
with Hitler," *New Hungarian Quarterly*, vol. IV. no. 11,
1963, pp. 174-191.

Tilkovszky, L., "Volksdeutsche Bewegung und Ungarische
Nationalitatenpolitik 1939-41," *Acta Historica*, vol. XII,
59-112, 319-346.

Vincent, S., "Carpatho-Ukraine in the International Bargaining of 1918-38," *The Ukranian Quarterly*, Summer 1954,
pp. 235-246.

Zsigmond, L., "Ungarn und das Munchener Abkommen." *Acta
Historica*, vol. VI, 1959, pp. 251-286.